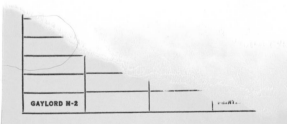

Musical Instruments
and their Symbolism in Western Art

By the same author

Musical Autographs from Monteverdi to Hindemith
Keyboard Instruments in the Metropolitan Museum of Art
Musical Instruments of the Western World

Musical Instruments and their Symbolism in Western Art

EMANUEL WINTERNITZ

Curator of Musical Collections,
Metropolitan Museum of Art

W. W. NORTON & COMPANY · INC · NEW YORK

Copyright © 1967 by Emanuel Winternitz
First Edition

Library of Congress Catalog Card No. 67-16617

Printed in Great Britain

In memory of Alfred Schütz,
thinker, musician, and noblest of friends

Contents

Illustrations

b. Above: Zampogna (Italy, 19th century). Length of longest drone, 4 feet. *Below*: Musette (France, 18th century). Length of chanter, 9½ inches; of bourdon cylinder, 5½ inches. Metropolitan Museum of Art, Crosby Brown Collection.

25. *a.* Bock (Germany, 18th century). Length of chanter, 2 feet 5 inches; of drone, 5 feet 4 inches. Metropolitan Museum of Art, Crosby Brown Collection.
    b. Bock with bellows (Germany, 19th century). Length of chanter, 1 foot 9 inches; of drone, 3 feet 6 inches; both are fitted with single beating reeds. Metropolitan Museum of Art, Crosby Brown Collection.

26. *a.* Musette player with other musicians, from Watteau's *L'Amour au théâtre français.*
    b. Watteau, *Fête champêtre*, detail showing musette player.
    c. Watteau, *L'Accordée de village*, detail showing musette and vielle played for dancing.
    d. Engraving after Watteau, showing Chinese musician with a vielle.

27. *a.* Angel playing a three-stringed hurdy-gurdy (c. 1500). St. Thomas Altar, Cologne.
    b. Van Dyck, *Portrait of François Langlois*. Private collection. Note the bellows straps on the right arm, and the single chanter.
    c. Player with zampogna.
    d. Street singer with hurdy-gurdy, from the case of a South Tyrolean psaltery (18th century). Metropolitan Museum of Art, Crosby Brown Collection.

28. *a.* Peter Bruegel, *Dance of the Peasants*, detail.
    b. Engraving after Peter Bruegel, *The Fat Kitchen*, detail.
    c. Vielle player from a woodcut (c. 1570) entitled *Les Noces de Michaud Crouppière: Histoire d'une drollerie facécieuse du Marriage de Lucresse aux yeux de boeuf et Michaud Crouppière son mary, avec ceux qui furent semouz au banquet.*

29. *a.* Page from Bordet's *Méthode raisonnée*, Paris, c. 1755.
    b. Cornemuse with ivory pipes (France, 18th century). Length of chanter, 10 inches; of drone, 7 inches. Metropolitan Museum of Art, Crosby Brown Collection.

30. *a.* Plaque for the musical scholar Ercole Bottrigari (early 17th century).
    b. *Orpheus in Hades*, after a bronze plaque by Moderno.

31. *a.* Examples of various lire da braccio and lire da gamba (after sketches by Disertori in *Rivista musicale italiana*, XLIV [1940]): (*a*) Lira da braccio, Brussels Conservatory, Mahillon Catalogue 1443. (*b*) Lira da braccio, Kunsthistorisches Museum, Vienna, Schlosser Catalogue 94. (*c*) Lirone, Heyer Collection, Kinsky Catalogue 780. (*d*) Lira da gamba, Heyer Collection, Kinsky Catalogue 784. (*e*) Lira da gamba, Brussels Conservatory, Mahillon Catalogue 1444. (*f*) Lira da gamba, Kunsthistorisches Museum, Vienna, Schlosser Catalogue 95.
    g. Lira da braccio by Giovanni d'Andrea, Venice, 1511: front and back views (same as (*b*) above).
    h. Lira da gamba by Wendelin Tieffenbrucker, Padua, c. 1590 (same as (*f*) above).

32. *a.* Bartolommeo Passerotti, *King David*. Galleria Spada, Rome.
    b. Raffaellino del Garbo, *Musician*. National Gallery, Dublin.

Preface

Most of the studies assembled here grew out of my work at the Metropolitan Museum of Art, for whose splendid collection of musical instruments I have, as Curator, been responsible since 1941. Preserving, repairing, and exhibiting instruments, studying purchases and gifts, and organizing museum concerts of forgotten masterworks using instruments of their periods, provided no end of incentive to research. Another stimulus came from the continual questioning by friends in the fields of the history of art and of music. In this age of intense interest in iconology, art historians seek information about instruments as traditional attributes of allegorical figures, as integral elements of mythical and religious beliefs and images, and as telling tools of social customs and traditions. In trying to answer these questions, it was necessary to view the instruments as objects invested with symbolic meaning beyond their musical significance. Music historians, in turn, having become increasingly familiar with the wealth of pictorial representations, have sought equivalent information for their purposes: more precise information about the nature of ensembles, playing methods, and practices of performance in general, in those many instances in which the answers could not be provided by surviving instruments.

This book does not aspire to be a comprehensive or systematic treatment of its subject. Nor is it only an anthology — that is, a conglomeration of essays chosen at random, unrelated to each other. When a selection from my articles on musical instruments was suggested to me, I was not sure that they would make a homogeneous group, but after some reshuffling, they seemed to fall into a natural order — reflecting what I suppose, or at least hope, has been an organic growth of thought.

That strange object the tool of music, a machine or technical contraption serving an art and often itself a work of art, pleasing the eye as well as the ear, opens up many vistas and approaches. It is obviously susceptible to investigation within its own esthetic realm, that of music. Among the problems to be studied here are: the function of the instrument in practical performance; the ever-changing rapport between the creative musician, striving for certain timbres, and the tools that best satisfied his imagination; and the ever-present antagonism between conservatism and the desire for change, and likewise between two other rival tendencies, individualization and standardization of musical instruments. But the interest in instruments is not confined to a consideration of them within a purely musical context. They carry meaning beyond their function as tools — that is, beyond their musical significance. And here we encounter aspects such as the function of the instrument within its social milieu, its role as bearer of allegorical thought, as product of the plastic arts, and so on. These aspects that are not strictly musical are, curiously, little investigated today, although much thought was given to them in earlier phases of culture — in the Renaissance and Baroque for instance — not only by scholars and poets, but also by artists. It was the painters, above all, who availed themselves of the symbolic character of musical instruments. A certain flute, or dragon trumpet, or drone fiddle, displayed in a mythological subject or *trionfo* or *fête champêtre* or genre scene, would often rapidly and accurately inform the initiated spectator of the meaning of the scene. It is for this reason that a large part of the articles selected for this book draw upon visual images as well as upon actual surviving instruments.

The function of the two introductory essays on the importance of co-operation between historians of art and those of music, hardly needs explanation here. The ensuing articles could perhaps be classified in three main sections, of which the first group, comprising Chapters 3 and 4, deals with the problem of evolution. In Chapter 3, 'The Survival of the Kithara,' some inconspicuous and non-functional elements of an instrument are revealed as atrophic remnants of parts that had been essential many centuries before, and the supposed revival of an ancient Roman instrument in the 15th century is seen as the final result of an actual survival. The chapter on 'Bagpipes and Hurdy-gurdies in Their Social Setting' is similarly concerned with gradual transformation: the strangely parallel history of instruments with wind and string bourdons is traced through the ages. Here the common bond is not their shape, but rather a functional musical device, the drone, whose characteristic sound possesses symbolic significance, especially within the bucolic and pastoral tradition.

The next group comprises studies of single instruments. Chapter 5, 'The Lira da Braccio,' deals with that exquisite improvisation instrument of the Renaissance. It is substantially an extract from an entry on the lira da braccio published in the German encyclopaedia *Die Musik in Geschichte und Gegenwart*, and I have placed it here as a focal point of factual information on this instrument, permitting me to eliminate repetitious references to its history and function in following articles, several of which touch on the lira da braccio. The sixth chapter tries to trace, in Lombard and Piedmontese pictorial documents, the still unknown early history of an instrument that was influenced by the lira da braccio — the violin. Chapter 7, the last of this group, seeks to interpret a fantastic harpsichord of Algardi's time as a typical Baroque allegory of two opposed branches of music, the learned and the rustic.

The remaining chapters deal with representations of musical instruments in various pictorial arts; most of these essays concern themselves either with the symbolic significance of the instruments for their time or with their significance as key to the interpretation of a particular work of art.

The index has been organized with special regard to iconological matters, and I hope that it may for this reason add to the usefulness of the book.

All the previously published articles assembled here were written during a span of twenty-two years: the first, '*Quattrocento* Science in the Gubbio Study,' in 1942, and the last, 'Muses and Music in a Burial Chapel,' in 1964. The chapter on 'The Knowledge of Musical Instruments as an Aid to the Art Historian' was written for this book. Some of the articles have been published in musical congress reports and in musicological journals and dictionaries. The greater part, those dealing chiefly with musical instruments represented in the visual arts, have appeared in periodicals that do not belong to the daily fare of musical connoisseurs: *The Metropolitan Museum of Art Bulletin, The Journal of the Warburg and Courtauld Institutes, The Art Bulletin,* and others. I sincerely hope that their appearance here will make them more readily accessible to students of music. The revision of the essays has consisted primarily in making excisions; occasionally, however, some repetition seemed unavoidable. My excuse — to borrow a phrase from William James — is that 'one cannot always express the same thought in two ways that seem equally forcible, so one has to copy one's former words.'

My sincere thanks go to Mrs. Eleanor Clark, my assistant at the Metropolitan Museum of Art, who with untiring devotion helped me in the preparation of my manuscript; to Mr. David Hamilton of W. W. Norton & Company, Inc., who brought to his editorial tasks the persistence of the gentle godfather towards the stubborn child; to Miss Mary McClane, for her assistance in compiling the index; and to the staff of Faber and Faber, especially Mr. Michael Wright for his supervision of the illustrations. I am also very much indebted to the John Simon Guggenheim Memorial Foundation for their generous grant, which made possible a substantial expansion of the picture section.

E. W.

Sources and Acknowledgments

Grateful acknowledgment is hereby made to the publishers of journals and books in which a number of the chapters in this book first appeared:

Chapter 1. *International Musicological Society Congress Report, New York, 1961.* Kassel: Bärenreiter Verlag, 1961.

Chapter 2. Published here for the first time.

Chapter 3. *Journal of the Warburg and Courtauld Institutes*, XXIV (1961), No. 3–4.

Chapter 4. *The Metropolitan Museum of Art Bulletin*, Summer 1943.

Chapter 5. *Die Musik in Geschichte und Gegenwart*, VIII, Kassel: Bärenreiter Verlag, 1960.

Chapter 6. *The Commonwealth of Music: Writings on Music in History, Art, and Culture, in Honor of Curt Sachs*, edited by Gustave Reese and Rose Brandel, New York: The Free Press, 1965.

Chapter 7. *The Metropolitan Museum of Art Bulletin*, February 1956.

Chapter 8. *Bericht über den siebenten internationalen musikwissenschaftlichen Kongress, Köln, 1958*, Kassel: Bärenreiter Verlag, 1958.

Chapter 9. *The Metropolitan Museum of Art Bulletin*, October 1942.

Chapter 10. *The Metropolitan Museum of Art Bulletin*, June 1958.

Chapter 11. *The Musical Quarterly*, XLIX (1963), No. 4.

Chapter 12. *Studies in the History of Art, Dedicated to William E. Suida*, London: Phaidon Press, 1959.

Chapter 13. *Mitteilungen des kunsthistorischen Institutes in Florenz*, XI (1965), No. 4.

Chapter 14. *Rendiconti della Pontificia Accademia Romana di Archeologia*, XXVII (1952–54).

Chapter 15. *The Burlington Magazine*, February 1958.

Chapter 16. *Les Fêtes de la Renaissance*, I, Paris: Éditions du Centre National de la Recherche Scientifique, 1956.

Musical Instruments
and their Symbolism in Western Art

There's meat and music here,
as the fox said when he ate the bagpipe.
— *Gaelic proverb*

1 · The Visual Arts as a Source for the Historian of Music

The history of music has concentrated, ever since its beginning, and for obvious reasons, on the most immediate and reliable embodiment of music, its notation. Therefore, those times and regions and forms that had no written music, or from which no written documents have survived, have been greatly neglected. Areas thus slighted include folk music, music of so-called 'primitive' civilizations, and even some of the most subtle forms of occidental music, such as improvisation. Contemporary verbal description, by its very nature, can give but little information about such music; it can mention the instruments, ensembles, places and conditions of performances, but can, at best, give only a faint reflection of the music itself — especially since such descriptions are most often written by musical amateurs or by persons unfamiliar with those aspects of music that would interest the future student. One might hope to find more reliable information in the musical treatises of the time, yet these latter too often focus on problems of theory and pedagogy and give us little idea of what the music actually sounded like. Flagrant examples of this are the ancient Greek treatises, despite their elaborate information on theory of harmony and other matters, and the great Italian theoretical works of the Renaissance which, had no written music survived from that period, would leave us speculating as to the content and emotional impact of the music which they treat. In short, these treatises take for granted many things that to later times are by no means obvious or self-evident.

Instruments themselves are, of course, most valuable documents, but from many periods few, or none at all, have survived. Egypt, with its dry climate and sealed burial chambers, is one of the exceptions, but northern climates, or those with great fluctuations in humidity, are destructive. Moreover, most instruments, and above all string instruments subject to tension, need perpetual care and repair; when they fall from public favour they are likely to disintegrate, if they do not happen to be ornate showpieces or parts of a *Kunst- und Wunder-kammer* or other public or private collections. The bodies of many lutes and harpsichords have survived only because they were rebuilt into hurdy-gurdies and piano-fortes.

In view of this situation, musical representations in painting, sculpture, and many other branches of the visual arts are of supreme documentary value to musical history.

It was not the historian of music who first indulged in the systematic collection of musical information from monuments of art. It was rather the artist himself who, during the early and high Renaissance, turned to the monuments of antiquity for models and inspiration, and borrowed what he needed for his own artistic purposes, including the images of ancient musicians and musical instruments. An enormous quantity of sketches and drawings of ancient Greek sculpture and Roman sarcophagi, many including musical subjects, have survived to our day from the 15th and 16th centuries. Raphael, to mention only one great name, employed draftsmen to obtain as many drawings as possible of ancient works of art, and he used the musical instruments of a Roman sarcophagus as models for those in his *Parnassus* in the Stanza della Segnatura.[1] Only later, when 16th-century humanism revived the ideal of recovering and, if possible, reconstructing ancient Greek music, did musical treatises begin to refer occasionally to Greek and Roman sculpture as authentic documents of ancient musical practice. At the same time, however, they referred also to contemporary — that is, Renaissance — works of art, sometimes naively crediting their creators with an exact understanding and imitation of the ancient originals. Ganassi (*Regola Rubertina*, 1542), in discussing whether the lute or the 'violone' is more ancient, refers to an ancient Roman marble relief in which one figure holds an instrument with a bow, 'una viola d'arco'(!), and the *Hiero-*

Fig. 1. Pseudo-ancient Roman altar with lire da braccio. Woodcut from Pierius Valerianus, *Hieroglyphica*, 1567.

[1] See Chapter 14 below.

glyphica (1567) of Pierius Valerianus includes a woodcut showing an 'ancient' Roman altar decorated on all four sides with lire da braccio in relief (see Fig. 1), a pseudo-archaeological imitation of an actual ancient Roman type of altar with four lyres, such as we find, for instance, in the Lateran Museum.[1]

Vincenzo Galilei, in his *Dialogo della musica antica e della moderna* (1581), repeatedly refers to the 'marmi antichi,' but he has few qualms about referring to works of art of his own time or of shortly before, trusting that these copies of ancient instruments were archaeologically correct, and being a true Florentine, he of course proudly refers to Florentine artists. In his chapter on the ancient lyre, he tells the reader to go to the court of the Medici palace, where he will find a statue of Orpheus, by Bandinelli, holding a lyre of ancient shape, and in his detailed discussion of the ancient plectrum, he cites the frescoes by Filippino Lippi in Santa Maria Novella, which include a large kithara flanked by two Muses, of which one is holding a plectrum. The Muses, by the way, had been copied by Filippino from a Roman sarcophagus.[2]

In the north, Praetorius, who obviously based the woodcuts of his *Organographia* (1618) on actual contemporary instruments, occasionally gives art objects as his source, as for instance in speaking of early kettledrums ('a type of kettledrum that is to be seen on old coins') and of one of the ancient lyres ('unknown and unusual types of lyres'; *Sciagraphia*, XL, 5; XLI, 9, 10).

Père Mersenne's *Harmonie universelle* (1636) also mentions the ancient Italian marbles and medals as important sources of information, but he broadens the horizon by at least mentioning the Egyptians (Bk. III, Prop. XXIV), and by including early Christian iconography. In his preface, Mersenne speaks of an illustration of the Redeemer in the character of a shepherd holding a 'seryngue' (or 'fleute pastorale'), which he found illustrated in a treatise called *La Roma soterranea*.

Kircher's *Musurgia* (1650) borrows, for one of its title pages, the schematic design of a lyre from an ancient gem, and a pseudo-ancient figure of Orpheus for another title page; but Book VIII contains a large engraving of a sort of filing cabinet with tabulations of the Greek *toni* and other theoretical information, as well as pictures of eleven instruments labelled 'Veterum Graecorum antiquis monumentis desumta,' though two Egyptian sistra are also included.

Buonanni, the learned student of Kircher, in his *Descrizione degli istromenti armonici* (1722), illustrates the instruments in a room contiguous to the Museo Kircheriano, today in the Collegio Romano in Rome. Buonanni's book is a curious mixture of lip service to the ancients from Pythagoras to Virgil and

---

[1] For more detailed information, see Chapter 14. Zarlino's *Istitutioni* (1558) confine themselves to mentioning that 'the Ancients had a statue of Apollo with a kithara on his knees' (Pt. II, p. 81).

[2] See Chapter 13 below.

astonishing carelessness in the illustrations. If he absorbed little from the Roman statuary in his immediate environment, ancient monuments are at least mentioned in his quotations from Mersenne, Kircher, and Strabo, who tells of having seen the statue of a kithara player in Calabria.

Padre Martini's classical *Storia* (1757–81) refers only occasionally to several 'Monumenta' (that is, illustrated editions of collections of classical antiquities), for instance that of Bernard de Montfaucon; and many of the charming vignettes with puzzle canons on Latin texts that are dispersed throughout his three volumes show musicians borrowed from ancient Roman reliefs. Volume III includes large engravings with ground plans of the Greek and Roman theatres.

Burney, manifestly affected by the English antiquarianism of his time, used his visit to Italy (1770) to good purpose. We may safely conclude, from his many explanations and illustrations of bas-reliefs, sculptures, vases, and frescoes, that he spent some time in Pompeii and Herculaneum, in museums at Rome, Portici, and Naples, and visited many of the Roman palaces that housed antiquities. Forkel's meagre iconographical references (*Allgemeine Geschichte der Musik*, 2 vols., 1788, 1801) are largely based on Burney.

As early as 1774, the first systematic exploration of medieval miniatures for the purposes of music history is found in Gerbert's *De Cantu et Musica sacra*, in which pictures from several codices are reproduced.

A review of 19th-century achievements would require an essay in itself, but among the most important contributions towards musical iconology there should be mentioned the works of Ambros (at home in the history of art as well as in that of music), Coussemaker, and the second volume of Viollet-le-Duc's *Dictionnaire raisonné du mobilier français* (1871).

Evidence of the rapidly growing interest in musical iconology, no doubt stimulated by the publication of illustrated art books and facsimile editions of illuminated manuscripts between 1900 and the outbreak of the First World War, are the many standard works of Buhle, Kinsky, Galpin, Schlesinger, Lütgendorff, Sachs, and the remarkable *Iconographie des instruments de musique*, organized by the Dutch collector of instruments, D. F. Scheurleer.[1]

Egypt and the ancient Near East abound in pictorial representations of musicians and instruments, and certain stylistic peculiarities in perspective and other mannerisms hardly hamper the recognition of actual shapes, fingerings,

---

[1] Readers interested in further information about the literature on musical instruments may consult the bibliographies given in the following:

Curt Sachs, *The History of Musical Instruments*, New York, 1940.

Nicholas Bessaraboff, *Ancient European Musical Instruments*, Cambridge, Mass., 1941.

Emanuel Winternitz, *Die schönsten Musikinstrumente des Abendlandes*, Munich, 1966; *Musical Instruments of the Western World*, London, 1967.

and embouchures, especially since so many depictions in reliefs and wall paintings are life-size or very nearly so.

Ancient Hebrew musical culture, with its disproportion between abundant references in the Scriptures and utmost scarcity of pictorial monuments, presents a problem too complex to pursue here.

The Greco-Roman world left us many visual records depicting musical scenes and instruments with admirable exactness. There are, above all, vase paintings, sculptures, reliefs, and coins, and from the Roman world an enormous quantity of frescoes, mosaics, and sarcophagi. Topics were mythological, as well as secular, including revelries, music lessons, and the like.

In the Middle Ages, subjects were for a long time limited to illustrations of the Scriptures (especially of apocalyptical themes), the Rex Psalmista, and the 150th Psalm. The apocalyptical subjects were:

(1) The seven angels with trumpets (Rev. 8: 2, 6).

(2) The seven holy men playing instruments in front of the Lamb ('numeri habentes cytharas').

(3) The two figures flanking each of the animals with the Lamb ('tenens cytharam' in Spanish Beatus MSS, represented with longnecked fiddles).

(4) The seven holy men 'stantes super mare vitreum habentes cytharas.'

(5) The twenty-four elders surrounding Christ in Glory (Rev. 4: 4; 7: 11; 14: 14). For the organologist this theme is by far the most rewarding of the apocalyptical scenes. Sometimes the elders are shown holding stereotyped, identical vielles (e.g., in the 11th-century Beatus MS of St. Sévère, Bibliothèque Nationale, Paris); later, the vielles often differ in shape and in the number of strings (Moissac); even later, other instruments, such as harps and organistrum, join them (Santiago di Compostela, Portico de la Gloria; Chartres, Portail Royal).

Carolingian illuminated MSS, above all the Utrecht Psalter, abound with portrayals of musicians (never angels) surrounding the Psalmist. These have been repeatedly — though not yet exhaustively — explored, especially in the works of Buhle, Schlesinger, and Panum. They represent an exceedingly complex problem in view of the fact that many of their illuminations are copied from, or at least influenced by, much earlier models, and therefore cannot be taken simply as depictions of contemporary practice. They may, however, throw new light on one of the great lacunae of musical history, the transition from the instrumental practice of late antiquity to that of the early Middle Ages, and especially on the rise, in the Occident, of instruments with fingerboards for stopping of strings, possibly due to the influence of performing practices in the Eastern Mediterranean.[1] Outstanding examples of the depiction of performance of secular music are the Manesse MS and, above all, the *Cantigas de Santa Maria*, with their enormous array of instrumentalists reflecting, side by side, both Christian and Moslem tradition. In Gothic art, when the sacred and the profane, even the vulgar, meet as close neighbours, a great number of wild and fantastic creatures, monsters, monks and nuns, jugglers and beggars, invade the margins of the pages of psalters, books of hours, and prayer books.[2] But while some of the instruments and ensembles are products of fancy, others are realistic depictions, rich in information about a period from which very few actual instruments have survived.

Musical angels, other than apocalyptical, enter the scene with the spread of the *Legenda aurea*, when legends of the saints and Marianic topics, especially the Assumption and the Coronation (the themes most conducive to the portrayal of large angel orchestras), prevail, and also appear later, chiefly in the Venetian realm, with the *sacre conversazioni* and their small ensembles or single angels playing the lute, the lira da braccio, and occasionally other instruments.

Of the biblical musicians, Renaissance imagery retains King David playing psaltery, harp, or, with the end of the 15th century, more often the lira da braccio. Of secular musical figures, the symbolic representation of Musica as one of the liberal arts is retained. At the same time, competing with the countless angel concerts, the mythological musicians of the ancient Greco-Roman world reappear on the scene: Apollo with the kithara; Hermes with the lyre he invented; Pallas Athena with her creation, the aulos;[3] Orpheus playing in Hades or for the beasts; and the Muses, particularly Erato, Euterpe, and Calliope. The publication of the *Ovidio metamorphoseos volgare* (Venice, 1497) stimulated countless portrayals of the contests between Apollo and his musical rivals Pan and Marsyas, in Lombard, Venetian, and Tuscan paintings, woodcuts, engravings, and plaquettes. The models for the instruments were found in ancient statues, sarcophagi, and other reliefs, greedily and systematically collected by the Renaissance connoisseurs, and copied, sometimes with great precision and thorough archaeological understanding, but more often misunderstood and distorted, or stylized and decorated with free pictorial fancy. True musical archaeology blended with strange misconceptions; Sappho, for instance, was credited with the invention of the fiddle bow, and etymology added to this confusion: 'lira' meant the ancient lyre as well as the lira da braccio,[4] and 'cetra' the ancient kithara as well as the contemporary cittern. Consequently,

---

[1] See Chapter 3 below.

[2] I have attempted an analysis of musical drolleries in the Hours of Jeanne d'Évreux, painted *c.* 1325 by Jean Pucelle, in Chapter 10 below.

[3] See Chapter 12 below.   [4] See Chapter 5 below.

Apollo, Orpheus, King David, and the allegorical Musica are now shown, more often than not, playing contemporary lire da braccio. Similarly, the diaulos is frequently replaced by contemporary wind instruments, usually double recorders, sometimes two shawms (as in a print by Giulio Romano), and the highest degree of pictorial fancy is reached in those paintings which evidently are renderings of scenes from stage plays or *intermedii*, and which portray fantastic instruments that are not functional, but rather, in all probability, stage props.[1] The greatest precision in the rendering of instruments is reached in the *sacre conversazioni* and the intarsias, the life-size portrayals of musical instruments in the choir stalls of Italian churches, in door panels of palaces, and especially in the studioli of Federigo da Montefeltro in Urbino and Gubbio.[2]

In reviewing 19th- and 20th-century achievements in musical iconology, it would be overly optimistic to believe that they are all better or more careful in method than their predecessors, although they are based on an incomparably greater wealth of source material. They often take pictures at face value, without critical discrimination between real and imaginary objects; without sufficient regard for successive styles, technical peculiarities, and mannerisms of pictorial representations; without an awareness of the artist's lack of freedom, during certain periods, in choosing his topic and often even in delineating his objects; without sufficient familiarity with the theological or political doctrines which controlled allegorical representation and therefore detracted from faithful adherence to the actual appearance of the object. Furthermore, they frequently take a pitiful handful of depictions as adequate evidence, ignoring the possibility that these may be atypical or that the rarity or profusion of certain pictorial representations may not at all correspond to the actual historical distribution of instruments and ensembles, or to actual performing practices. Last, but not least, they do not take sufficient account of the fact that the image of an object may not have been drawn directly from the object itself, but copied from a picture of it, and this again from another, resulting sometimes in a chain of successive copies reaching back, often through centuries, up to the point of complete denaturalization of the original object (see Pl. 1, a–d).

An enumeration of typical pitfalls and misunderstandings may help to illustrate these flaws in method.

In the interpretation of medieval illuminated manuscripts, two diverging

---

[1] See Chapter 16 below.

[2] See Chapters 8 and 9 below; also my article *Alcune rappresentazioni di antichi strumenti italiani a tastiera*, in *Collectanea historiae musicae*, II (1956), 465–73.

lines coming from a person's mouth, with a horned head issuing from the open end of the tube thus formed, have been taken for a wind instrument, when actually they symbolize a curse — in the fashion of the balloon in modern comic strips — and the horned head is none other than Satan's.

Likewise, in ignorance of traditional allegories, wind instruments have been seen in the four corners of illuminations in 12th-century Beatus MSS, where actually the artist was suggesting the airstreams issuing forth from the mouths of 'the four winds of the earth held back by angels' (Rev. 7: 1).

Angel orchestras depicted in *trecento* and *quattrocento* art have been accepted as true ensembles, whereas often the traditional requirements of compositional symmetry have led to the mirror-like duplication of such visually conspicuous shapes as trumpets, organetti, and the like. For instance, in Pl. 1e the representation of four trumpets pitted against a few soft string instruments should be taken *cum grano salis*.

Similarly, homogeneous angel orchestras consisting of musicians all playing the same type of instrument — for instance, all lutes, or all organettos — have been taken at face value, whereas actually the depiction was of an allegorical nature. Similar misconceptions were provoked by the frequent allegorical representation of Psalm 150, of which Luca della Robbia's cantoria in the Museo del Duomo in Florence is a famous example. There, the various groups of angels, one playing trumpets, another psalteries, and so forth, are literal illustrations of the verses of the psalm, 'Laudate eum in sono tubae, laudate eum in psalterio,' and have nothing to do with actual ensembles. Even the combination of portative, lute, and harp is only an illustration of the words 'Laudate eum in chordis et organo.' Nevertheless, Arnold Schering accepted this relief as the depiction of an actual ensemble.[1]

Sometimes even the most crucial questions of organology have been 'solved' by erroneous interpretation of pictorial evidence. A flagrant case in point is the attribution of the first fiddle bow in the Occident to the Carolingian period by Curt Sachs and, following his lead, Georg Kinsky and, still more recently, even *Die Musik in Geschichte und Gegenwart*.[2] The basis for this dating is the illustration of Psalm 108 in the Utrecht Psalter (Pl. 17a). Here the psalmist carries two instruments: a long-necked cittern in his left hand and a harp on his left shoulder. The long stick is not a bow, but a measuring rod — 'exsurge psalterium' (the harp) 'et cythara' (the long-necked cittern) 'et dividam Sicimam et convallem tabernaculorum dimeciar' (I will divide Sichem and mete out the valley of the tabernacles). Regrettably, the Latin text has been ignored, and the

---

[1] *Studien zur Musikgeschichte der Frührenaissance*, Leipzig, 1913, p. 59.

[2] Sachs, *Handbuch der Musikinstrumentenkunde*, Leipzig, 1920, p. 171; Kinsky, *Geschichte der Musik in Bildern*, Leipzig, 1929, p. 32; *Die Musik in Geschichte und Gegenwart*, IV, 158, Ill. 4.

incorrect interpretation made plausible by showing only one-third of the meting rod in the illustrations.[1]

The illustrations in the Utrecht Psalter, as well as in a great many other psalters and illuminated manuscripts, have also been erroneously accepted as evidence of 'contemporary' instruments, whereas these manuscripts are often links in a long chain of successive copies. The Utrecht Psalter, though written in Carolingian times, is derived from a manuscript pre-dating it by three hundred years. No botanist would uncritically accept literally the evidence of *herbaria* — again, copies of copies — but organologists do just this. Even today the precise dating of many early medieval manuscripts is controversial, and caution is required in accepting their illuminations as illustrations of contemporary life.

One might perhaps expect that this practice of copying copies, with its resulting accumulation of distortions, would have come to an end with the invention of the printing process, which offered, for the first time in the history of civilization, the means of reproducing visual statements with a high degree of accuracy. However, while this invention was of enormous value to scientific publications, it did not have the same impact on the arts for the simple reason that the exact repetition of a particular object or, in a more general sense, of so-called visual reality, is not necessarily the artist's goal. Even those prints which copied frescoes or paintings soon after their completion often simplified or distorted certain objects for the sake of popularization. I will mention here only two outstanding examples among many: Raphael, in his *Parnassus* in the Stanza della Segnatura, based the rendering of Sappho and the Muses on thorough archaeological research, and borrowed their instruments from the famous Sarcophagus of the Muses, which was long in the Palazzo Mattei and is now in the Museo Nazionale in Rome. But when Marcantonio Raimondi made an engraving of it, he preferred to replace the true ancient musical instruments with banal and stylized specimens.[2] Similarly, Raphael's famous painting of Saint Cecilia in San Petronio in Bologna appears distorted in Marcantonio's engraving and deprived of its original meaning. In Raphael's painting, the instruments lying at the feet of the saint have been broken and the angels in heaven engage solely in vocal music, while in the engraving, the instruments are intact and the angels blast away blithely with fiddle and harp.

Even after the invention of the printing process, distortions of illustrations

---

[1] Friedrich Behn's *Musikleben im Altertum und frühen Mittelalter*, Stuttgart, 1954, reproduces, in Tafel 95, a larger section of the page from the Utrecht Psalter, showing the whole length of the rod, which is substantially longer than the player himself. Nevertheless, in the text (pp. 162–63), he regards this as the first evidence of bowing in Europe; from the excessive length of the clumsy bow, he concludes that 'in the middle of the 9th century, that is, at the time of the origin of this Psalter, bowing had just been introduced.'

[2] See Chapter 14 below.

accumulated through successive copies, due to the fact that woodblocks and copper plates for engraving wear out and must be replaced or reworked; too, authors borrowing illustrations from earlier treatises had to employ draughtsmen, and their drawings were again inevitably altered by the engraver. Examples of this progressive distortion may be seen in Pls. 88a, 88b, 82a, and Fig. 2.

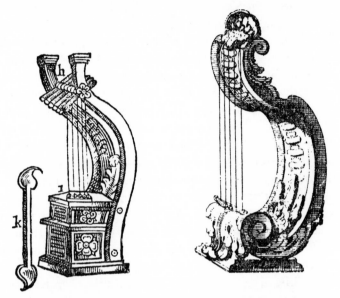

Fig. 2. LEFT: Kithara. From Mersenne, *Harmonie universelle*, 1636. RIGHT: The same kithara, in a later stylized version. From *Gravures en lettres, en géographie, et en musique*, in the *Encyclopédie ou dictionnaire raisonné*, 1751–65.

The study of Egyptian instruments and music through their pictorial representations has been comparatively free of such misinterpretations, because Egyptian archaeology began much later than classical archaeology, and with the immediate unearthing of an enormous wealth of precise representations in sculpture, relief, and wall paintings, as well as the excavation of a substantial number of well-preserved actual instruments from dry, sealed burial chambers. Of course, musicologists had been interested in the music of the Egyptians long before the large bulk of excavated treasures was available; Athanasius Kircher (*Oedipus aegyptiacus*, 1652, Bk. IV, Ch. 13, p. 426) mentions a 'lyra triangularis, von einem egyptischen Basrelief genommen'; and Burney, in his *General History of Music* (Vol. I, p. 204 ff.), includes a very large engraving of an Egyptian 'lute,' reporting that he had seen this instrument on the Egyptian obelisk lying in the Campus Martius in Rome, and that he had a drawing of it made under his very eyes. He also devotes almost two pages to the explanation of this instrument. This drawing then found its way into Forkel's *Allgemeine Geschichte der Musik*

(Vol. I, Ch. 2, p. 83). This 'lute,' however, is nothing else than a very common Egyptian hieroglyph, meaning 'good,' which uses an ideogram based on the shape of the windpipe joined to the heart!

One extremely frequent misnomer concerns ancient woodwind instruments. One can hardly blame classical archaeologists for calling ancient oboes 'flutes,' as they do when confronted with auloi and diauloi, but the same is often done by historians of music; even in Robert Haas's admirably illustrated *Aufführungs-praxis der Musik*, Potsdam, 1932, double-reed pipes in Egyptian paintings are captioned 'Doppelflöte' (p. 5, Ill. 4; p. 9, Ill. 6).

Another source of bewilderment, a veritable *richesse d'embarras*, are pictures of early reed instruments, which are often interpreted as brass instruments — or, to use the more pretentious term, lip-vibrated aerophones — whenever the reeds are invisible. In the playing of early double-reed instruments with pirou-ettes, such as the shawms, the reeds were sometimes held, not between the lips, but rather in the cavity of the mouth, producing the same stiff tone that is peculiar to instruments with wind caps, such as the crumhorn. It is obvious that such a misinterpretation leads to a total misunderstanding of the timbre of these instruments.

Other frequent misunderstandings have arisen in the case of the flood of allegorical subjects in engravings of the late Northern Renaissance and the early Baroque, as for instance in the many religious musical allegories engraved by Antwerp artists beginning with the end of the 16th century, and above all, in the *Encomium musices* (Antwerp, c. 1595). Exact reproduction of the instruments is not the main concern of the draughtsman; the more striking or interesting the shape of the instrument, and the more varied and colourful the ensemble, the more attractive the composition. Yet such prints are frequently accepted as the gospel truth concerning both the instruments and their combination. Robert Haas reproduces one of these engravings, *Die Musik* by Philipp Galle, in his chapter on *Verzierungspraxis* (*op. cit.*, p. 115). The 'lutes' are downright fantastic; the 'zink' is no zink, but apparently a shawm, but with its protective cylinder in the wrong place, close to its bell; the harp has one of those undulating 'scrolliferous' frames, lacking any soundbox; and the strings care neither whence they come, nor where they go.

Finally, one of the most widespread misinterpretations of instruments in pictorial representations should be mentioned: that of small keyboard instru-ments. Surprisingly, this happens even with woodcuts and engravings, although as a rule the printmakers take the trouble to indicate such unmistakable features as the jackrail[1] of a virginal or spinetto and the typical curvature of the keys of

---

[1] See the *Musica* engraved after Frans Floris, reproduced in R. Haas, *op. cit.*, p. 132, Ill. 55, where the virginal is called a clavichord.

a fretted clavichord.[1] Amusingly enough, the reverse also occurs; an author, though himself entirely at home with the intricacies of a clavichord, employs for the illustration a draughtsman unfamiliar with the real mechanism, who copies another illustration and produces a jumble of incoherent curves (Fig. 3).

Fig. 3. LEFT: Woodcut suggesting a clavichord. From Virdung, *Musica getutscht*, 1511. RIGHT: Nonsensical copy of the same woodcut. From Martin Agricola, *Musica instrumentalis deudsch*, 1528, and used later as an illustration in Fétis, *Histoire générale de la musique*, 1869–76.

The information furnished by pictorial sources is by no means restricted to the field of performance practices, and, for the sake of brevity, a tentative tabulation of such data may not be amiss.

A) PERFORMANCE and PERFORMERS (Habits and methods of performance) — 1) Instruments, their shape and construction. 2) Playing methods. 3) Ensembles: *a*) vocal, instrumental and mixed groups; numerical proportions between the constituents; 'loud' and 'soft' instruments; the rules formulated for his time by Praetorius for the grouping of instruments in 'Accorts' or 'Stimmwerke' — these can be reconstructed to some extent by a comparative study of the visual sources. *b*) Use of written music for performance (choir books, part books, scores). *c*) Spatial disposition of performing groups (*cori spezzati*), polychoral music, placing of continuo instruments, etc. 4) Methods of conducting.

B) THE LISTENER — Placement of the audience in church or theatre; habits of acclamation; audience participation in the performance.

C) THE SITE OF PERFORMANCE AND THE ACOUSTICAL ENVIRONMENT — Here, pictures of rooms and halls, palaces and churches, theatres and even gardens no longer in existence are often the only source of information we have about the acoustical conditions of performance.

D) STAGE SETTINGS — Depictions of settings and decorations of church plays,

[1] See the admirably precise woodcut *Die Geschicklichkeit in der Musik* by Hans Burgkmair, in the book *Der Weisskunig* (*c.* 1516), in which the clavichord is seen chiefly from the back, yet sufficiently indicated by just a few curved lines for the keys.

intermedii, and operas are of significance to the modern performance and interpretation of these works.

E) SOCIAL STATUS AND ENVIRONMENT — 1) The social status of performers and instruments; social connotations of certain types of instruments and ensembles (typical high- and low-class instruments and ensembles).[1] 2) The role of the musician in society: court musicians, troubadours, minnesingers, jugglers, and beggars in early illuminations; the poet-musician, the humanist-reciter, and musician portraits in Renaissance art; the virtuoso as the centre of social circles in 18th-century and Romantic art; the professional, the amateur, the dilettante. 3) Types of ensembles and instruments associated by custom or tradition with various public occasions (weddings, funerals, receptions, festivals, *fêtes champêtres, serenate, notturni, cassazioni,* etc.) in contemporary imagery.

F) SYMBOLISM AND ALLEGORY (mystical, religious, erotic, political symbolism) — Here again, the overwhelming wealth of topics makes a systematic tabulation nearly impossible, but a few promising directions of research may be suggested: 1) Association of musical instruments with religious and cosmological beliefs; magical instruments in 'primitive' and Far Eastern art. 2) Instrumental concerts on the walls of Egyptian burial chambers. 3) Instruments symbolic of passion and reason in Greek mythology, philosophy, and educational doctrine (the instruments of Dionysus and Apollo; the symbolic implications of the musical contests between Apollo and Marsyas, Apollo and Pan, between the Muses and the Sirens; the significance of the invention of the aulos by Pallas Athena).[2] 4) Medieval and Renaissance representations of biblical musicians (King David and the elders, with their 'appropriate' instruments; King David with, successively, the lyre, rotta, harp, and lira da braccio). 5) The allegories of Musica from the late Middle Ages to the Baroque, and the instruments in the representation of the *Artes Liberales;* Pythagoras and Tubalcain with their instruments as traditional accompaniment of the allegorical Musica; the organ, clavichord, and harp as the instruments of Saint Cecilia in successive periods of painting.

Pervading all musical cultures is the erotic symbolism of musical instruments, especially of wind instruments and idiophones, traceable in their music and visual representations alike. The following are some outstanding examples: the aulos as the instrument of passion, urges, instincts; the aulos in the entourage of Dionysus, in the hands of satyrs, in drinking parties (Greek vase painting); the Dionysiac connotation of woodwind instruments (reed pipes, vertical flutes) in Renaissance art (as for instance in the woodcuts in the *Hypnerotomachia;* engravings by Marcantonio, Zoan Andrea, Girolamo Mocetto; numerous *trionfi*

---

[1] On instruments gaining and losing caste due to changing fashions, see Chapter 4 below.

[2] For a discussion of some of these questions, see Chapter 12 below.

d'amore; Francesco Cossa's Schifanoia frescoes in Ferrara; the numerous flute lessons, for instance in drawings by Lodovico Caracci (Uffizi), and other music lessons on the lute, theorbo, and virginal in Baroque genre paintings.

A special section of the broad field of the symbolism of musical instruments concerns their specific timbre as indicative of character, temperament, mood, and many other things. A few obvious examples are: 1) the timbre of reed instruments, often with drones, associated with the Nativity, both in painting and in music; 2) the 'heroic' connotation of the trumpet, traceable in the visual sources long before its absorption into oratorio, opera, and symphony; 3) the musical equivalent of the visible halo (for instance, Christ's halo suggested by string timbre in Bach's *St. Matthew Passion* and in the cantatas).

In many periods of art, the portrayal of the visible world, including musical scenes, is not a simple mirror, reflecting objects with photographic precision; rather, it renders or suggests them through various 'stylizations.' The artist is subject to many influences and factors that may interfere, in some measure, with the 'realistic' portrayal of the object. Some of these factors are of a psychological nature, others are rooted in traditions of technique or style, and still others are the result of the social environment in which the artist works. More precisely: 1) he is style-bound, born into a definite tradition with all its pictorial devices, tricks and mannerisms; 2) he is often limited in the choice of his subject, and in the manner of delineating it, by church or secular authorities and by the tastes and predilections of his sponsors and critics; 3) he is limited by his media and tools — stone or terra cotta, canvas or paper, brush or pencil, stained glass or needlework. Also, the two- and three-dimensional realms restrict 'realism' of portrayal in different ways. Depictions on the two-dimensional surface can represent the object from only one angle, and the various types of perspective used by different periods of art to create the illusion of depth must then be interpreted by the style-conscious beholder. Sculpture, on the other hand, does not easily permit the rendering of strings, the hairs of bows, and the like, and either omits these features entirely or suggests them in simplified form (Pl. 11b).

These are truisms, but perhaps worth repeating in view of a certain naiveté often betrayed in the 'reading' of pictures and the exploration of their 'objective content' by historians not steeped in the tricks of illusion that are part and parcel of the visual arts. The aim of the musical iconologist is to 'read' the work of art as a document, to concentrate on its material content and thereby see beyond the devices of stylization; to abstract, as it were, from the work of art just those elements which make it art. To formulate this paradox even more pungently, he should be an art historian, not for art's sake, but for the purpose of concentrating on the core and body of the image by consciously eliminating the subjective, 'disturbing' elements of style.

In selecting some outstanding examples of exact renderings of musical subjects in two-dimensional representations from the last five hundred years of Occidental art alone, one could mention the schools of Van Eyck and Memling; virtually all the Italian painters of *sacre conversazioni*, such as Giovanni Bellini, Carpaccio, Montagna, Fra Bartolomeo, and many more; Holbein's *Ambassadors*, with the famous likeness of a lute, in the National Gallery, London; Jan Bruegel's *Allegory of Hearing* in the Prado, with its nearly complete inventory of early 17th-century instruments; the many still-lifes by Baschenis composed entirely of musical instruments — not to mention the enormous wealth of Netherlandish genre paintings with their virginals, lutes, citterns, and theorbos. Though they all excel in their attention to minute detail and consistent use of linear perspective, they are yet surpassed, if this be possible, by the wood intarsias of 15th- and 16th-century Italy, with their many beautiful instruments.

The problem for the fact-finder is then to interpret the pictures 'correctly,' that is, for his practical purposes, and it may be useful to attempt an approximate tabulation of those factors which cause an image to deviate from 'reality.'

1) *Limitation of the medium of depiction.* For instance, in sculpture, strings are often not detached from the soundboard or fingerboard, or are omitted altogether. In woodcuts, the number of strings is frequently reduced, and other elements, such as pegs, are disproportionately large.

2) *Pictorial style of the period or of the individual painter.* An example would be the finger positions of the musician angels in the Isenheim altarpiece by Mathias Grünewald; an example of typical *chinoise* transformation can be found in Watteau's depiction of a vielle à roue (Pl. 26d).

3) *Carelessness or lack of mechanical or musical understanding.* Pseudo-lyres and harps, non-functional pipes, and many other acoustically impossible instruments, as well as ensembles composed at random and at the painter's fancy, are all too frequent.

4) *Requirements of pictorial composition.* One case in point is symmetry, often imposed by pictorial convention; for instance, the symmetrical duplication of instruments, particularly those of striking appearance such as organettos,[1] trumpets,[2] etc., or even of all instruments,[3] in order to achieve visual balance, at the expense of musical balance. Many examples are found in 14th- and 15th-

---

[1] As, for example, in the *Coronation* of P. and G. Veneziano (1358), Frick Collection, New York.

[2] As in the Florentine choirbook, *c.* 1350, in the Cleveland Museum, where the convincingly balanced string ensemble is overpowered by the flanking pairs of trumpets (Plate 1e).

[3] As in Bernardo Daddi's *Coronation of the Virgin*, Altenburg.

century angel concerts celebrating the Assumption and the Coronation of the Virgin.

5) *'Prettification.'* Rubens, who has no qualms in showing the puffed-out cheeks of a satyr playing the double recorder in his *Silenus* (National Gallery, London), prefers to show the fingers of Saint Cecilia elegantly hovering over the clavichord keys, rather than in the contracted position required. The problem confronting the painter in the conflict between the pleasant and the realistic was already clearly formulated by Giovanni Paolo Lomazzo in his *Trattato dell'arte della pittura, scultura, ed architettura* (1584; Bk. II, Ch. VIII). He recommends reckless realism at the expense of prettiness, an attitude quite remarkable in view of his manneristic leanings.

6) *Symbolic or allegorical significance of the painting.* This is a vast field, whose magnitude can only be suggested by a few examples. Number symbolism is frequent; Apollo's lira da braccio in Raphael's *Parnassus* has nine strings (7 stopped plus 2 open) instead of the customary seven (5 plus 2), thus alluding to Apollo's function as leader of the nine Muses, and possibly referring to the nine modes. Seven identical instruments are found in the hands of the apocalyptic angels and holy men. Number also plays a role in the numerous symbolic depictions of the nine angel choirs, and usually each of the nine groups is homogeneous — that is, devoted to singing or to playing the same type of instrument. In these paintings, the instruments are usually the exact images of contemporary ones, yet the 'homogeneous' ensembles offer no information as to usual ensemble practices. I have already mentioned the role of musical instruments as traditional attributes of mythological figures and saints; a main source of these symbolic connotations is the illustrated emblem books of the late Renaissance.[1]

Under this heading can also be grouped many of the allegorical and fantastic instruments and musical scenes in those paintings that represent or reflect actual stage performances (church plays, *intermedii*, etc.). The function of these instruments can frequently be clarified by the examination of contemporary instructions for the theatre workshop. Among the most important musical allegories in the visual arts are the representations of Musica, Poesia, Harmonia, and Auditus, all with more or less stereotyped attributes. To mention only one: a stag head made into a lyre in Filippino Lippi's *Allegory of Music* (Berlin Museum; Pl. 96b), evidently a variation on that traditional attribute of Musica, the stag, which symbolized velocity of sound.

7) *Archaic aims.* In periods of revival such as the Carolingian era and the 14th and 15th centuries, the artist will often fuse ancient models with actual objects taken from his contemporary environment. A characteristic case is that of the

---

[1] For the symbolism of the lira da braccio, see Chapter 5; for that of the bagpipe, see Chapter 4.

wind instrument held by Euterpe in Raphael's *Parnassus* (Plate 83). To comply
with the archaeological ambitions of the time, it has the typical protuberances of
the ancient Roman tibia, but at the same time it has the mouthcup and bell of a
trumpet, the traditional attribute of Fama. This purposeful blending of two
different mythological notions is, of course, acoustical nonsense.

8) *The fantastic.* Bizarre performances and instruments abound in the drolleries
found in illuminated prayer books of 13th- and 14th-century Flanders, France,
and England, and later in the Italian grotesques of the *cinquecento*. The works of
Bosch and Peter Bruegel teem with demonic and humorous musicians and
instruments. These depictions are often symptomatic of popular customs. One
should also mention at this point musical caricatures, as well as satirical
paintings and prints, pamphlets, and broadsides, some of which are full of
information about the social status and political connotations of certain instruments.

In Italian Renaissance painting, especially in the large angel concerts, one
often finds instruments that appear fantastic, and it sometimes requires more
than a glance to establish whether they are: *a*) actual but rare instruments; *b*)
common instruments, but smothered in Renaissance decor; *c*) instruments
created *ad hoc* by the painter's brush, but nevertheless acoustically feasible (e.g.
Pl. 21c); or, *d*) instruments which are grotesque inventions with no basis in
reality. All of these types occur simultaneously, for instance, in Gaudenzio
Ferrari's magnificent angel concert in the cupola of the Santuario in Saronno.

Other important factors that may blur the reliability of the visual document
are spoiling due to time, and falsification due to inept restoration. Many telling
details are often distorted or overpainted through a lack of understanding or a
desire to 'prettify.' Unfortunately, the more famous the work of art, the greater
the chance that it has been restored and possibly altered. The organologist in
search of accurate documentation would often do better to go to out-of-the-way
museums, which have less money for restoration, and see the correct shapes
through layers of time-darkened varnish.

In addition to these factors impeding accuracy of portrayal, we must be
aware that the popularity of certain instruments and musical practices is not
necessarily reflected by their frequency of depiction in art. This is particularly
true of periods in which most of the visual arts were of a religious nature. In such
periods, folk music or secular court music had fewer chances of representation.
Furthermore, large quantities of sculpture and painting have been destroyed by
iconoclasm, war, and natural catastrophe.

In conclusion, and in view of the rapidly growing availability of pictorial
sources, I should like to suggest at least a few *desiderata* for iconological research:

1) Critical interpretation with awareness of all the factors that might possibly have blurred the faithful delineation of the objects depicted.

2) Methodic evaluation of pictorial evidence, not in single isolated instances, but on the widest possible comparative basis, taking into account a reliable number of parallel cases, and making due allowance for contemporary local or regional variations in instrument building or playing habits.

3) Systematic distinction between functional and non-functional elements of instruments, and between those non-functional ones that are derived from decorative fashions or from atrophic remnants of once functional elements (carried through the centuries by the sheer force of habit or tradition).[1] Such distinction might help to pave the way for a morphological view of instruments throughout their gradual evolution.

Finally, I might suggest a few topics for research and discussion:

1) A comparative study of Near-Eastern parallels to the musical scenes in illuminations of the Carolingian period, especially in the Utrecht Psalter.

2) A new search for the origin of bowing in the Occident.[2]

3) The survival or revival of double-pipes in the Middle Ages and the Renaissance, and the question of the perpetuation of aulos practice in the double-oboe and double-recorder.

4) A study of the irruption of large and varied angel concerts into painting and sculpture with the rising popularity of Marian subjects (especially the Assumption, Ascension, Coronation, Mary in Glory), and a systematic investigation of the extent to which their instrumental ensembles are symptomatic of the contemporary evolution of polyphony.

5) The examination of Renaissance and early Baroque paintings to establish those scenes which are based upon actual or planned stage performances.

6) Re-investigation of the early history of the violin, especially through its documentation in frescoes and other art media, long before its regular production in more or less standardized shapes by the dynasties of the famous builders.

---

[1] I have tried to follow this method in Chapter 3 below.

[2] Since this was written, the excellent book of Werner Bachmann, *Die Anfänge des Streichinstrumentenspiels*, Leipzig, 1964, has filled this gap.

2 · The Knowledge of Musical Instruments as an Aid to the Art Historian

Nearly all the studies assembled in this book deal to one degree or another with musical instruments and instrumental practices as illustrated in painting and the other visual arts. In some instances, the paintings furnish valuable documentation for the organologist, showing instruments and the way in which they were played during periods from which few or no instruments have survived, or instruments which are valuable for comparison with specimens still existing. In other instances, the paintings permit us to draw conclusions about the current popularity of instruments, their religious significance, or their function as embodiments of symbolic meaning — for instance, the mythological connotations of certain instruments relating to Apollo, Dionysus, and others.

But whereas the visual arts present a gold mine of information for the organologist, the art historian, on the other hand, can draw manifold information for his purposes from the kinds of instruments, their players, their grouping, etc. Often the instruments represented provide trustworthy clues for dating a picture, since the invention of many musical instruments can be dated precisely — a fact which, fortunately, has been often unknown to even the most prudent and knowledgeable of forgers. One striking instance may be mentioned here. During the last war, the owner of a beautiful Dutch painting, apparently by Vermeer, came to my office at the Metropolitan Museum to ask advice about it. If anything was wrong with the picture, it was that it was too much Vermeer. It showed an old bearded beggar in a cloak whose folds half concealed a coiled metal horn. But the horn had valves, and valves, as any connoisseur of wind instruments knows, were invented in the 1830s. If the owner of the picture had publicized this information, the Van Meegeren scandal might have broken several years earlier than it did. Likewise, the inexpert stringing of a harp may contradict the attribution of a painting to an artist who is known to have been a connoisseur of music. Or the appearance of a drone string on a half-hidden instrument may reveal it as a lira da braccio, that aristocrat among polyphonic instruments — and reveal its player, dressed as a peasant, to be Apollo, participating in a pastoral masquerade. Or, to mention still another example, the appearance of pseudo-ancient instruments may prompt the interpretation of a Renaissance painting as one actually representing a stage performance of a mythological subject.[1]

An instrument depicted in a work of art may offer a clue to its interpretation if the instrument is an accepted attribute, or symbol, of the identity or status of a figure in the representation. Characteristic features of such instruments are often quite small or inconspicuous, but still, to the contemporary eye, the merest hint sufficed. We who come later need to acquire the knowledge that the artist took for granted. Beginning with the last decades of the *quattrocento*, most gods and heroes with a musical education, and likewise humanists and reciting poets, would have disdained anything other than the noble polyphonic lira da braccio. The same is true of the most elevated and sophisticated angels in the Venetian *sacre conversazioni*, and also of King David (King David with a psaltery, as in Raphael's *Disputà*, is one of the rare exceptions). There were many historical reasons for this, not the least important of which was the name 'lira,' harking back to the lyre of antiquity; in addition, its free-running, unstopped strings recalled those of the ancient lyre. The fact that bowing was unknown in Greek and Roman antiquity did not disturb Renaissance painters, stage designers, or musical historians because at that time the invention of the bow was attributed to Sappho; and did not statues and reliefs of Apollo and the Muses show them using large plectra — something, one might think, like bows?

The most outstanding functional characteristics of the lira da braccio are the drone strings (*bordoni*), which run outside the fingerboard and are held away from it by a little piece of wood that projects from one side of the peg box.[2] In Giovanni Bellini's *Feast of the Gods*, we can see only the small and rather inconspicuous shoulder of a string instrument held by one of the feasting peasants (Pl. 2). Yet the drone strings of a lira da braccio are clearly visible (Pl. 3a). No peasant plays a lira da braccio — the player must be Apollo, the only god who has this attribute. Thus a minute line, or a double line, can reveal a masquerade of the gods.[3]

In a drawing by Luca da Cambiaso (No. 13726F, Gabinetto dei Disegni, Uffizi), a naked youth holds a fiddle and a bow, the instrument only cursorily drawn and with no strings marked (Pl. 3b). But a short dark little line appears above the upper rim of its head. A word to the wise . . . ; it is the wedge for the

[1] See Chapter 16 below.

[2] See Chapter 5 below for a full description of the lira da braccio.

[3] See my article, *A Lira da Braccio in Giovanni Bellini's 'Feast of the Gods,'* in *The Art Bulletin*, XXVIII (1946), 114, where I tried to unfold the meaning of the whole painting as a feast of the gods, basing this interpretation on the presence of a lira da braccio. Later, two books concurred with my interpretation: Edgar Wind, *Bellini's Feast of the Gods*, Cambridge, Mass., 1948; and John Walker, *Bellini and Titian at Ferrara*, London, 1956.

drones of a lira da braccio. The youth is Apollo, since Orpheus is excluded for other iconological reasons.

If a little projection on the head of an instrument is the clue to its identification, this is because of the functional importance of this projecting part. But even a non-functional part of an instrument may be the salient feature for its correct symbolic interpretation. This is the case with a string instrument represented in Agostino di Duccio's reliefs in the Cappella delle Arti Liberali and the Cappella dei Planeti in the Tempio Malatestiano in Rimini. The instrument, a *quattrocento* cittern or cetra as revealed by the two little projections where the neck meets the body, appears in almost identical shape three times,[1] twice carried by gods and once by an allegorical figure, Musica.[2] One of the gods in the Chapel of the Planets is Mercury (Pl. 4a). Besides the cittern, he has all the attributes associated with him in traditional iconography:[3] the caduceus with the serpents, the winged feet, the rooster, and (less conventionally) the souls whose guide he is; they crawl between his feet and even try to climb the caduceus.

If we turn to the Chapel of the Liberal Arts, we find an instrument similar to that of Mercury, here held by Apollo (Pl. 4b). The god appears well equipped with his traditional attributes: bow and quiver, one arrow, and the birds. His instrument, however, differs in some respects from that of Mercury. Its head, decorated by a little carved *putto* face, is hidden by leaves, in fact by a whole cluster of laurel leaves, from which emerge the naked figures of the three Graces.[4]

Also in the Cappella delle Arti Liberali is the wonderful Allegory of Music. She is singing and holding two instruments, one a flute à bec and the other, again, a cetra (Pl. 5a). So here all the main realms of music are represented: voice, string instruments, and wind instruments. This cetra is the most elaborate and beautiful of the three represented in these reliefs (Pl. 5b). Its upper end terminates in a carved boy's head, and the soundboard is decorated in elegant,

[1] In the literature on Duccio, the instrument is not mentioned or is misunderstood, not only in Andy Pointner's *Die Werke des florentinischen Bildhauers: Agostino di Duccio*, Strasbourg, 1909, but also in the excellent description of Duccio's reliefs in Amico Ricci, *Storia dell'architettura in Italia*, Macerata, 1834. Pointner calls all these instruments, anachronistically, 'mandolins' (p. 97). Ricci calls them — in spite of their obvious identity — once a lyre in the shape of a viola (p. 467), another time 'cetra in forma di mandola' (p. 529), and finally simply 'mandola' (p. 533).

[2] Jean Seznec, in *La Survivance des dieux antiques*, London, 1940, p. 120, quotes from the *Comentarii* of Pius II the reproach directed to Sigismondo Malatesta about the paganism in the Church of San Francesco da Rimini (Tempio Malatestiano): 'He filled it with pagan works to such an extent that it appears to be a temple not so much of Christians as of infidels who worship demons' (*Comentarii*, p. 51).

[3] See, for instance, Natalis Comes, *Mythologia*, Bk. V, Ch. 5; Vincenzo Cartari, *Imagini dei dei degli antichi*, in the chapter 'Mercurius.'

[4] The Graces in Apollo's hand are taken over by Cartari, *Imagini*, 1571 ed.

extremely flat relief,[1] with tendrils among which are set two medallions having profile views of Sigismondo Malatesta and Isotta (whose glory, more than that of God, the whole temple appears to celebrate).

The iconologist, guided by the emblematic literature of the Renaissance and the results of modern scholarship,[2] may wonder what these strange little long-necked instruments have to do or to say when they appear in the hands of mythological personages, especially since they seem to be a world apart from the authentic and genuine instruments that were associated with certain gods and muses in antiquity — the kithara and the lyre. The cetra, as we have seen it in the hands of these three figures, was, in Duccio's time, a small instrument that, unlike the lute, had a shallow body made with a flat soundboard, a flat back, and side walls whose depth diminished from top to bottom. The body, in fact, recalled that of an ancient kithara, even to the projection at the lower end, corresponding to the more pronounced base of the kithara. The strings ran in pairs, and were usually struck with a plectrum. We mentioned above the two little projections at the shoulders, and one is tempted to ask what their function was. The answer is that they had no musical function whatever. They did not help in the playing nor in carrying the instrument. They are atrophic remains of the arms that carried the yoke or crossbar in the ancient kithara, and to which were fastened the upper ends of the strings.

It may seem strange, if not fantastic, to consider these two little pieces of wood as a sort of crystallized memory of a past at least nine centuries back. Yet an exploration of the history of the cittern, especially in its pictorial representations, reveals a gradual transformation of the arms of the ancient Roman kithara.[3] It was, in fact, a process of gradual shrinking, down to the inconspicuous remnants that survive in Duccio's citterns. These projections are not the only reminiscences of the ancient kithara. The instrument was struck by a plectrum, in the ancient kithara technique, and it often had a rudimentary base, as we mentioned above. Last but not least, there was the name, derived from the Latin 'cithara.' 'Cetra' thus meant cithara (kithara) to the *quattrocento*; a cetra in the hands of mythological persons was the legitimate substitute for the kithara, just as the lira (later, in the *cinquecento*, called lira da braccio) was the substitute for the lyre of the ancients.

---

[1] Such carving of the soundboard is not altogether imaginary. Actual instruments with such decoration existed, although there was always the danger that a soundboard thick enough for such modelling would not easily vibrate. An outstanding example, with no noticeable acoustical handicap, is the richly carved lira da braccio by Giovanni d'Andrea, now in the Kunsthistorisches Museum, Vienna (Pl. 31g).

[2] For the literature on iconology, see:
Erwin Panofsky, *Meaning in the Visual Arts*, New York, 1955; *Studies in Iconology*, London, 1939.
Jean Seznec, *La Survivance des dieux antiques*, London, 1940; English transl. by Barbara F. Sessions, as *The Survival of the Ancient Gods*, New York, 1953.

[3] For the history of the cittern, see Chapter 3 below.

If visual representations of musical instruments can be helpful in dating works of art, they share this quality with many other artifacts such as pottery, costumes, and carpets, all of which are reliable guides. But musical instruments can be helpful in still another way. They are often depicted not just as isolated decorative objects, but are held in the hands of players; and there are certain methods and fashions of blowing, plucking, bowing, and stopping strings or fingerholes, characteristic of various phases in the history of instrumental music. The contemporary painter is, of course, familiar with these methods; he may have been a musician himself, or have watched performers. Here I would recall the delineation of the bowing and stopping hands in Raphael's famous drawing of a player of the lira da braccio (possibly the famous virtuoso San Secondo; see Pl. 84b) as a study for the Apollo in the *Parnassus* of the Segnatura; or the finger position of the keyboard player in Titian's *The Concert* (Pitti Gallery, Florence).

One word of caution must be added here. 'Erroneous' instruments or playing methods can not always be taken as contradicting the authenticity or dating of a painting: one need only recall the mannered, theatrical, and highly 'unrealistic' way in which the angels in Mathias Grünewald's Isenheim altarpiece bow their fiddles, or the reversed shape of the beautiful organetto which seems to glide out of the hands of Saint Cecilia in Raphael's altarpiece in San Petronio in Bologna. (Normally the upper contour of an organetto descends from the longest bass pipe, at the left, towards the smallest treble pipe at the right, but this oblique line would have disturbed Raphael's composition.) Often, too, the art historian has to bear in mind that what looks unnatural to us may have been functional at some earlier time. A modern organist would never be called upon to bend his wrist sideways as players of Renaissance organettos do. They could not help it; in order to pump the bellows with the left hand, they had to hold one end of the instrument (that with the bass pipes) against their chests, and this in turn caused the awkward bend of the right hand pressing the keys or pushing the buttons, as in the case of the angel playing the organetto in Hans Memling's altarpiece for Najera.

The representation of a player's hand and fingers is a delicate task, requiring absolutely fastidious exactness and scrupulous observation; even a slight deviation in the design may result in functional nonsense. Unmusical distortions of this kind may be warning signals to the art critic, and perhaps lead to an investigation. An interesting allegorical painting attributed to Jan van Hemessen (Pl. 91) includes a musician with fiddle and bow. His right hand, holding the bow, is stiff and awkwardly bent, with the knuckles of three fingers resting on the ground and the index finger rigidly extended along the stick of the bow. No fiddler, even pausing in playing, would hold the bow in such a way. The suspicious art historian will look for an explanation, and with good fortune he will find that the whole figure is borrowed from that of the shepherd in Titian's *Three Ages of Man* (National Gallery, Edinburgh; see Pl. 90); there the shepherd, holding a little recorder, rests his right hand leisurely on the ground. Hemessen grafted the bow into a hand originally bent for quite a different purpose.[1]

Apart from musical instruments as mythological attributes, or as symbols of the social level (such as instruments belonging to angels, courtiers, peasants, beggars and jugglers), sexual symbolism is involved, especially with certain wind instruments. Such symbolism is based on their suggestive shapes, often on their intoxicating sounds, and frequently on both. From defloration and initiation flutes, taboo to women in the so-called primitive civilizations,[2] up to the intoxicating, reedy saxophone of our days (or nights), there runs an unbroken tradition of magic, religious, or poetic notions, all crediting certain wind instruments with sexual connotations and regarding them as symbols of fertility, birth, and rebirth.[3] The rapidly growing modern literature on primitive civilizations, especially on the ethnology of musical instruments and on folk music, is full of cases in point. The *locus classicus* in antiquity is Plato's warning against the use of the aulos in education.[4] And Hemingway, in *A Farewell to Arms*, reports on serenades in the Abruzzi in which flutes were forbidden: 'Why, I asked. Because it was bad for the girls to hear the flute at night.'[5]

Although these facts are well known and have been amply discussed, it seems curious how little modern iconology has drawn on them for the interpretation of paintings. The auloi in hundreds of scenes of revelry on Greek vases, and the countless vertical flutes represented in paintings of music lessons in Italian, French, and Dutch genre painting up to the Rococo, speak an eloquent and rather obvious language. But still, art historians have often misunderstood or even disregarded the meaning and importance of the flute in some very famous paintings of the Italian Renaissance. While the flute is not part of the official, conventional, pictorial idiom or language of symbols as codified in the iconological, mythographical, and emblematic treatises such as those by Ripa, Cartari, and Natalis Comes, it nonetheless appears so frequently as a conspicuous and unequivocal accessory in paintings with amorous topics that there can be no doubt about its connotation.[6]

[1] See Chapter 15 below.

[2] André Schaeffner, *Origine des instruments de musique*, Paris, 1936, p. 240 ff.

[3] See, for instance, Curt Sachs, *Geist und Werden der Musikinstrumente*, Berlin, 1929; the various investigations of Jaap Kunst; Schaeffner, *op. cit.*

[4] See Chapter 12 below.

[5] This passage was quoted in Curt Sachs's classic chapter on early flutes, in *The History of Musical Instruments*, New York, 1940, p. 45.

[6] 'Lascivious sound' has occasionally been imputed to other wind instruments as well; for instance, to the cornetto, a wind instrument that consisted of a wooden tube with side holes like a flute and a cup-shaped mouthpiece like that of a trumpet. Benvenuto Cellini, in his *Auto-*

Whether the representation of pipes implies an intentional borrowing from ancient sources, a case of humanist revival of ancient customs (as, for instance, instruments taken over from aulos scenes), is not an easy question to answer. Sometimes it is the aulos itself that appears in Renaissance painting and sculpture, copied from Roman sarcophagi. More often, this instrument is represented in mythological scenes by such substitutes as a pair of trumpets or a pair of *pifferi* (early Italian reed pipes) — that is, by instruments that were part of contemporary musical life in the Renaissance, but which could be arranged in the composition so that they gave the impression of double pipes diverging in aulos fashion.[1] They were represented as being played by two different people, or sometimes by a single person — which, in the case of trumpets, was of course nonsense. But most frequent of all substitutes for the aulos was the *flauto dolce* (also known as the recorder, or fipple flute), which happened to be a bucolic[2] as well as an art instrument.[3] We will restrict ourselves here to the flauto dolce and to three groups of examples that may interest art historians because they are well-known paintings: one of the Schifanoia paintings, Titian's Arcadian paintings, and an allegorical *tondo* by Veronese.

Among the *trionfi* from the frescoes by Francesco Cossa in the Palazzo Schifanoia, in Ferrara, is one of Venus.[4] It is filled to the brim with traditional astrological and mythological symbols, medieval as well as pagan — swans, rabbits, the Graces, Cupid — so many of them that it is almost surprising that they enhance rather than disturb the complex and graceful composition. In the foreground at the extreme right is a group of young people (Pl. 6a) — a pair kneeling in a tender embrace while the large group of their companions, young men and women, stand in a half-circle around them, watching seriously and curiously.[5] The girls at the extreme left and right each carry a lute, but the girl in the centre is holding, directly over the amorous couple, a pair of flauti dolci,

---

biography, reports that his father, an experienced maker of wind instruments, tried unsuccessfully to instruct his son in the use of the 'lascivissimo cornetto.'

[1] See, for instance, Filippino Lippi (Pl. 94c), or the *tondo* showing a sacrificial scene by Giulio Romano in the Sala dei Venti of the Palazzo del Tè, Mantua, where two large pifferi, blown by two men side by side, produce the appearance of a double pipe.

[2] See, for example, the satyr playing a recorder in double aulos fashion in Rubens's *Triumph of Silenus* (London, National Gallery).

[3] On the recorder as an art instrument, see Sachs, *The History of Musical Instruments*, p. 302 ff. Sachs mentions that King Henry VIII, in 1547, left no less than 77 recorders in a collection of 381 instruments.

[4] On the importance and symbolic content of the Schifanoia frescoes, see Aby M. Warburg, *Italienische Kunst und internationale Astrologie im Palazzo Schifanoia zu Ferrara*, in his *Gesammelte Schriften*, Leipzig, 1932, II, 471; and Jean Seznec, *op. cit.*, p. 175. However, neither author deals with the musical instruments.

[5] Philipp Fehl, in a very interesting article, *The Hidden Genre: A Study of the Concert Champêtre in the Louvre*, in *Journal of Aesthetics and Art Criticism*, XVI/2 (Dec. 1957), 153, refers briefly to this

reminiscent of the auloi. The iconophile, confronted by the attributes of Venus in the same fresco, will not regard the flauti dolci as accidental.

Among bucolic scenes with flauti dolci are Titian's Arcadian landscapes and one of his paintings of Venus. In the centre of his Giorgionesque *Concert champêtre*, in the Louvre (Pl. 7), two youths in rich apparel are in conversation. In the foreground at their left and right are two nude women. The youth at the left holds a lute, but he is not playing it. Of the women, only the one on the right holds an instrument, a flauto dolce, and, again, she is not playing it. The young men do not pay any visible attention to the women.[1] It seems remarkable that it is one of the men who holds the noble lute, while the less decorous, not to say unladylike, wind instrument is held by a girl.

In Titian's *Three Ages of Man*, a pair of flauti dolci, in aulos fashion, forms the centre of the group in the foreground (Pl. 90). In the background an old man, sitting among skulls, symbolizes the evening of life. The infants at the right, in the middle ground, indicate the beginning. The two lovers in the foreground, gazing raptly into each other's eyes, represent the climax of life. Again, perhaps surprisingly, it is the girl who holds or plays a pair of flutes. Has the girl taken them from the young man? Vasari says that the girl offers the flutes to him,[2] but it would seem that he did not look closely enough. First of all, the young man himself has a flute, again a recorder, held in his right hand — a fact that has never been noticed by the interpreters of this painting and that alone excludes the assumption that the girl is offering her flutes to the boy. Furthermore, both of her recorders have their characteristic mouthpieces pointing upward towards her mouth, and she has the fingers of both hands on the fingerholes of the

---

group in the Schifanoia frescoes as 'an outing of young gentlemen in the company of courtesans' (p. 156). I would defend the young ladies against such a classification. This is, after all, a triumph of Venus; her power, we know, is irresistible, and making love in her presence is by no means a sign of professional activities.

[1] Philipp Fehl, *op. cit.*, p. 157, suggests that these women are 'not human but nymphs of the wood who, having been attracted by the music and the charm of the young men, have joined their concert. They are as invisible to the young men as they are, in the full beauty of the landscape which they represent, visible to us.' His explanation of the flute is that 'the music of the recorder recalls the sound of the birds' (p. 158), and that the recorder was an attribute of Poesia in the *tarocchi* (the Italian equivalent of the *tarot* cards). But the allegorical air of the *tarocchi* seems to me a world apart from the down-to-earth symbolism in the *Concert champêtre*. It is for similar reasons that I cannot quite concur with Patricia Egan's interesting interpretation of this painting [*Poesia and the Fête Champêtre*, in *The Art Bulletin*, XLI (1959), 303], in which she relates the two women in the painting to the *Poetics* of Aristotle and the Poesia of the *tarocchi*, and says that 'the meaning of the two nude figures must in some way have developed from that of the earlier one,' suggesting therefore as a title of the painting: *Allegory of Poetry*. If we take cognizance of all the girls with flutes in the pastoral scenes of the Giorgione-Titian orbit, it is hard to believe that these painters would have transplanted the respectable art of poetry into their sensuous Venetian Arcady.

[2] 'che gli offre certi flauti' (Vasari, *Le Vite*, ed. Milanesi, Florence, 1906, VII, 435).

instruments. Therefore, she must have just paused in playing. The flutes, connecting the two bodies as it were, have a twofold significance. They are the symbols of the amorous union; and the simultaneity of their sounds signifies the harmony of souls.[1]

The *Bacchanal*[2] in the Prado Museum (Pl. 8), Titian's rhapsody on wine, women, and song, has often been discussed and does not need a detailed description here. We will focus only on the role of music in it. The central place among the revellers is given to two women in the foreground (Pl. 9). In front of them, conspicuously in the middle, lies a music sheet with notation and the words 'Qui boyt et ne reboyt le ne scet boyre soit' ('He who doesn't have more than one drink doesn't know what drinking can be'). The music is a four-part canon.[3] However, no one is singing,[4] but each of the two women in the centre foreground holds a flute.[5] Curiously enough, the presence of these flutes, as far as I know, has not been given due attention before. The instruments are actually recorders, and those in the hands of the women are held so as to be in close and conspicuous proximity. A third flute is partially visible near the foot of the fair-haired woman in the centre.[6] Again, as in the other Arcadian pictures discussed, they are not being played. There can hardly be any doubt that these flutes symbolize an

[1] It is of this painting, and of the *Divine and Profane Love* (Villa Borghese, Rome), that Burckhardt says: 'Lastly, Titian painted two pictures without any mythological precedents, mere allegories, if you will, but of that rare kind in which the allegorical meaning that can be expressed is quite lost by comparison with an inexpressible poetry' (*Cicerone*, Basel, 1860, p. 975). One never turns to Burckhardt in vain. Although the genius of Titian seems 'inexplicable' to him, he is inspired to sum it up in perhaps the most monumental words ever written of a painter: 'The divine quality in Titian lies in his power of perceiving in things and men that harmony of existence which ought to be in them according to the natural tendency of their being, or which still lives in them, though dimmed and unrecognizable; what in real life is broken, scattered, and limited, he represents as complete, happy, and free. This is probably always the task of art; but no one any longer fulfills it so calmly, so unpretentiously, with such an appearance of necessity. In him this harmony was a pre-established one, to use a philosophical term in a special sense' (*Cicerone*, p. 967).

[2] Representing the feast of the Andrians after Philostratus (*Imagines*, I, 25), as Franz Wickhoff pointed out in *Venezianische Bilder*, in *Jahrbuch der königlich Preussischen Kunstsammlungen*, XXIII (1902), 118–20.

[3] It has been deciphered by Gertrude P. Smith in an excellent study, *The Canon in Titian's Bacchanal*, in *Renaissance News*, VI (1953), 52–56.

[4] Fehl, *op. cit.*, p. 167, attempts to identify the two youths in the left background as singers and points out the similarity of their dress to that of the two youths in the *Concert champêtre*. However, it is not quite apparent that they sing; they seem to be, rather, in quiet conversation with one another. Fehl does not mention the flutes.

[5] See also the sacrifice to Priapus in Francesco Colonna's *Hypnerotomachia Polyphili*, Venice, 1499, where three ladies accompany the cultic scene with wind instruments, two recorders and one piffero.

[6] This third recorder is difficult to make out in the shadows of Titian's canvas, but it is very clearly delineated in Castiglione's drawing after Titian (Bibliothèque Nationale, Paris), and Rubens's copy (Nationalmuseum, Stockholm).

utter abandonment to the senses. Also, by the way, a substitution of instruments for some of the four vocal parts of the canon would be quite in line with the performance practice of the time.

If we wish to focus on the symbolic connotation of the flute in the Italian Renaissance, we must deal with at least two different sources. One is of an intellectual and rational nature: the impact of the ancient authors, read, translated, and commented upon by the humanists. The other source is not humanist but human; not intellectual or literary; not an artificial graft. It stems not from a humanist revival of articulated legal, moral, or aesthetic preferences of the ancient world for certain kinds of music and instruments, but from the perennial underground stream of universal magic signs or symbols for elementary powers in human life.

These symbols are not attributes or conventional signs pedantically attached to the scene like explanatory labels, but are organic, self-evident elements of the life depicted by Titian. It is the golden glow of nostalgia for an Arcady far back in antiquity, and yet transposed into the vivid present; not an archaeological reconstruction, and not paying lip-service to the pagan past, but living fully, in a new harmony of lines and palpitating colours — the summer day of human existence, with the vibrating landscape and the sensuous flesh of the body all permeated by an inaudible music. And if this music is made visible by the representation of its tools, the musical instruments, these are organic elements of the magic substance conjured up by the master. Here we have no replicas of the pagan past, no renascence of ancient modes and moods of life, but a new unity of emotion — an artistic expression of *joie de vivre* stimulated perhaps by the recollection of ancient pictorial and literary models, but experienced in its fullness and in its own right. It is not a mosaic of humanist findings but a return into a paradise that was never wholly lost.

A study of flute symbolism should perhaps also include paintings which are not Arcadian or rural concerts in the strict sense of the word. Titian's *Venus and the Lute Player* (Metropolitan Museum of Art, New York) includes no less than four musical instruments (Pl. 10). The young cavalier sitting at Venus's feet plays the lute; Venus holds a recorder; a tenor viola da gamba leans against her couch; and, far back in the landscape, a bagpiper plays for the dancing crowd. Here we have no country girl, but a majestic woman bejewelled and crowned, with a winged *putto* in attendance. (This painting and a variant in the Fitzwilliam Museum in Cambridge are the only ones among a number of versions[1] that show so many instruments. The others have only one instrument, a large positive organ played by the cavalier.)

[1] Otto Brendel, in his very interesting study, *The Interpretation of the Holkham Venus*, in *The Art Bulletin*, XXVIII (1946), 65 ff., gives a complete list of all existing variants and old copies.

Of the instruments depicted here, only the viola da gamba has no player. Who played or is to play it — perhaps another admirer to whom Venus (if she is Venus at all) turns her far-away gaze? Or is it another instrument for herself? But no Venus is known to play a viola da gamba, or indeed any instrument.[1]

So much for flute symbolism in Titian's paintings, particularly the pastoral ones. A substantial number of contemporary engravings, though hardly suitable for reprinting, would readily confirm our interpretation of it. Thus, no literary evidence seems to be needed. The Greek and Roman bucolic literature was, of course, fashionable in the Renaissance. But apart from lip-service to the ancients, what description of actual life exists from that time? Living customs, like the air we breathe, were not usually topics of discussion or explanation. Cultural history is commonly written by later generations. Still, our problem of the etiquette of the flute was discussed at length, with humanist trimmings of course and yet with a half-hidden smile and in most elegant, suggestive language, by a great connoisseur of mores, Baldassare Castiglione:

> The human voice adds its charm and grace to all these instruments with which, I believe, the courtier should be acquainted. But the more he excels in them, the more he should stay away from those that once were rejected by Minerva and Alcibiades because they seem to have something disgusting about them.
>
> The appropriate time at which one can make use of that kind of music [the pipes] is, I believe, when a man finds himself in private and dear company and when he is not concerned with any other pursuits; but above all in the presence of women, because the appearance of these instruments softens the listener and makes her penetrable to the sweetness of this music and, at the same time, arouses the spirits of the one who makes the music. And, as I have said before, I like to avoid the crowds of indelicate people. But let it be understood that all this must be accompanied by tact and good judgement, for it is, after all, impossible to imagine all the things that can happen. . . .[2]

[1] Brendel, *op. cit.*, is rightfully puzzled by the fact that Venus holds a recorder, since this instrument is not among her attributes. In his search for the meaning of musical instruments and music, he quotes various passages from Marsilio Ficino, Leone Ebreo, Pietro Bembo, and Baldassare Castiglione on the relation between the different senses, specifically between that of the eye and that of the ear. They all concentrate on general aesthetic problems and do not seem to throw much light on the presence of a recorder in a nude woman's hand. The passage that Brendel quotes (p. 69) from Castiglione mentions the possibility that the woman may be a musician: 'Likewise with his [the courtier's] hearing let him enjoy the sweetness of her voice, the concord of her words, the harmony of her music (if his beloved be a musician). Thus he will feed his soul on sweetest food by means of these two senses. . . .'

[2] '. . . Dà ornamento, e gratia assai la voce humana a tutti questi instrumenti, de quali voglio che al nostro Cortegian basti haver notitia; e quanto più però in essi sarà eccellente, tanto sarà meglio senza impacciarsi molto di quelli, che Minerva rifiutò, et Alcibiade, perchè pare che habbiano del schifo. Il tempo poi, nel quale usar si possono queste sorte di musica, estimo io che sia sempre che l'huomo si trova in una domestica, e cara compagnia, quando

In passing, we should perhaps mention a symbolic flauto dolce in a Romanino fresco in the Castle of Trent (Pl. 11a). There we find an unmistakable antithesis between the allegories of sensuous love and chastity. Two representations are juxtaposed. The lower part of the fresco shows a beautiful woman, evidently Castitas, caressing a unicorn whose oblique horn is a conspicuous element of the composition. The upper part also shows a young woman in a pose parallel to that of Chastity. But this woman is extravagantly if not provocatively over-dressed; free strands of hair fall on her deep décolletage, and her expression is clearly seductive. All these features are eloquent enough to characterize her sufficiently as the opposite of Chastity. And to crown it all, there is one more piquant detail: the large recorder that she holds — but does not play — and which corresponds, within the composition, to the horn of the unicorn.

We should not conclude these remarks on the study of musical instruments as an aid to the art historian without citing an example of how a celebrated art historian, with considerable musical knowledge, managed to see in a picture things that are not visible, and to overlook others that were there. The art historian was Vasari, who was deeply interested in music. This interest of his appears not only in the cheerful frescoes with which he decorated his palazzino in Arezzo, but even more strikingly in his *Vite*, where he rarely misses an opportunity to refer to music whenever the painting he is describing gives him a chance. And he does not content himself by merely mentioning instruments or musicians, but often points out what only a connoisseur of musical practice would have known, describing accurately and with visible relish the musical importance of poses and gestures of players.[1]

How Vasari's musical knowledge helped him to describe and actually in-terpret — evidently from memory — a painting he could have seen only briefly during his visit to Venice, may be seen from his biography of Paolo Veronese (*Vite*, ed. Milanesi, VI, 373). The painting is Veronese's charming *tondo* for the

altre facende non vi sono; ma sopra tutto conviensi in presentia di donne, perchè quegli aspetti indolciscono di chi ode, e più, il fanno penetrabili dalla soavità della musica: et anchor svegliano i spiriti di chi la fà. Piacemi ben (come anchor ho detto), che si fugga la moltitudine, et massimamente de' gli ignobili. Ma il condimento del tutto bisogna che sia la discretione: perchè in effetto saria impossibile imaginar tutti i casi, che occorrono . . .' (*Il Cortegiano*, Book II).

[1] One good example of this is found in Vasari's life of Fra Bartolomeo, in the discussion of the latter's painting of the mystic betrothal of St. Catherine for San Marco in Florence (*Vite*, ed. Milanesi, IV, 185–86): '. . . two boys, one of whom plays a lute and the other a lira. The former is shown as he bends his leg to put the instrument on it, with one hand placed on the strings to stop them, an ear concentrating on the harmony, and his head turned up with the mouth slightly open, in such a manner that anyone who looks at him can almost hear the voice. In a similar way, the other boy, sitting next to him with one ear bent towards the lira, appears to perceive the harmony produced by the voice and the lute while he provides the tenor part; with downcast eyes, he listens to his companion who plays and sings. What an ingenious and understanding observer he is!'

old library of San Marco and which is to be seen today in the Palazzo Ducale (Pl. 6b). It is an allegory of music; we quote Vasari's lively description:

> There are depicted three beautiful young women; one of them, the most beautiful, plays a large lirone da gamba, looking down at the fingerboard of the instrument. Of the two women, one plays a lute and the other sings from a book. Near to the women is a cupid without wings who plays a gravecembalo,[1] showing that Amor is born from Music, or that Amor is always in the company of Music. And because Amor never tears himself away from her, he is shown without wings. In the same picture, the painter represented Pan, the God of shepherds according to the poets, together with certain flutes made of tree bark consecrated to him by the shepherds who had been victorious in the musical contest.

A comparison of this description with the picture reveals discrepancies. The lady with the 'lirone da gamba' (it is a viola da gamba rather than a lirone) gazes not down at its neck, but directly into the onlooker's eyes. The lady who 'sings from a book' has no book, or at least none appears in the painting. Likewise there is no 'gravecembalo' visible in front of the 'cupid without wings.' What we see is a small part of a box, and the awkward right hand of the cupid there does not give us a definite clue.

Yet Vasari's defective memory is not altogether wrong, and it is guided by a sound musical knowledge. The singer at the left, who evidently leads the three instrumentalists, appears to be reading her words and vocal part from a written page. Her glance seems to concentrate on a sheet or book hidden from our eyes.[2] A keyboard instrument would go well with voice, lute, and viola da gamba, and would conform to the musical practice of Vasari's time, although an instrument as large as a gravecembalo would less likely be found there in the open air than a spinettino. When Vasari saw the picture, he evidently perceived it in musical terms, and in his recollection pictured the ensemble as it could have been. (We won't argue too severely with him about the wingless cupid, although his reason for the absence of wings strongly recalls the assumption that the Egyptians must have had wireless because no telephones were found in their tombs! To dabble in mythology was fashionable in the *cinquecento*.)

Strange, however, is Vasari's attitude toward the flutes, and here he seems to have missed a point. The flutes may well be votive gifts from shepherds who were victorious in musical contests; indeed, Vasari knows his bucolica. But Pan would have welcomed a syrinx or two. The flutes in the picture are actually fipple flutes — recorders or, in the suggestive Italian term, flauti dolci. The

---

[1] Equivalent to clavicembalo, i.e. harpsichord.

[2] The seven instrumentalists in Veronese's *Marriage at Cana* (Louvre) all seem to be looking at written music, although only five have music books visible before them.

smaller is of square construction like a wooden organ pipe; the larger round one, in its oblique position, shows the fipple in profile. It does not require a Renaissance eye or imagination, nor a reminder of Giovanni da Udine's innuendoes in the fruit garlands of the Villa Farnesina or of the general fashion for more or less delicate pictorial allusions, to recognize here a discreet supplement to the figure of Pan-Priapus who, transcending his caryatid existence, squints amiably down at the ladies. Was the learned author of the *Vite* too solemn to mention frivolities, or was the serious Tuscan blind to Venetian mirth?

3 · The Survival of the Kithara and the Evolution of the English Cittern: a Study in Morphology

The history of the cittern, often called the English cittern, has been clearly traced back to Elizabethan times, when it was one of the most popular instruments, available in every self-respecting barber's shop for the convenience of the waiting customer.[1] England's claim to the invention of the cittern dates back to the Renaissance: as erudite a humanist and music historian as Vincenzo Galilei writes in 1581 in his *Dialogo della musica antica e della moderna*: 'fu la Cetera usata prima tra gli Inglesi che da altre nationi,[2] nella quale isola si lavorano già in eccellenza . . .' But Galilei cannot have read his Dante well, for in the *Divina Commedia, Paradiso,* Canto XX, the cetra figures in a wonderful metaphor comparing the formation of sound in an eagle's neck with that of a cittern:

> *Eccome suono al collo della cetra*
> *Prende sua forma, e si come al pertugio*
> *Della sampogna vento che penetra;*
>
> *Cosi, rimosso d'aspettare indugio,*
> *Quel mormorar dell'aquile salissi*
> *Su per lo collo, come fossi bugio.*

(And as the sound takes its form at the
cittern's neck, and as the vent of the
bagpipe enters its neck, so the sound
rose up through the neck of the eagle.)

Cetera (cetra) means here, of course, the cittern, not the kithara of antiquity (which was also called *cetera* in Dante's time, as it still is today), since the neck is described as the place where 'the sound takes form,' that is, where the stopping

---

[1] Thurston Dart, in his interesting essay *The Cittern and its English Music*, in *Galpin Society Journal*, I (1948), 46 ff., does not follow the literature of the cittern back further than the middle of the 16th century. He mentions the remarkable number of instruction books for solo cittern and suggest good reasons for the replacement of the lute by the cittern.

[2] Claims for Italy and for Flanders are mentioned in Dart, *op. cit.*, p. 50.

of the strings takes place. The metaphor could not be more telling! The names for old musical instruments are very confusing. The same instrument often had many names, and one name often indicated various instruments. The medieval vocabulary alone includes kithara, citola, cistôle, sitole, cuitole, sytole, cycolae, and later we find gittern, getern, kitaire, quitare, guiterne, guitarra. Which are actually the prototypes of the cittern and which those of the guitar? And are all of them children of the ancient kithara? Johannes de Grocheo (*c.* 1300), enumerating instruments, mentions the kithara and the gitarra side by side, and the *Speculum musices*, attributed to Johannes de Muris (1290–1358?), and recently to Jacques de Liège, groups together in a list of *instrumenta artificialia* cytharae, psalteria, and cycolae.

I will therefore confine myself chiefly to visual evidence; the representations of musical instruments in the visual arts tell a more reliable and, I trust, convincing story. I shall relate the story of the cittern in cancrizans, from its more recent, well-known forms back towards antiquity, on the assumption that it is certain non-functional features of an instrument — as of other artifacts — that reveal its evolution, if we can look at them from a sufficiently detached point of view. Musical instruments, like other tools, have to adapt themselves to constantly changing conditions and demands. They may develop new features and organs; usually, however, the outdated, useless features are not abandoned right away, but are retained through the centuries, and may survive, in atrophic form, for an incredibly long time. Instrument builders, and other artisans, like to continue to do what their fathers and grandfathers did, and so they preserve shapes, patterns, and features that once served a purpose, even though that purpose may now have disappeared, without giving the matter further thought. They may, of course, also be influenced by the fact that their customers expect the merchandise to have its traditional, time-honoured shape.

In Père Mersenne's *Harmonie universelle* (1636), although we find not a single word about the origin of the sistre — that is, our cittern — there are no less than three different woodcuts of citterns.[1] Mersenne concentrates on the different ways the instruments are tuned and played, but we are here more concerned with their shape. In Pl. 12a, showing the three illustrations, the middle instrument has a small, inconspicuous buckle at its shoulders, which otherwise rise smoothly enough from the neck. The cittern on the left has shoulders that terminate abruptly at right angles to the neck; the lower end of the body has a slight protuberance to which the strings are fastened. The cittern on the right has large scrolls at the shoulders and a larger projection at the bottom of the body which almost forms a base. All these minor features seem to be merely decorative; certainly they have nothing to do with the playing or with the

[1] *Harmonie universelle, Traité des instruments à chordes, Livre second*, Prop. XV, pp. 97, 98*r* and *v.*

musical function of the instrument. We find the same mysterious little buckles long after Mersenne, as for instance in Jan Steen's *Merry Company on a Terrace*, in the Metropolitan Museum of Art, New York, painted near the end of his life in the 1670s (Pl. 12b).

Tracing back the history of the instruments, we may single out certain specimens or depictions of citterns that have survived as examples revealing its evolution. Plate VII of the *Theatrum instrumentorum* in Michael Praetorius's *Syntagma* (*Tomus secundus de organographia*, 1618) shows two different citterns, the larger one with twelve double strings, the smaller with six double strings (Pl. 13a). Both are depicted in front and in side view and show clearly the small buckles. The same shape is shown in the cittern in the foreground of Frans Floris's famous allegorical engraving of *Musica*. Sebastian Virdung, in his *Musica getutscht* (1511), does not mention the cittern at all; nor does the versifier of Virdung's work, Martin Agricola, in his *Musica instrumentalis deudsch* (1528). Nevertheless, all throughout the 16th century the cittern was a fashionable instrument. One of the most beautiful and most lavishly decorated citterns to have been preserved is that made in 1574 by Girolamo de Virchis of Brescia (the town praised at exactly the same time by Vincenzo Galilei for its beautiful citterns), now in the Vienna collection (Pl. 12c). The buckles of this instrument have been skilfully absorbed into the Renaissance décor, while the neck terminates in a small figure representing Lucretia stabbing herself, and beneath her, at the rear of the neck, a fantastic mask impudently thrusts forth a large nose; this is the hook, which we will find now in larger and larger form, the farther back we go towards the early Renaissance.

Similar, but simpler, is a cittern in the collection of the Paris Conservatory. Here the nose of an animal head provides the hook, and the buckles stand out sharply from the smooth side walls of the shoulders. Several paintings of the early *cinquecento* (for instance, the little Giorgionesque painting of a boy in a landscape, attributed to Palma Vecchio, Lorenzo Lotto, Correggio, and others, now in the Munich Pinakothek) show citterns with more marked buckles and larger hooks.

The Italian *quattrocento* is an unparalleled gold mine for the organologist, for it abounds in extremely accurate depictions of instruments, often life-size or nearly so, in reliefs, in paintings of angel concerts and mythological scenes, and above all in the hundreds of intarsias in the choir stalls in Verona, Monte Oliveto Maggiore, in the doors of the Stanze of the Vatican, and many other places.[1] One of the most interesting representations of citterns is in the famous cantoria by Luca della Robbia (Pl. 13b). Since the panels of the cantoria all

[1] See Chapter 8 below; also my article *Alcune rappresentazioni di antichi strumenti italiani a tastiera*, in *Collectanea historiae musicae*, II (1956), 465–73.

illustrate the verses of the 150th Psalm, most of the panels are devoted to one instrument, which is then represented by several specimens, an allegorical grouping into ensembles which bears no relation to the actual grouping in performance. The relief with the citterns shows two specimens: in both of them the buckles are replaced, or rather 'preceded,' by large ears; the frets extend far out on one side of the neck; and the base has reached considerable dimensions.

These features are even more sharply defined in intarsias. One example is from the choir stalls in Monte Oliveto Maggiore, near Siena, made by the great *intarsiatore* Fra Giovanni da Verona. In the upper of the two half-opened shelves, there leans a large, bulky cittern (Pl. 13c) with a rather deep body of strongly curved outline, and a beautiful gothic sound-hole rose. The shoulders are set sharply away from the body, and two wooden 'wings' reach out from there into space. The seven frets are arranged in steps of slightly different height, and the hook behind the neck is emphasized in yellow-white wood. The strings are not depicted. Earlier in time is the other intarsia, or rather part of an intarsia, from the studiolo of Duke Federigo da Montefeltro, once in the ducal palace in Gubbio and now in the Metropolitan Museum of Art in New York.[1] This elegant cittern (Pl. 53a), casually resting upside down on a book, has a more shallow body with nearly straight sides that begin to curve near its lower end, and also a large base. Striking features are the large hook, the six frets in steps, and the nine strings minutely rendered in inlay. The horizontal line of the shoulders is much broader than that of the Monte Oliveto cittern and supports large 'wings.' If we turn this instrument over and rest it on its base, we can hardly fail to see behind its shape the spectre of the ancient kithara with its arms extending from the body: these arms have shrunk into the 'wings' of the more modern instrument.[2] Yet a thousand years still separate this *quattrocento* spectre of the ancient kithara from the time in late antiquity when the kithara was still in vogue. From now on visual evidence will be rarer and we must begin leaping from stone to stone.

We might well be tempted to think that our search ends here, and that the invention of the modern cittern should be ascribed to the early Renaissance, which took a direct interest in the culture and the arts of antiquity. Indeed the treatises of Renaissance archaeologists are full of theories about the ancient lyra and kithara. But rather than quote from treatises I would prefer to point out the impact of musical archaeology upon instrument building, as it is reflected in the visual arts. I shall cite only three or four examples out of hundreds of bronzes, reliefs, paintings, and prints. Sometimes the kithara shape is only slightly hinted

[1] See Chapter 9 below.

[2] The bulky, large-based cittern in the hands of Terpsichore in the frescoes by Spagna in the Pinacoteca of the Capitoline, Rome, also strikingly resembles the body of the ancient kithara.

at by indicating the 'ears,' as in the small pseudo-kithara held by the sorrowful Damon in the little Giorgionesque painting in the London National Gallery (Pl. 13d), or in a similar instrument with the 'ears' playfully suggested by the tips of decorative leaves in that largest of all angel concerts by Gaudenzio Ferrari in the cupola of the Santuario in Saronno (Pl. 14b). But this was only one of many ways in which the shape of the ancient kithara was borrowed and, with more or less fantasy, transformed by the artists of the *quattro-* and *cinquecento*. Filippino Lippi, who had deep archaeological interests and borrowed much from Roman sarcophagi, not only shows kitharas in his frescoes for the Capella Strozzi in Santa Maria Novella, Florence (Pl. 74c), but also invents lyre-guitars by adding a neck for the stopping of strings to the shape of a kithara (Pl. 74b); and Lorenzo Costa does the same in his mythological paintings now in the Louvre (Pl. 96a). A similar pseudo-guitar is seen in the hands of one of the angels in Raffaellino del Garbo's *Madonna* in the Dahlem Museum, Berlin (Pl. 14c).

The interest of artists in ancient instruments is manifest also in many drawings of such instruments taken from ancient statues, reliefs, and especially from sarcophagi: for instance, the drawing by Francesco di Giorgio of Erato holding an ancient kithara, in which both the instrument and the plectrum are rendered with the utmost accuracy. The model for this drawing is one of the Muses in the famous Sarcophagus of the Muses, formerly in the Palazzo Mattei, now in the Museo Nazionale in Rome. It was Raphael who later borrowed not only the figure of this Muse and her kithara but also all the other instruments for his *Parnassus* in the Stanza della Segnatura.[1]

As a matter of fact, this revival of ancient forms, and especially of the shape of musical instruments, in the *quattro-* and *cinquecento* was only one of many such revivals which have occurred throughout the evolution of occidental art. One, which we will discuss later, occurred during the Carolingian era. Another found expression during the first Napoleonic empire in the feminine vogue for instruments which were made to look like kitharas, but were actually played by stopping the strings against a fingerboard grafted on to the traditional shape (Pl. 14d).

These 'renaissances,' produced by deliberate and conscious selection from antiquity, are not the only form of borrowing from the past. There is also the hidden underground stream of tradition, unbroken since classical antiquity. And with this in mind, let us continue our voyage back towards antiquity.

The Queen Mary Psalter in the British Museum, dating from the early 14th century, illustrates numerous musicians, many of whom are playing citterns (called mandoras in the facsimile edition of 1912). We observe that the wings

[1] See Chapter 14 below.

are bigger again, and rounded now in true gothic style, while the bases take the form of the gothic trefoil shape. The instruments are plucked with a plectrum; this brings us one important step nearer to the ancient kithara. Pl. 14a shows one of these citterns side by side with a bowed vielle,[1] adequate proof of the absurdity of the old hypothesis that 'the cittern is probably a plucked descendant of the vielle of the tenth to twelfth centuries.'[2] We are fortunate in being able to compare this design with large representations of the cittern in sculpture. One of these, made about 1290, is in the middle section of the west portal of Strasbourg Cathedral (Pl. 15c). The fiddle played by the musician at the left in our illustration is a modern reconstruction; the cittern on the right, however, damaged though it is, corresponds exactly, with its large wings and trefoil base, to those in the Queen Mary Psalter. One century earlier, about 1180, we encounter the wonderful *David* by Benedetto Antelami in the Baptistery of Parma (Pl. 15d). David carries a large plectrum, and the shape of the whole instrument is now, except for the neck, precisely that of a small kithara. We have now reached the point where we can align this necked kithara with the type of instrument appearing in the Utrecht Psalter; the many string instruments illustrated in this Psalter were brilliantly analysed fifty years ago by Miss Kathleen Schlesinger in her studies of the precursors of the violin family.[3]

When we turn to the 10th and 9th centuries (the approximate date at which the Utrecht Psalter was written), we find rich pictorial evidence of the transformation of the ancient kithara into an instrument with stopped strings. The famous Bible of Charles the Bald, of the 9th century, shows in one full-page miniature King David surrounded by musicians. One of them plays a strange instrument (Pl. 15a): the bulky body has wings, and a neck over which run three strings. These wings carry merely decorative kithara arms, and the kithara yoke is replaced by a large ornamental and non-functional superstructure. The addition of a neck was one way in which to turn the open-string kithara into a stopped-string instrument; another way was to fill in the air space between the kithara arms with a massive solid wooden soundboard. One of the many examples of this latter form is in the Stuttgart Psalter of the 9th century, originating in northeastern France (Pl. 15b).[4] Here again the decorative superstructure is reminiscent of the yoke of the kithara, and the curving arms are retained in enormous ornamental wings. This, like the other illustrations of the Stuttgart Psalter, reflects contemporary musical usage; that is, native, barbaric — or, rather, pagan — tradition soon after it was modified by the

---

[1] Facsimile edition, London, 1912, Pl. 219.

[2] *Die Musik in Geschichte und Gegenwart*, II (1951), 1451.

[3] *The Instruments of the Modern Orchestra and Early Records of the Precursors of the Violin Family*, London, 1910.

[4] Facsimile edition, ed. Ernest De Wald, Princeton, 1930, f. 40r.

spread of the gospel, while our previous example from the Bible of Charles the Bald leans on earlier pictorial representation, thus reflecting an earlier stage of the transformation of the instrument.

The Utrecht Psalter is of the greatest value in this investigation because it depicts an unusually large variety of instruments, and also because it frequently shows the ancient kithara side by side with an instrument that has the body of a kithara, but a neck in place of the yoke; in other words, a cittern — that is, if we want to project this term as far back as the 9th century. The frets are usually carefully indicated on the neck, and the graceful curvature of the wings corresponds precisely to that of the arms of the kitharas near by.

Among the most important representations, we find:

a) in Psalm 147, the psalmist with a kithara urging numerous musicians, 'Psallite Deo nostro in Cythara'; on either side of him is a group of musicians, and in each of them appear both a kithara and a pseudo-kithara with fingerboard (Pl. 16a). On these fingerboards, or necks, one can clearly see the frets for stopping the strings.

b) in Psalm 150 (which we have seen before illustrated by Luca della Robbia, see Pl. 13b), on either side of the famous hydraulic double organ, are wind and string instruments, among which we again see these same instruments (Pl. 16b).

c) in Psalm 71, 'veritatem tuam . . . psallam tibi in cythara . . . ,' the psalmist himself holds the fingerboard kithara, and behind him a large kithara leans against what appears to be a roughly drawn hydraulis (Pl. 16c).

d) in Psalm 92, 'in deca cordo psalterio cum cantico in cythara . . . ,' we can relate the names of the instruments to the drawings: 'psalterium' indicates the harp, and 'cythara' our pseudo-kithara with fingerboard (Pl. 16d).

e) in Psalm 43, 'emitte lucem tuam et veritatem tuam . . . confitebor tibi in cythara . . .'; with only one instrument depicted (Pl. 17b), its identification as a 'cythara' is beyond doubt.

f) in Psalm 108, the psalmist carries two instruments: our fingerboard kithara in his left hand, and a harp on his left shoulder (Pl. 17a). The long stick is not a bow, but a measuring rod: 'exsurge psalterium [the harp] et cythara [our fingerboard instrument] . . . et dividam Sicimam et convallem tabernaculorum dimeciar' (I will divide Sichem and mete out the valley of the tabernacles). Regrettably, German organological literature has ignored the Latin text, and this incorrect interpretation is made plausible by showing only one-third of the meting rod in the illustration.[1]

As mentioned above, Miss Schlesinger has made a brilliant analysis of the instruments in the Utrecht Psalter, though I cannot follow her in considering these necked kitharas to be ancestors of the modern violin. At any rate, this

[1] See Chapter 1 above.

assumption seems less absurd than the hypothesis of Curt Sachs, still retained
in *Die Musik in Geschichte und Gegenwart* and also followed by Friedrich Behn in
his recent book, *Musikleben im Altertum und im frühen Mittelalter*,[1] that the cittern
is probably a plucked descendant of the vielle of the 10th to 12th centuries.
However this may be, the crucial question remains: do the drawings of the
Utrecht Psalter reflect contemporary usage — that is, are these instruments of
the 9th century? If they are, we now have reached the point where the technique — probably oriental — of stopping strings against a fingerboard had
begun to rival and to replace the method of plucking open strings in kithara
fashion. But, as is well known, the Carolingian era was an era of renaissance, of
revival of 'classical' culture, and in all probability also of musical usage. On this
basis, therefore, we would have to interpret at least the orthodox kitharas in the
Utrecht Psalter not as a survival, but rather as a revival, of the Roman kithara
abandoned centuries before.

However, there is still another, more convincing, possibility. Modern investigations have shown, with almost general consent, that the drawings of the
Utrecht Psalter are based on much earlier models, probably Eastern and quite
possibly Alexandrian, antedating the conquest of Alexandria. These drawings
would then reflect, not 9th-century, but 6th-century or even 5th-century
musical usage. This interpretation of the Utrecht Psalter, however, is based
chiefly on the visual style of the drawings. If we had but one more reliable
representation of a fingerboard kithara from the 6th century! It would not only
push back the origin of the European cittern to the threshold of the ancient
world, when kithara and lyre were still in use, as we know from other sources;
it would also support the dating of the origin of the Utrecht Psalter in this
earlier period. Recent work by British archaeologists has enabled me to find this
missing link; an unmistakable cittern with atrophic kithara features (Pl. 17c)
appears in one of the fifty panels in a large mosaic discovered in 1957 by the
British School of Archaeology in Qasr el-Lebia, generally known today as
'Castle Libya,' fifty miles west of Cyrene, in Libya.[2]

This large mosaic occupied part of the nave of a church, but includes figures
which are still quite un-Christian: for instance, a leaping satyr and the nymph
Castalia. The panel which interests us here represents a musician holding an
instrument with a long neck. The description in the supplement of the *Illustrated
London News*, December 14, 1957, is perhaps a little naive: 'Everyday life is
represented by a shepherd seated on a rock playing his lute, with a dog beside
him, and his dinner-pot hung on a nearby tree. Despite the rusticity of the scene,

---

[1] See fn. 1, p. 33, above.
[2] I am indebted to Professor John Ward Perkins for kindly making available to me a photograph of this panel.

the musician uses a plectrum'! I won't argue with the dinner-pot, but I fail to see why an open-air occupation should exclude the use of a plectrum. Actually, the figure strongly recalls similar ones representing Orpheus. The instrument has four large pegs, although the mosaic technique allowed only two strings to be shown. What interests us most, however, are the atrophic wings curving away from the body in kithara fashion, and the large base. Thus, it is here, in the *6th century*, when the Roman kithara was still alive in Byzantine-Alexandrian civilization, that we can conclude our voyage, recognizing precisely the same atrophic features which puzzled us in the citterns of Mersenne and in 17th-century Dutch genre painting.

4 · Bagpipes and Hurdy-gurdies in their Social Setting

Every builder of musical instruments combines different roles: he observes, as an acoustical engineer, the invariant properties of vibrating matter, whether revealed by his own research or handed down by the tradition of his craft; he follows, wittingly or not, the vogue of his day; and, finally, he obeys his own personal taste, musical and decorative.

But these are not the only factors that determine the production of musical instruments. There are, also, different social levels: we see the instruments gaining and losing caste, passing from street singer or shepherd to courtier and perhaps back again. There is, moreover, the unequal pulsation of inventive life in the different dwelling places of men: centres of creative energy, courts and cities fermenting with competition and consequently with novelties, and quiet, remote mountain valleys where a hundred years are like a single day. There are, finally, the cultural migrations such as the infiltration of oriental civilization into Europe through its main gates, the Balkans, southern Italy, and Spain.

But above all, one is struck by the enormous influence that the beaten path of custom has. If the other factors form the fleeting and shifting surface pattern, the curls of foam, tradition is the regular beat of the heavy waves. Structural devices, playing techniques, even small decorative patterns such as the shape of soundholes are retained for centuries. Having seen a flute in an ancient Egyptian tomb, we recognize the same instrument in the hand of a fellah; just as we recognize in Torre Annunziata the very same wall scrawls, kitchen utensils, and children's toys that we had noticed half an hour before in Pompeii, four feet, or rather two thousand years, lower in the ground.

Among the most versatile instruments — at the same time stable and protean — are the bagpipe and hurdy-gurdy. Both are of remarkable age. Though at first glance they are as different as possible, after an adventurous history their fates intertwined, and they became so assimilated that they could replace each other in the same score. But before taking up their evolution, let us examine their structure.

In its simplest form the bagpipe consists of *a*) a bag, *b*) a short blowpipe through which the player inflates the bag with air, and *c*) one or more reed pipes through which the air leaves the bag, thus producing sound. The bag, which serves as a flexible wind reservoir, is made of the skin or bladder of an animal, usually a goat or a sheep; the pipes are inserted into the natural holes of the skin, where the animal's neck or feet were, by means of cylinders of wood (the so-called stocks) round which the skin is tightly fastened with a cord. The blowpipe, where it enters the bag, is fitted with a leather flap valve that prevents the air from passing back. The sounding pipes — primitive oboes or clarinets — differ in structure and function. One, called the chanter, is fitted with fingerholes that shorten the vibrating air column within the pipe and thus permit the playing of a melody. The other, which is usually larger, has no fingerholes and is therefore capable of only one tone — the continuous and invariable bass called the drone (a name also given to this pipe). The playing position of the bagpipe is well known: the player holds the blowpipe in his mouth, fingers the chanter in front of him like an oboe or clarinet, and squeezes the bag under one of his arms, thus regulating the air pressure (Pl. 20a).

The elements just described are only the minimum components of the typical bagpipe. Throughout its history the instrument has been subjected to various modifications, improvements, and complications: more drones have been added (producing the octave and the fifth of the first drone); the chanter has been doubled; the blowpipe, so hard on the lungs, has been replaced by the more comfortable bellows. In the British Isles even greater intricacies have been invented, one of the most complex instruments being the Uilleann pipe, also called the Irish organ.

As the bagpipe is an eccentric member of the woodwind family, so the hurdy-gurdy, being a sort of mechanized fiddle, is a capricious member of the great family of string instruments. The sound box may be that of a lute, guitar, or fiddle (Pls. 18a & 18b), but the strings stretched along it are neither plucked nor bowed, being set into vibration by a wooden wheel revolving in the middle of the sound box and turned by a crank at its tail end. The smooth edge of the wheel, which is coated with resin, serves as an endless bow. Like the pipes of the typical bagpipe, the strings differ in kind and function: there are stopped ones (the melody strings, or *chanterelles*) running along the middle of the sound box and open ones (the drones, or *bourdons*) running on either side. The melody strings are stopped by a primitive key mechanism, a set of stopping rods — naturals and sharps — equipped with little projections that press inward against the strings when the rods are pushed in (Pl. 19, and Fig. 4). Thus a full scale can be produced. When released, the rod falls back of its own weight. Consequently, as Pl. 20b shows, the hurdy-gurdy is played with the keyboard down. As the two melody strings are tuned in unison, each rod has two projections simultaneously stopping both strings. When there are two drones, they

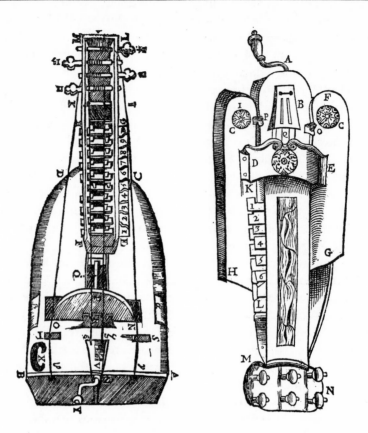

Fig. 4. Woodcuts from Mersenne, *Harmonie universelle*, 1636. LEFT: Hurdy-gurdy with open peg box and lateral pegs. RIGHT: Diagram of a hurdy-gurdy (compare with the identical instrument in Pl. 20b).

are tuned in octaves; when there are more, the octave is strengthened by an added fifth.

Thus it appears that our two instruments, so different in appearance and structure, have much in common musically. First, both are highly mechanized. In other instruments, such as the clarinet or lute, the player's lips or fingertips are in immediate contact with the heart of the instrument — that is, the agent of vibration: the reeds on the clarinet mouthpiece or the strings of the lute. But in our instruments mechanical devices intervene, the windbag in the bagpipe, the friction wheel in the hurdy-gurdy. True, this results in obvious handicaps: no such direct control of timbre and dynamics is possible as a clarinet or a lute permits, or even the bow of a violin, so responsive to the fingers. On the other hand, bag and wheel make possible something which neither lute or violin nor any pipes (at least in the Occident) can render — a continuous sound. This is the second analogy between our instruments: the bag overcomes the pauses between breaths, the wheel the pauses between the single strokes of plucking or bowing. The third, and musically the most important, analogy between the bagpipe and the hurdy-gurdy is that both employ the drone principle — that is, the accompaniment of a melody by an invariable bass. This principle is a very ancient one in the music of western Asia, where many instruments such as fiddles and pipes are based upon it. It has also played an important role in the development of occidental polyphony. We find it in the tuning of early occidental fiddles and, to mention the most notable example, in the open strings of the lira da braccio — the graceful instrument seen in the hands of Apollo and of so many angels in the Italian *quattro-* and *cinquecento*.

We have no means of knowing what emotional responses were evoked by music in distant periods; the habits of the musical ear follow the changes in musical styles. But the archaic contrast between a lively melody and a mono-tonously humming bass still affects us strongly and, strangely enough, with varying emotions. Sometimes it may be felt as restful, as in 19th-century music when it is used to convey a pastoral atmosphere, sometimes as exciting, as in the battle tunes of the Highland pipes. In the pedalpoints in classical and con-temporary music there seems to be a similar ambiguity of expression.

It was particularly the principle of the drone that later brought about the most intimate relations between members of such distant families, but curiously enough neither the hurdy-gurdy nor the bagpipe had drones when they first appeared in occidental history. There is no mention of drone pipes before 1300. The hurdy-gurdy adopted drone strings even later — the precise date we do not know.

The bagpipe is much the older instrument of the two. The first traces of it go far back into remote antiquity in the Orient and in those parts of Africa which were subjected to the Persian-Arabian civilization. It seems that the idea of combining pipes with a bag must have been natural to herdsmen who had plenty of goats and little water and to whom the hide was familiar as a water bag.

Martial mentions the bagpipe, and from Suetonius we learn that Nero played the *tibia utricularis*. In the Middle Ages we find the bagpipe all over Europe, from the Mediterranean to Ireland, which indeed proudly claims to have invented the instrument independently of the Romans. Numerous manuscript illuminations bear witness to its popularity.

The hurdy-gurdy is exclusively the child of the Occident. When it first appeared in the 10th century, under the name of organistrum, it was an ungainly two-man affair (Pl. 23a), not less than five feet long and usually with three melody strings. The stopping mechanism was clumsier and slower than that described above for the later hurdy-gurdy. Instead of teeth, the small stopping rods had bridges which lay beneath the strings. To raise a bridge one had to take the end of a rod between his fingertips and revolve it a quarter circle. This was an awkward procedure, requiring two hands to achieve even a slight degree of speed, and thus a second player was needed to turn the crank. Moreover, with this method of stopping, the handles of the rods had to point upwards towards the player and so could not fall back of their own weight as in the later hurdy-gurdy.

It seems very likely that this stopping mechanism was an improvement on the

Fig. 5. Monochord for studying consonances; the two stopping bridges permit two tones to be produced simultaneously on a single string. Woodcut from Lodovico Fogliano, *Musica theorica*, 1529.

monochord, that venerable scientific instrument of the Pythagoreans and of the learned medieval monks for studying on one string the mathematical ratios of the consonances. The string of the monochord was originally stopped by means of a bridge that could be shifted back and forth. As this was awkward, several bridges were sometimes used (Fig. 5), and finally these were fixed in the proper positions to be raised by hand when necessary. One more improvement, the addition of handles to the bridges, would give us the key mechanism of the organistrum. It is worth noting that the great scholar and friend of Descartes, Father Marin Mersenne, found the hurdy-gurdy reminiscent of the monochord, which, of course, must have been an important tool in his acoustical experiments. In his *Harmonie universelle* (1636) he says of the melody strings that 'they act as an ever-ready [*perpétuel*] monochord, because they make all sorts of tones by means of the keys.' How the strings of the organistrum were tuned we have no detailed information, but there is reason to believe that the outer strings were tuned in octaves, the middle a fourth or fifth above the lower. This, at least, would be in line with the early forms of polyphony developed between the 9th and the 13th centuries. The beginnings of polyphonic music must have left their mark on the instruments of the time, particularly on their tuning. Unfortunately we do not know much more of that instrumental music than we can gather from depictions of the instruments. The early writers on polyphony deal mainly with vocal music. Their subject was the tabulation of rules for accompanying the traditional melodies of Gregorian chant with a second melody. Following those rules the singer had to improvise an accompaniment called the descant. The rules changed through history, but, very roughly, two main methods can be distinguished. One was the 'organum' found in the writings of the Flemish monk Hucbald (840–930); it prescribed an accompaniment in fourths and fifths — sometimes with the octave also added. The other, as found in Scotus Erigena (9th century) and again later in Guido d'Arezzo (about 1020), directed that the chant be accompanied by an improvised melodic line below, which started and finished in unison with the chant and often held the same note for some time with the chant moving above. The first method would correspond with the tuning of the organistrum described above, and the second method with the drone principle as found in bagpipes with drones. It might even be, though no documentary evidence exists, that at some time one of the strings of the organistrum was used as a drone, being touched by the wheel but not by the stopping bridges. This is the more probable as we know that early medieval fiddles had a drone string in the oriental tradition. It is worth noting in this connection that Scotus Erigena, the first writer on polyphony, was a son of Eire, where drones in bagpipes were supposedly used early. Indeed, Irish historians trace the beginnings of medieval polyphony directly to the Irish bagpipe. In any case, there is food for thought in the conjecture that the development of polyphony in theory and practice was connected with the introduction of drones to the bagpipe and hurdy-gurdy.

It was perhaps because of its harmonic, chordal capacity, as well as for its use in sacred music and in instruction in the cloisters, that the hurdy-gurdy was frequently given the place of honour in the assemblage of the twenty-four elders in so many French and Spanish tympanums of the 11th and 12th centuries. We find the organistrum with its two players at the summit of the 'rainbow' which — according to Revelation 4: 3–4 — arches over Christ, the organistrum thus being just above Christ's head (Pl. 23a). The elders, it seems, preferred the apparently nobler instruments, the stringed ones, perhaps because of the string instruments mentioned in Revelation 14: 2–3; as far as the writer can see, they did not touch a bagpipe.

In the 13th century the organistrum shrank to more elegant size and received the easier pushing rods, which could be managed with one hand, freeing the other for the crank. So we see it later in the hands of the graceful angel from the Saint Thomas Altar in Cologne (Pl. 27a). It is now called symphonia, or in old French, *chifonie*, from its being able to produce a concord of sound.

Hurdy-gurdy and bagpipe appear side by side in secular music and, if not in church music, at least in the hands of angels. Unlike the elders, angels seem to have no social prejudices whatever; like playful children they do not hesitate to take a juggler's or beggar's instrument for the greater glory of the Lord or his saints. In the *Glorification of Saint Francis* in Pistoia, by pupils of Giotto (Pl. 23b), we find several groups of angels before the throne of the saint, the middle group with string instruments, the flanking groups with winds. There is a bagpipe of considerable size, with an enormous oboe chanter and even a drone. To the right of the piper group an angel plays a hurdy-gurdy with six strings. It cannot now be ascertained whether this painting has been retouched, but if the six strings are authentic some must be drones, as the stopping rods could not very well have stopped six strings simultaneously.

We also find our two instruments in the miniatures of the *Cantigas de Santa Maria* of Alfonso the Wise of Castile (1252–84) in the Escorial. These form the richest collection of popular Spanish music of the 13th century and present important evidence of the influence of Arabic civilization, including music, on Christian Spain (though it should not be overlooked that Arabic music in its turn then carried a good deal of European, notably Byzantine, contagion). After having reconquered Seville from the infidels, King Alfonso became enthusiastic about the Moslem civilization and kept Moorish musicians at his court. Besides occasional musical scenes, the *Cantigas* contain a whole gallery of musicians — forty illustrations, most of them showing two players. In some of the pictures Moslem and Jewish musicians compete with Christian Spaniards. Lute and rebec still appear in their Arabic shape alongside instruments of occidental origin, such as the portative organ. The instruments and their manipulation are drawn with great care. Among them we find the bagpipe and the hurdy-gurdy. The latter is represented by two similar specimens (Pl. 22a). They have the form of oblong boxes, the stopping mechanism extending over the entire length of the box and the rods now placed away from the player, unlike those of the organistrum. Bagpipes appear here in an amazing variety. One form, the simplest (Pl. 22c), has only one chanter, elegantly decorated with a carved head and a slightly flaring bell, possibly of oxhorn. Another (Pl. 22d) is furnished with double pipes, of which the outer one seems to be a drone. This is the more probable as multiple pipes without a bag occur in other miniatures of this set. A third, the largest form (Pl. 22b), is fitted with two separate pairs of drones besides a double chanter — an unusually complex combination for a bagpipe of that time.

The Loutrell Psalter (14th century) also shows the bagpipe and the symphonia in friendly proximity (Pl. 21a). The symphonia has the form of a simple rectangular box. The stopping rods are of the older, clumsy type turned from above, though here with only one hand.

In the 15th century the hurdy-gurdy lost caste, but later it was still played by angels, as in the greatest angel concert ever painted, the famous fresco at Saronno by Gaudenzio Ferrari. Like his contemporary Leonardo, Ferrari was also a musician and, moreover, an imaginative inventor of instruments, as appears from the Saronno fresco and other paintings of his. Of the total of a hundred and sixteen angels glorifying God the Father, no less than fifty-seven play instruments. The fingering is depicted with the greatest precision and

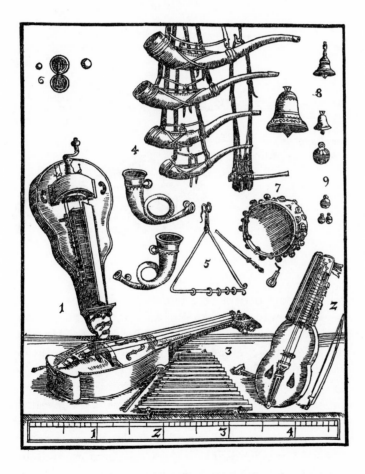

Fig. 6. Hurdy-gurdy and related instruments. From Praetorius, *Syntagma musicum*, 1618.

alone would reveal the hand of a painter musician. Plate 21b shows an elegant hurdy-gurdy, with three strings, to conclude from the pegs; Plate 21c a fantastic bagpipe with two one-hand chanters and two conical drones; it must have been capable of exceptional harmonic effects. A slightly later French woodcut, in the Rabelaisian vein, shows the hurdy-gurdy *déclassé* in the hands of a '*vielleur des maulx vestus*' (Pl. 28c).

It is interesting to observe how the earliest treatises on musical instruments evaluate the hurdy-gurdy. Sebastian Virdung in his *Musica getutscht und ausgezogen* ('Treatise on Music Put into German and Condensed'), published in

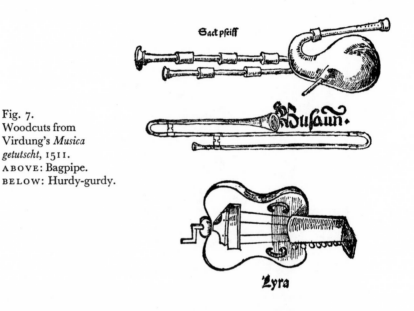

Fig. 7.
Woodcuts from Virdung's *Musica getutscht*, 1511.
ABOVE: Bagpipe.
BELOW: Hurdy-gurdy.

1511 in Basel, gives a woodcut of a four-stringed hurdy-gurdy (Fig. 7) but apparently does not consider it worth discussing in the text. The same is true of Martin Agricola, who reprints Virdung's woodcut in his *Musica instrumentalis deudsch* (Wittenberg, 1528), calling the instrument 'Leyer.' In the ominous year 1618, the first year of the Thirty Years' War, appeared the first comprehensive, systematic treatise on the subject, Michael Praetorius's *Syntagma musicum*, with many admirably precise woodcuts. Among them we find a five-stringed hurdy-gurdy (Fig. 6, upper left) and two of its relatives, a fiddle with a wheel but no stopping rods (lower left) and a keyed fiddle with a stopping mechanism but a bow instead of a wheel (right). The latter is still used as a folk instrument in Scandinavia under the name *nyckelharpa*. The caption for all three instruments says, somewhat deprecatingly, 'Some peasant lyres.' The text, without any discussion, merely mentions 'the peasants and vagabond women's lyre.' Shortly after this, in 1636, Mersenne expressed the same evaluation, though in more graceful and tolerant terms:

> If men of distinction usually played 'la Symphonie,' which is called *vielle*, it would not be as scorned as it is. But because it is played only by the poor, and especially by the blind, it is less esteemed than others that give less pleasure. This does not prevent my explaining it here, since skill does not belong to the rich more than to the poor and since there is nothing so base or vile in nature or in the arts as to be unworthy of consideration.

Two woodcuts from his *Harmonie universelle* are reproduced in Fig. 4, one showing an instrument identical with that in the hands of Georges de la Tour's *Hurdy-Gurdy Player* (Pl. 20b), the other interesting because of the open peg box with lateral pegs, a rather rare form obviously taken over from the rebec or the viol.

The bagpipe retained its status longer, particularly in the country of exceptions, the British Isles. We have reports that it enjoyed royal favour from Edward II to Henry VIII. On the Continent, too, it was used at courts and in the free cities, but on the whole it was the folk instrument which it has always been, played by beggars and at folk dances. The famous *Dance of the Peasants* (about 1568) by Peter Bruegel the Elder shows a large bagpipe with two drones (Pl. 28a). Its structure remains the same as that of the instrument played by Dürer's *Bagpiper* (1514) (Pl. 20a) and of the instrument illustrated by Virdung in 1511 (Fig. 7). A simpler instrument, with only one drone, is shown in Bruegel's *Fat Kitchen* (Pl. 28b). There can be no doubt about the social standing of the skinny piper, thrown out of the well-stocked kitchen by its well-fed inhabitants and their equally corpulent dog.

So far we have considered chiefly Western Europe and Italy; we should now glance at Eastern and Central Europe. There another type of bagpipe was in use and still prevails unaltered in the Balkans. It is the old Persian-Arabian type having a small double chanter formed of two cylindrical clarinets but no drones. Among the most striking decorative features are the animal horns attached to the chanter and serving as bells (Pl. 24a). Sometimes each pipe has its own horn, sometimes one horn embraces both pipes.

These East European instruments of old oriental type must have exerted a decisive influence in Central Europe, particularly in Germany, through the mediation of the Slavs. From a comparison of Virdung's (1511) and Dürer's bagpipes (1514) (Fig. 7 & Pl. 20a) with those in Praetorius (1618) (Fig. 8), it seems likely that this influence was exerted in the 16th century; for, besides the bagpipe shown in Virdung (Fig. 7), with a conical oboe chanter that reappears practically unaltered in Praetorius (Fig. 8, left, no. 7), we find there three new forms (nos. 6, 8, and 9) with small cylindrical chanters apparently identical with Eastern clarinet chanters. In Germany the instrument now underwent a strange transformation into the satanic grotesque. It grew, often into weird size; the hide retained its black fur; the pipes — not joined in the same stock but separated — were enormously expanded and with them the oxhorns which were attached as bells, the latter being sometimes lengthened even more by the addition of metal cones (Pl. 25a & b). This bagpipe was called the *Bock* ('billy goat'), and frequently the upper end of the melody pipe was fitted with a carved-wood head of a goat, which looked out convincingly enough from the dark fur. The old cloven-footed Pan, or as we might call him now, Satan, must have enjoyed this development. As the devil smelled of goat, so the bagpipe now smelled of the devil — 'Forthwith the devil did appear, for name him and he's always near.' The *Bock* played for peasant dances that must have been coarse enough. We recollect the even coarser dance of Walpurgis Night, when witches rode on goats to the Blocksberg to hold revels with the Prince of Hell in the

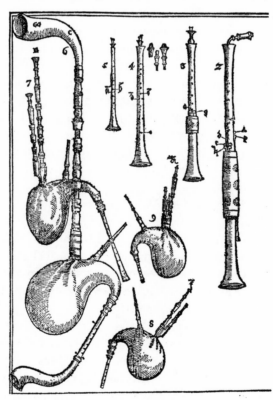

Fig. 8. Various bagpipes, From Praetorius, *Syntagma musicum*, 1618.

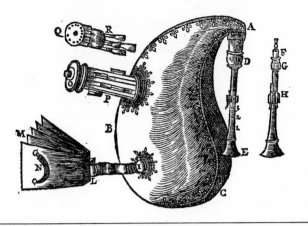

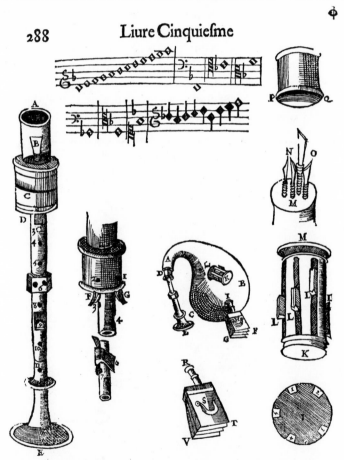

Fig. 9. Diagrams showing the construction of the musette. From Mersenne, *Harmonie universelle*, 1636. In upper diagram under R, and in lower diagram under N and O, note the four oboe reeds corresponding to the four drone channels concealed in the bourdon cylinder. In lower diagram, note the layettes marked L. The chanter shown is the form in use before Hotteterre's invention of the *petit chalumeau*.

guise of a gigantic goat — and all this in the heart of a Germany depaganized, we are told, long before.

The *Bock* had a sturdy life. Even in Viennese prints of Mozart's time we find street musicians with this instrument. Much earlier, in the time of the Reformation, the archfiend did not disdain to play the bagpipe himself. It was, however, a rather dainty one, a monk's head, apparently supposed to lure the faithful (Fig. 10). This woodcut is one of the grim political broadsides against the Church.

Turning again to Western Europe, we have to deal with one of the most decisive stages of the development leading to the assimilation of the bagpipe and hurdy-gurdy. It was the absorption into the pastoral fashion — or rather the pseudo-bucolic fashion — which put shepherd and peasant instruments in a refined and prettified form into the hands of the courtiers of Versailles. Two events at the end of the 16th century are of consequence for our story: the appearance of Giovanni Battista Guarini's pastoral drama *Il Pastor fido*, and the addition of bellows to the bagpipe.

The bellows is a very ancient tool; its story contains a good deal of the history of civilization. It was originally connected not with music but with fire, serving

Fig. 10. German woodcut, c. 1535.

forges, furnaces, and foundries. It helped to melt metal in Thebes in 1500 B.C. Pyramidal bellows were known to the Romans. Bellows were added to bagpipes in the last quarter of the 16th century, either in Ireland, as the Irish claim, or probably before, in Central Europe, as a bagpipe with bellows still in existence is mentioned in the inventory of the collection of Duke Ferdinand of Tyrol (Schloss Ambras in the Tyrol) taken after his death. It may seem almost absurd that bellows found their way to the bag that late; they are so convenient and besides they had been connected with a musical instrument, the organ, for almost two thousand years. But technical inventions, as history proves, must be timely; if they do not fill a pre-existing need, they are not absorbed by their age.

This need, in our case the application of bellows to bagpipes, was brought about by the pastoral fashion in the Latin countries of Europe. The story of conventional bucolics cannot be written here: a few reminders must suffice. Nature as the subject of fashion is by no means peculiar to the 17th and 18th centuries. Every advanced epoch of urban civilization has had its *retour à la nature* as an antidote. Old Pan never died. It is the legendary herdsman, Daphnis, of whom Thyrsis sings to his goatherd in Theocritus's *Bucolics*. There is an almost uninterrupted chain of attitudes toward nature from Virgil's *Eclogues* to the French Rococo: mystical, philosophical, or merely recreational retreats to the innocence of nature. We may mention at random Saint Francis's praise of Brother Wind and Sister Water; Petrarch's wonderful descriptions of the Bay of Spezia and the woods of Reggio; Boccaccio's *Ninfale fiesolano*; the landscape backgrounds of Antonello da Messina, Giovanni Bellini, Filippo Lippi.

The most influential early work of the *poesia boschereccia* was Sannazzaro's *Arcadia* (1504). It presents contests on the *humile fistula di coridone* ('the humble pipe of Corydon') and, as an epilogue, a 'Farewell to the Zampogna' — the bagpipe of the South and Central Italian mountain people. Then follow in Western Europe, to mention only the most outstanding, Remi Belleau's *Bergerie* (1565), Tasso's *Aminta* (1573), Spenser's *Shepheardes Calender* (1579), and Cervantes's *Galatea* (1584). True, there is much imitation of the ancient classics in these works. But on the other hand we feel in them a good deal of real nostalgia for nature, just as we find it later in the Aeolian harps of the dying 18th century, the romantic horns of Weber's *Freischütz* and Mendelssohn's music for *A Midsummer Night's Dream*, French *plein-air* painting, and Debussy's *Après-midi d'un faune*. We cannot help recalling how much our own time is also imbued with an innocent longing for nature, to be satisfied, it is true, in the mill of mass amusement by *Ersatz*, by jungle and South Sea pictures and cartoons, by Tarzan and his Jane.

A quite different spirit permeated the French pastoral fashion of the 17th and 18th centuries. It was rustic life conventionalized as a pleasant game for the nobility. Its upbeat was Guarini's *Pastor fido* (1590), strangely enough the very same poem that was the finale of pastoral poesy in Italy. *Il Pastor fido* is a pastoral drama, its stage in Arcadia, but in it country life is far from being naive or innocent shepherdry. It is rather a slightly veiled satire contrasting the corruption of the court of Ferrara with blameless rural life, and it was this which made *Il Pastor fido* the enormous literary success that it was. It mirrored its time, decadent and dissolute, and became the textbook of feigned innocence, and probably it was no gross exaggeration for a contemporary voice to state that it had done more harm to Christendom by its blandishments than Luther by his heresy.

Of this brand was the rustic fashion that pervaded the court life of France. What a spectacle — a noble society that has conventionalized even its vices! There is some grandeur in it, no doubt: classical balance is carried to extremes, with Apollo entertaining Dionysus. It may be a triumph of civilization to rationalize even passion, but this triumph is dangerous, for moral boundaries are blurred when sins become socially acceptable.

The fashionable shepherds, smelling rather of perfume than of the stable, took over the pastoral bagpipe along with the hats and ribbons. This folk instrument, as it then was, did not, of course, fit the hands of courtiers. It had to be refined: its most awkward, heavy parts, particularly the drones, were reduced; the chanter became smaller in size and sweeter in tone and received more conveniently spaced fingerholes and, later, even keys; and, as mentioned before, the blowpipe, unbecoming to a lady's mouth, was replaced by bellows. Thus arose the musette, which remained in vogue from the early 17th century until almost the end of the *ancien régime*. The story of its gradual refinement would form a chapter in itself. How great a reduction in size took place one can realize by comparing the musette (Pl. 24b) with the gigantic Italian zampogna still played in the Abruzzi (Pl. 27c).

The contraction of the long drones of earlier bagpipes was achieved through the adaptation of an ingenious instrument, the rackett, also called ranket or sausage bassoon. This instrument, which can be traced back to the late Renaissance, consisted of a short wooden or ivory barrel within which a cylindrical bore of remarkable length was bent several times in U-shape and fitted with an oboe reed. Now it was constructed so as to enclose the drones of the bagpipe: instead of a single bore, there were several independent ones, each fitted with an oboe reed. This is the drone cylinder, or bourdon, which is found in the musette. Mersenne's woodcuts show four drones concealed in the bourdon (Fig. 9). Later the number grew to six. Each of the drones could be tuned by an ivory slide (*layette*) running in a groove along the bourdon. About 1650 Jean Hotteterre, the founder of a dynasty of instrument makers and virtuosos (flutists, oboists, and hurdy-gurdy players), added to the chanter of the musette a smaller chanter which ran alongside the other and extended its compass upwards. The chanters were now called *le grand* and *le petit chalumeau*. This fully developed form of the musette appears regularly in Watteau's *fêtes champêtres* (see Pl. 26a & b). The earlier form is found, for example, in Van Dyck's portrait of a French nobleman (Pl. 27b). Nothing was spared in decorating the musette with the finest material. The leather bag was covered with brocade or velvet; rosewood and ivory were used for the pipes; ribbons and tassels were added.

These refinements affected another, simpler type: the cornemuse, a bagpipe that still retained its blowpipe but reduced its drone, so that it lay alongside the chanter in the same stock (Pl. 29b).

The importance and diffusion of the musette were enormous and perhaps comparable to those of the saxophone and the jazz trumpet in our times. In *fêtes rustiques* and in the ballet it was indispensable. Lully soon took it into his opera orchestra. Its most rapid rise took place under Louis XIV: the king himself danced to the musette in the court ballet; it was used in the orchestra of the Grand Écurie. Learned treatises were written on it. The first systematic method appeared anonymously in 1672 in Lyons, the *Traité de la musette*, 'with a new method for easy and quick self-instruction.' Its author was the jurist Charles Emmanuel Borjon, 'avocat au parlement de Paris,' known for his *Compilations du droit romain, du droit français, et du droit canon*. A characteristic passage from the *Traité* runs as follows:

> There is nothing so common nowadays as to see the nobility, especially those who spend much time in the country, finding enjoyment in playing the musette. How many worthy men of science and affairs relax their minds by this charming exercise, and how many women make the effort to add to their other good qualities that of playing the musette.

Later, in 1737, there followed the *Nouvelle Méthode pour la musette* by Jacques Hotteterre Le Romain, the grandson of Jean Hotteterre, inventor of the *petit chalumeau*. The number of compositions for the musette is legion: it suffices to mention those of the three brothers Chédeville, who wrote for this instrument *concerts champêtres, symphonies, sonates, duos gallantes, fêtes pastorales, gallanteries amusantes*, as well as *Les Pantomimes italiennes dansées à l'Académie royale de musique, mises pour la musette, vielle, flute traversière, et hautbois*.

The rise of the hurdy-gurdy (in French, *vielle à roue*) followed that of the musette. The climax, it seems, came under Louis XV. Two wandering virtuosos,

Janot and La Rose, excited the nobility. The queen herself, Marie Leszczynska, was a famous amateur of the vielle. In the arts it is found even in chinoiseries; an engraving after Watteau shows a chinoiserie vielle probably never built in reality (Pl. 26d).

The vielle did not have to undergo such essential changes as the musette to become courtly and convenient. It had shrunk in size in the 13th century, as we have seen, but its range now had to be expanded. The famous virtuoso Charles Baton increased the number of stopping rods to twenty-three, that is, two tones less than two octaves. This made the range of the vielle equivalent to that of the chanter of the musette. In 1757 Charles Baton published a *Mémoire sur la vielle* in the *Mercure de France*. In 1741 the Abbé Terrasson, professor of Greek and Latin philosophy at the Collège de France, had published his learned *Dissertation sur la vielle*. In 1763 there appeared a *Méthode pour jouer la vielle, instrument agréable, brillant et bon pour jouer seul et faire danser*, by Michel Corette. We have reports that innumerable lutes, theorbos, and guitars were rebuilt into vielles by adding a wheel and stopping mechanism. One can only guess how many magnificent Renaissance instruments fell victims to this fashion.

In Watteau we find occasionally the two drone instruments, vielle and musette, side by side (Pl. 26c), but their gradual convergence is evident from the increasing number of scores first with parts for both and later parts to be played by either one *ad libitum*. Already the great Antonio Vivaldi had composed *Il Pastor fido, Sonates pour la musette, vielle, etc.* (Op. XIIIa). About 1700 Esprit Philippe Chédeville, known as le Cadet, the second of the three brothers mentioned before, published *Les Déffis, ou l'Étude amusante pour la musette ou* [!] *la vielle*. We quote from the dedication:

> As for you, gentlemen, whom the god of war drafts to his colours, I have your applause if I have the ladies'. The clash of arms will not make you forget my concerts, and the blare of trumpets that proclaim your laurels will not render you insensible to the soft harmonies of the sweet musette.

How far is the pastoral musette of France from the martial bagpipe of Britain!

About 1755 there finally appeared a treatise that to a particular degree reveals the complete assimilation achieved between the vielle and the musette. This was the *Méthode raisonnée pour apprendre la musique d'une façon plus claire et plus précise à laquelle on joint l'étendue de la flute traversière, du violon, du pardessus de viole, de la vielle et de la musette. . . . Ouvrage fait pour la comodité des Maîtres et l'utilité des Écoliers*, by M. Bordet, 'Maître de flute traversière.' On page 23 of Bordet's book (Pl. 29a), the tuning and the compass of the two instruments are set against each other. At the left is shown the complete coincidence between the tuning of the drone strings of the vielle (*chanterelles, trompette, mouche, bourdon supprimé*, and *bourdon de sol*) and that of the drone pipes of the musette. At the right is shown the close analogy in the compass of the two instruments, which is now almost identical.

Before the French Revolution, the vielle had passed its zenith and returned to the street, where it had meanwhile maintained a humble existence (Pl. 27d). But at the same time, and for the last time, a great master wrote for it, Joseph Haydn. King Ferdinand IV of Naples, an ardent admirer of Haydn's art, had been inspired to play the vielle by a secretary at the Austrian Legation at the Court of Naples, Norbert Hadrava, who must have been one of those numerous and cultivated Czechs in the diplomatic service of the Austrian monarchy. Haydn, commissioned upon Hadrava's suggestion, wrote five concertos for the vielle and later several *notturni*, each of three movements, for two vielles and orchestra, magnificent pieces that found enthusiastic reception when they were performed again — with the vielle parts executed by flute and oboe — at the famous Salomon concerts Haydn gave in London. Even in the *notturni* the vielles are treated as typical solo instruments, successively alternating, imitating, and uniting. It was a magnificent finale for the vielle in art music.

But still the drone went on humming. Bagpipe and hurdy-gurdy had early been imitated by other instruments, such as the organ or the harpsichord, or by groups of instruments, whenever it was desirable to create a pastoral atmosphere. From many suites of the 17th and 18th centuries we know dance forms which were based completely or partly on a drone bass, often strengthened by its fifth. Among them was the graceful 'musette,' in calm three-four time. It had received its name from the bagpipe musette, just as about five hundred years earlier the organistrum had probably been named after the harmony it was fitted to perform, the organum. Another drone dance, in two-four time, was the 'tambourin,' derived again from the instrument of the same name, which is a stringed drum producing a drone bass in the tonic and dominant of the melody of a little one-hand pipe. There are countless 'musettes' and 'tambourins' in the harpsichord and orchestra suites of the Rococo. Anyone who wants a vivid idea of the vigour of the drone in typical tunes for the vielle may find imitations of this and other drone instruments in the *11ième Ordre* of Couperin's *Pièces de clavecin*. One of these is *Les Fastes de la grande et ancienne ménestrandise*, in five acts — a clever satire, by the way, on the clashes between the musicians' unions of that time. The second act is called *Bourdon* and carries the subtitle *Les Vielleux et les gueux*. It consists of two 'airs de vielle.' The third act, which introduces jugglers with their animals, is a characteristic pipe tune upon a drone bass in the tonic and dominant, suggesting a drum accompaniment.

The drone effect is also found in numerous pastorales of the middle of the 17th century. These are idealized shepherd tunes retaining the six-eight or twelve-eight rhythm and frequently the drone bass. Such tunes were played in South and Central Italy by the *zampognari* and *pifferari* who surrounded the cradle of the Child, a custom still alive. Thus it came about that pastorales were used in Christmas music, for example, the 6th movement of Corelli's *Concerto da Natale* and the *Sinfonia* in Bach's *Christmas Oratorio*. Handel must have heard the *pifferari* when he lived in Rome, and he used this effect in the *Sinfonia pastorale* of *Messiah*, in his oratorios *Semele* and *Acis and Galatea*, and in many other pieces. Other pastorales occur in works by the Scarlattis, Couperin, Pachelbel, Telemann, and so forth. One of the most famous is the great organ Pastorale in F major by J. S. Bach. Joseph Haydn, whose art was so deeply rooted in the fertile ground of folklore, employs drone tunes of all sorts, from literal quotations of bagpipe melodies to faintly suggestive uses of the drone effect. We mention only two examples, the finale of his Symphony No. 82, *L'Ours* (1786), based upon a real bagpipe tune, and the main theme in the finale of his 'London' Symphony, No. 104.

Not before Beethoven was there an entire symphony entitled *Pastorale*. In one of his sketch books it is called *Sinfonie caracteristica: Die Erinnerungen von dem Landleben*, or, as we might translate today, 'A programmatic symphony: Reminiscences of rural life.' Beethoven, moreover, took the utmost care to explain to the hearer what he wanted to express. Each movement is given a title suggesting the rustic scene it depicts. Was this necessary at the time? When the symphony started, with the violoncellos and violas droning the tonic and dominant as pedal point and the violins followed with their characteristic capering melody, the audience, we may safely assume, understood the connotation. In another mood, it seems that Beethoven himself took this response for granted, for a second note in his sketch book says, 'It is left to the hearer to find out the situations.' No doubt he did.

Today, however, a hundred and thirty years farther from the musette, the situation is different. Many listeners, more familiar with 19th-century music than with earlier music, may draw their interpretation of the drone as rustic from the mere fact that the drone occurs in a symphony which is entitled *Pastorale*.

Strange, indeed, are the mechanics of style. In the beginning there was a shepherd, his instrument the bagpipe, which happened to acquire a drone. The shepherd became fashionable; so did his drone. Thus the drone in art music became the symbol of the pastorale. Later generations, finding such effects used in music entitled *Pastorale*, learned its connotation from the name; they might never have seen a shepherd or heard a bagpipe. A short cut is formed: where grandfather knew the whole story, we react and interpret automatically. Thus a fashion hardened by tradition becomes second nature. So crystallize the habits of the ear.

The hurdy-gurdy as a folk instrument has not yet entirely died out. An imitation of a characteristic vielle tune is found in Schubert's melancholy *Der Leiermann*, the last song in the *Winterreise* cycle, ending with the words,

> Strange old man, say, will you go with me,
> Crank your lyre to my melody?

In our time it has been manufactured for the people of the Auvergne and Bourbonnais, of Berry, and of Savoy.

The bagpipe, however, is still very much alive, not only as a folk instrument in many mountain valleys of Europe but as a military instrument in the British Isles. The mechanical peculiarities of English and Irish bagpipes are beyond the scope of this article. They belong in a world of their own. Two facts only may be stressed: while the French musette symbolizes peace, for many centuries past the Highland pipes have led men to battle and still sound all over the globe where British troops are stationed. Secondly, the Scotch bagpipes reveal their oriental origin more strikingly than do other occidental bagpipes. It has been pointed out that the Piob Mor, the great Highland bagpipe, is not based on our equal-tempered scale, but that its scale, as determined by the spacing of the finger-holes on its chanter, is actually based on the Arabian. The sound of the Piob Mor on the North African battlefields during World War II thus closed a cultural circle of thousands of years.[1]

[1] In *The New York Times* for May 16, 1943, an American officer, First Lieutenant Daniel G. Kennedy, asked for bagpipes and discussed the value of this instrument for a soldier's morale. 'Even in the African campaign,' he said, 'they were reported to be a factor in the dogged, relentless drives at El Alamein and the Mareth line. Here at this infantry replacement center where the American doughboys train we have long wanted to add bagpipe music to our band.' Perhaps on some such occasion was heard again that fine old bagpipe tune so irresistible in 1702: 'The Day We Beat the Germans at Cremona.'

5 · The Lira da Braccio[*]

The lira da braccio was one of the most important string instruments of the High Renaissance, the instrument of the recitalists who improvised polyphonic accompaniments for their singing, and therefore one of the most characteristic implements of the intended revival of the rhapsodic art of the ancients. Its use remained primarily restricted to Italy.

In its fully developed form, the instrument consisted of a flat sound box with a broad fingerboard, a slightly rounded bridge, and a peg box on the front of which were seven pegs for fastening strings: five melody strings running over the fingerboard and two bass strings running parallel to the melody strings but apart from the fingerboard; there were no frets. Larger forms, such as the lirone and the lira da gamba, had a correspondingly greater number of strings, up to a total of fifteen, including four free-running strings.

Tracing our instrument in the treatises of the Italian Renaissance is no easy task, because it had a variety of names, some of which referred also to instruments of Greek or Roman antiquity, or were given indiscriminately to other different Renaissance instruments. Although sometimes also called 'lira da spalla,' it was generally called simply 'lira' in contemporary literature,[1] or occasionally 'lira moderna' to distinguish it from the ancient lyre; Ganassi speaks of the 'lira di sette corde.'[2] The invention of the lira was ascribed to the ancients by authors of the 15th and early 16th centuries, and even by Bernardi in 1581,[3] while 16th-century emblematic literature,[4] when discussing the lira, quotes indiscriminately from both ancient and contemporary sources, and regards both the 'lira con l'archetto' and the 'lira toccata dal plettro' as instruments of antiquity. Bronze plaques of the late 16th and early 17th centuries show Apollo with an ancient lyre and a modern bow. Ganassi describes a discovery of antiquities in Rome, among them the figure of a player

---

[*] The original article on the *Lira da Braccio*, published in *Die Musik in Geschichte und Gegenwart*, VIII (1960), contained several long sections concerning matters such as the morphological evolution of the lira da braccio, various methods of tuning, the history and evolution of its bow, various playing methods, the employment of the lira da braccio and of the lirone in intermedii, and others. Since these sections were of a predominantly technical nature, they did not seem sufficiently pertinent to warrant their inclusion here.

[1] For instance, in Giovanni Maria Lanfranco, *Scintille di musica* (1533), and Pietro Cerone, *El Melopeo y maestro*, Naples, 1613.

[2] *Regola Rubertina* (1543).   [3] *Ragionamenti musicali*, Bologna, 1581.

[4] E.g., P. Abb. Picinelli, *Del Mondo simbolico ampliato*, Bk. XXIII, Ch. V.

holding in his hand 'a viola d'arco, which should be called lira or lirone, rather than viola or violone,'[1] and Pierius Valerianus's *Hieroglyphica* (Basel, 1567) even illustrates an 'ancient' altar decorated with reliefs of lire da braccio (Fig. 1 in Chapter 1 above).[2]

This assumption that the lira da braccio was an ancient instrument was apparently based on several facts. The number of strings — seven — recalled that of the classical ancient lyre. Moreover, the lira da braccio had, in addition to its stopped strings, unstopped strings which always sounded their full length, just as did all the strings of the ancient kithara and lyre. Finally, it was widely believed that the ancient plectrum for the kithara and lyre was actually something like a fiddle bow, and it was only as late as 1581 that this assumption was energetically refuted by Vincenzo Galilei.[3]

For a long time, the lira da braccio was also called 'viola.' In the second half of the 16th century the usage still varied: Vasari, for example, speaks of the lira da braccio played by one of the angels in Carpaccio's *Presentation in the Temple* (Accademia, Venice; Pl. 33b) as 'una lira ovvero viola,' but calls the same instrument, in Fra Bartolommeo's *sacra conversazione* for San Marco in Florence, simply a 'lira.'[4] Galilei, in his *Dialogo*, maintains that only recently had the viola da braccio been called 'lira,'[5] and, in another passage, that it had been called 'lira' only in his own time ('modernamente').[6] The fact that earlier sources generally refer to the lira da braccio by the name 'viola' is not without importance in view of the many musicians with the nickname 'della viola'; as we know, during the reign of Alfonso II, the court of Ferrara employed Francesco di Viola, a pupil of Willaert, as chapelmaster, and also the madrigal composer Alfonso della Viola. Further evidence for the use of the name 'viola' for the lira can be seen in the terminology of the period, which frequently speaks of 'viols with frets' when referring to members of the viol family, obviously to distinguish them from the fretless lira da braccio; thus, Ganassi's *Regola Rubertina* speaks expressly of the 'viola d'arco tastada' in the title of its first part, and of the 'violone d'arco da tasti' in its second part, while Lanfranco's *Scintille* mentions 'violoni da tasti & da Arco.'

The names for the larger forms, with more than seven strings, were *lirone*, *lirone perfetto*, *lira da gamba*, and *arciviolatalira* (probably a corruption of *arciviola da lira*). The *Organographia* of Praetorius uses distorted names, *Arce violyra* and *Arce-viola telire*, while Mersenne calls the lira da gamba which he describes in his *Harmonie universelle* simply *lyre*.

---

[1] *Regola Rubertina*, Pt. I, Ch. VIII.

[2] For further information about this pseudo-archaeology, see Chapter 14 below.

[3] *Dialogo della musica antica e della moderna*, 1581, p. 130.

[4] *Vite*, Milan, 1564, III, 642.   [5] *Dialogo*, p. 147.   [6] *Ibid.*, p. 130.

The literary evidence from authors of the early and high Renaissance should be combined with what we can learn from extant specimens. Unfortunately only a very few pieces have survived, and of them hardly a handful are in their original or approximately original condition. The oldest, and certainly the most beautiful, is the magnificent instrument by Giovanni d'Andrea da Verona, dated 1511, now in the Kunsthistorisches Museum, Vienna (Pl. 31b & g). Its soundboard is of a warm brown colour, while the back and sides have a dark reddish varnish. The fingerboard and the string holder are decorated in typical North Italian style, 'alla certosina' — that is, by a colourful combination of ebony, ivory, bone which has been stained green, and brown wood. The most striking feature, however, is the carving of belly and back, which give the impression of human forms. The belly is shaped like a male torso and, correspondingly, the front of the peg box shows a grotesque male face. The back shows, in stronger relief, the form of a female torso with breasts and nipples strongly marked and, accordingly, the back of the peg box shows a woman's face. But this is not the end of the sculptural fantasy: acanthus leaves encroach upon the female torso and on its middle region is a large moustachioed *mascherone* that overlaps the undulations of the female form.

The sound-holes in the belly are unusually large, of tendril shape; the peg box can be closed, and it is remarkable how cleverly the pegs are inserted so as to disturb as little as possible the grimace of the grotesque face. A little ivory plaque inserted into the back bears the somewhat miswritten Greek inscription: '*ΛΥΠΗΣ ΙΑΤΡΟΣ ΕΣΤΙΝ ΑΝΘΡΩΠΟΙΣ ΩΑΗ*' ('Men have song as the physician of pain'). This is an adaptation of an ancient monostichon (326) in which, for obvious reasons, ῷδή (song) replaced the original λόγος (*logos*), and in quoting it respect is paid to humanist learning, so important in Venetian culture of the time.

How far this masterpiece of applied sculpture is from the standardized forms of string instruments of later ages! And how much it helps us to visualize other Renaissance instruments, such as the lira da braccio that Leonardo built in the shape of a horse's skull — a shape so beloved by that great connoisseur of animal anatomy!

The Heyer Collection in Leipzig includes a lirone by Ventura di Francesco Linarol, Venice, 1577 (Pl. 31c). A lira da braccio in the Ashmolean Museum, Oxford, by Joan Maria, and a somewhat larger one in the Museum of the Brussels Conservatory (Pl. 31a) are undated, as are the following lire da gamba: one with four free and nine melody strings in the Vienna collection, by Wendelin Tieffenbrucker, Padua, c. 1590 (Pl. 31f & h), which is related by its complex contour to the lira da braccio shown in a painting by Bartolommeo Passerotti in the Galleria Spada, Rome (Pl. 32a); a later example in the

Brussels Conservatory Museum with a round sound-hole, nine melody strings, and frets (Pl. 31e); and a very late one from the mid-17th century in the Heyer Collection, which also has frets, a round sound-hole, and two free and fourteen melody strings. Two further examples in the Heyer Collection had been made into violoncellos before their restoration.

Since only very few examples, of comparatively late date, have survived, the pictorial sources for the lira da braccio are indispensable. There is a profusion of contemporary representations, especially in the art of Venice, Lombardy, and Tuscany — frescoes, paintings, woodcuts and engravings, sculptures, reliefs and plaques, wood intarsias, book vignettes, frame carvings, and so on. The most numerous depictions are in mythological and allegorical scenes, and in angel concerts.

In the mythological scenes, both Apollo and Orpheus are often shown playing the lira da braccio. Apollo appears both in his contests with Marsyas and Pan (of which the earliest illustrations are probably the woodcuts in *Ovidio*

Fig. 11.
King David in prayer, with a lirone
in the foreground. From a 1497
edition of the Office of the B.V.M.

Fig. 12.
Fifteen-stringed bass lira
('lyre'), with bow and
tuning. From Mersenne,
Harmonie universelle, 1636.

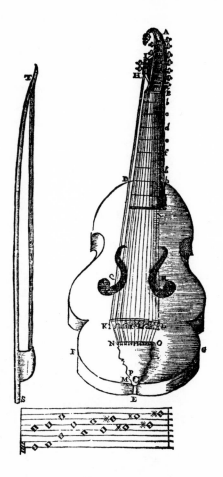

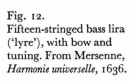

metamorphoseos volgare, Venice, 1497 and 1501; see Figs. 20 & 21 in Chapter 12)
and as leader of the Muses (most notably in Raphael's *Parnassus* fresco in the
Vatican, which was endlessly copied and varied; see Chapter 14 below).
Orpheus appears playing among the wild beasts (as in the engraving of
Benedetto Montagna), subduing the demons of hell (as in Signorelli's fresco
cycle in the Chapel of San Brizio in the Orvieto Cathedral, and in Peruzzi's
frescoed frieze in the Villa Farnesina in Rome), or leading Euridice (in Marcantonio Raimondi's engraving, for example). Concerts of the Muses, among them
Tintoretto's numerous examples, also include the lira da braccio, and Homer
and the royal psalmist David (Fig. 11) are frequently shown with it. It is,
therefore, the celebrated recitalists of the ancient world and of the Old Testament who accompany their singing with the lira da braccio.

In angel concerts of the Renaissance, the lira da braccio appears both in the large instrumental ensembles surrounding the Coronation of the Virgin and in the small groups of angels (usually two or three, but sometimes only a single one) before the throne of the Madonna in the *sacre conversazioni*, especially those of the Venetian school (see Pls. 33, 35, & 37b).

Curiously enough, portraits of musicians with the lira da braccio are uncommon; an early one, attributed to Raffaellino del Garbo, is in the National Gallery, Dublin (Pl. 32b). Musical treatises contain few pictures of this instrument, and only from the last phase of its popularity; they are also sometimes unreliable, such as those in Praetorius's *Syntagma*[1] and in Buonnani's *Gabinetto armonico* (Rome, 1722). Mersenne's *Harmonie universelle* (1636) shows only one, a very precise woodcut of an atypical bass lira ('lyre'), with frets and side-pegs inserted in a sickle-shaped head (Fig. 12).

The accuracy of representation is greatest in the almost life-size depictions in Venetian altarpieces, and in the numerous, though heretofore largely ignored, still-lifes in wood intarsia (most importantly those at Monte Oliveto near Siena, in Verona, Padua, and the ducal palaces of Urbino and Mantua; see Pls. 34a, 52a, and Chapters 8 & 9 below), which excel in their use of accurate geometric perspective. The reliability of paintings is often impaired by inexpert restoration (ignorant restorers were likely to paint over the free strings), while often in sculpture and reliefs, for obvious reasons, the strings are simplified, their number is reduced, and the free strings are entirely omitted.

Pictures and reliefs often show lire da braccio of fantastic forms or with profuse ornamentation; among these are the lira in Cima da Conegliano's *tondo* in the Uffizi showing the contest of Apollo and Pan; that in the engraving by the Master of the Sforza Book of Hours, showing the Virgin with two musical angels; and the one in Gaudenzio Ferrari's *Madonna* in the Pinacoteca in Turin (Pl. 34b). The belief that the exquisite instrument shown in Passerotti's *King David* (Pl. 32a) really existed is made plausible by a comparison with the lira da gamba in the Vienna collection (Pl. 31g).

In general, one must keep in mind that it is not always easy to distinguish between the exuberant imagination of the painter and the decorative fantasy of the instrument maker, especially since the manufacture of musical instruments was by no means standardized at that time, and because solo instruments 'in the ancient manner' such as the lira da braccio were often built to satisfy the purchasers' desire for showpieces of unusual form and decoration; examples are Vasari's report of the lira built by Leonardo da Vinci in the form of a horse skull (not 'Pferdekopf' — horse head — as in much German art-historical literature, but 'Pferdeschädel'), and the lira of Giovanni d'Andrea described earlier.

[1] *Sciagraphia*, XVII, 4 and XX, 5.

In addition to its importance as a solo instrument, the lira da braccio and the lirone are frequently mentioned in reports of Renaissance intermedii, in which they were used for the accompaniment of madrigals, sometimes as a substitute for the harpsichord, or occasionally in such combinations as: 1 lirone, 4 violoni, and 4 tromboni.[1] Lire were also used in the famous Florentine intermedii of 1589; a solo madrigal was accompanied by a lute, a chitarrone, and an arci-violatalira, which latter was played by Alessandro Striggio himself. The performance of Peri's *Euridice* in 1600 used a 'lira grande' in the orchestra. Two short examples of tablature for the lira da gamba have been preserved: Mersenne reproduces three bars of a *Laudamus te* with an accompaniment of four- and five-part chords,[2] and a similar example is found in Cerreto's *Della prattica musica*.

It is characteristic of the great interest in archaeology prevailing in Italy that an instrument regarded — though erroneously — as a descendant of the ancient lyre achieved its greatest importance and popularity in the 'terra sacra'; outside Italy, the lira da braccio is seldom found. Mersenne emphasizes the scarcity of the 'lyre' in France.[3] Praetorius, in his *Theatrum instrumentorum*, specifically designates both forms illustrated as 'italienische,' and the few representations found in German art all seem to be derived from Italian models. This is the case

P   O   E   S   I   A.

Fig. 13. Allegorical representation of Poesia with a lirone. From Cesare Ripa, *Iconologia*, 1618.

[1] For further information, see Otto Kinkeldey, *Orgel und Klavier in der Musik des 16. Jahrhunderts*, Leipzig, 1910, Chapter 6.

[2] *Harmonie universelle*, p. 207.   [3] *Ibid.*, p. 206.

Fig. 14. Two representations of Jupiter, one holding a lira da braccio (described in the text as nine-stringed). From Vincenzo Cartari, *Le Imagini dei dei degli antichi*, 1580.

with Peter Vischer's Orpheus plaque, which is inspired by a similar plaque by Moderno (see Pl. 30b); a marginal vignette in Dürer's prayerbook for the Emperor Maximilian; and a small Orpheus playing the lira da braccio among the Muses, found in the decoration of a processional car for Maximilian illustrated among the woodcuts of Burgkmair. In Italy, the instrument seems to have survived until after 1600, and the larger forms even until after 1700; the inventory of instruments at the Medici court of 1716 includes three lire with twelve, thirteen, and fourteen strings — thus apparently bass lire — but not a single lira da braccio.

Although the lira da braccio was often, as mentioned above, referred to as 'viola' in the contemporary sources, it remained quite distinct, in structure, tuning, and playing technique, from the viola da gamba family which evolved at the same time. Occasionally, hybrid forms appeared, such as instruments combining the characteristic stringing of the lira da braccio with the scroll and lateral pegs of the viola da gamba; an example can be seen in the anonymous early 16th-century Italian portrait of a youth with a string instrument, in the Kunsthistorisches Museum, Vienna.

In shape, the later examples of the lira da braccio gradually approached that of the violin, and its characteristic tuning in fifths and lack of frets (as opposed to the viol family) clearly influenced the development of the violin. On the other hand, Gaudenzio Ferrari's cupola fresco in Saronno (*c.* 1534) shows a fully developed four-string violin alongside various forms of the lira da braccio, and therefore Hajdecki's hypothesis of a gradual but direct evolution of the violin from the lira da braccio cannot be maintained without some modification (see Chapter 6).

The musical treatises of the Renaissance that mention the lira da braccio focus primarily on technical questions such as tuning, rather than on its central position in the musical life of the period, a matter they take for granted. However, other writings give occasional hints to fill out a sufficient picture. Vasari, in his discussion of the musical interests of Leonardo, emphasizes the latter's predilection for the lira da braccio as that of a man 'who by nature possessed a spirit both lofty and full of grace which enabled him to improvise divinely in

Fig. 15.
A poet with lira da braccio. From *Epithome Plutarchi*, 1501.

Fig. 16. A humanist with lira da braccio. From Quintianus Stoa, *De Syllabarum quantitate*, 1511.

singing and playing the lira da braccio,'[1] and a similar remark is applied to Raphael's teacher Timoteo Viti, who also played the lira da braccio.[2] Castiglione, in the second book of his *Cortegiano*, distinguishes between two forms of making music: 'Good music means to me singing well and securely and in good style from the score; but much more still the singing to one's own *viola* accompaniment'[3] — the 'viola' being the lira da braccio, which we find depicted several times in the ducal palace of Urbino, whose court and culture are the subject of Castiglione's treatise. Baccio Ugolino, the celebrated protagonist in the Mantua performance of Poliziano's *Orfeo* in 1471 and later bishop of Gaëta, earned the applause of Lorenzo de' Medici by his singing 'ad Lyram.' From these and many other passages emerges the significance of the instrument as a favourite of virtuosos and dilettantes. At the courts of Ferrara and Milan, virtuosos of the lira da braccio were employed. According to Vasari, Leonardo, when introduced to the Milanese court in 1494, was presented to the Duke as a player of the lira da braccio.[4]

As a rule, reports speak of 'cantare sopra' or 'su la lira,' which corresponds exactly to the conception that Renaissance musical archaeology had formed of ancient musical practice; Zarlino, for example, devotes an entire chapter in the

[1] '... che della natura aveva spirito elevatissimo e pieno di leggiadria, onde sopra quella cantò divinamente all' improvviso' (*Vite*, ed. Milanesi, IV, 18).

[2] *Ibid.*, IV, 498.

[3] 'Bella musica ... parmi il cantar bene a libro sicuramente, et con bella maniera: ma anchor molto più il cantare alla viola'.

[4] *Vite*, ed. Milanesi, IV, 28.

fifth book of his *Istitutioni harmoniche* to the ancient poets and rhapsodists and their recitation to the 'lira' and 'cetra.' Sometimes the lira da braccio appears with the player not singing or reciting, particularly in depictions of angel concerts. In the larger ensembles shown in Coronations of the Virgin, it always appears only once, never doubled, while in *sacre conversazioni* it appears with one or two other instruments (lute, rebec, occasionally also a recorder or cromorne). There are, however, paintings in which it appears as the sole instrument; such a painting as Palma Vecchio's *Sacra Conversazione* in San Zaccaria, Venice (Pl. 36), where one angel sits alone before the throne of the Madonna and between the groups of saints playing the lira da braccio, is an eloquent testament to the rank and importance of the instrument.

More than any other instrument of the Italian Renaissance, the lira da braccio is associated with the attempted revival of ancient musical practice. The facts of its name, its supposed antique origin, and its specific or imagined similarities to the ancient lyre, mentioned above, all contributed to endow it with a kind of allegorical significance that is clearly mirrored in the visual arts and in the allegorical and emblematic literature of the period. As early as the *quattrocento*, it appears as the symbolic attribute of the great poets and musicians

Fig. 17. Lute player, with lira da braccio in background. Title page of Lorenzo de' Medici, *Selve d'amore*.

of classical mythology and of the Old Testament: Apollo, Orpheus, Homer, King David — and also in the allegorical representations of Poesia, Musica, and Harmonia (see Fig. 13), in the famous mythological treatises of Lilio Gyraldi (*De Deis gentium varia et multiplex historia*, Basel, 1548), Vincenzo Cartari (*Le Imagini dei dei degli antichi*, Venice, 1556), Cesare Ripa (*Iconologia*, Rome, 1593), and others. In Cartari's book, even Jupiter is shown with a lira da braccio (see Fig. 14), while Valerianus, in his *Hieroglyphica*, 1567, shows it as an attribute of Mercury.

In the allegorical representations of the Liberal Arts, the lira da braccio frequently characterizes Musica, as in Pinturicchio's fresco in the Borgia Apartments in the Vatican, and in Pollaiuolo's decorations for the bronze tomb of Sixtus IV in St. Peter's. Later, even Tintoretto assigns it a prominent place in the foreground of his concerts of the Muses, and Jan Bruegel the Elder gives it the place of honour in the foreground of his *Allegory of Hearing* in the Prado (Pl. 37a), one of the last representations of the instrument.

In the numerous depictions of Apollo's contests with Marsyas and Pan, Apollo usually plays the lira da braccio, a symbol of the noble 'mathematical' music as opposed to the guttural and lascivious music of the various reed instruments played by his opponents (see Chapter 12); most of these use as their iconographical models the woodcuts of the first edition of the *Ovidio metamorphoseos volgare* (Venice, 1497). Later examples are found in the paintings of Schiavone, and in the picture by Correggio (or Bronzino?) in the Hermitage, originally the lid of a harpsichord. A small section of a lira da braccio can be detected in Giovanni Bellini's *Feast of the Gods* (National Gallery, Washington), a painting whose meaning can be deciphered by the presence of this very instrument (see Chapter 2).

In the miniatures and woodcuts of the late *quattrocento*, the lira da braccio begins to replace the harp and psaltery of King David, and the pictures and prints of the 16th century nearly always show him with this instrument (see, for example, the Passerotti painting in Plate 32a, and also Fig. 12).

Frequently, the number of strings is given symbolic significance — the number seven, for example, referring to the seven known planets (in Zarlino's *Istitutioni*, p. 21, and in Lanfranco's *Scintille di musica*). The nine strings of the instrument played by Apollo in Raphael's *Parnassus* evidently refer to the nine Muses and perhaps also to the nine Greek modes supposedly established by Gaudentius and later cited by Zarlino.[1]

---

[1] Zarlino, in the second table of contents for his *Istitutioni harmoniche* (Venice, 1558), states that 'Gaudentio filosofo numera nove modi nella Musica' and enumerates them in the text (part IV, p. 367) as follows: Mistolidio, Lidio, Frigio, Dorio, Hypolidio, Hypofrigio, Commune, Locrico, Hypodorio.

As an attribute of humanists, the lira da braccio appears in numerous book illustrations and frontispieces, to characterize the poet or philosopher, crowned with laurels and writing or teaching. Examples are the frontispieces of the 1501 Ferrara edition of Plutarch (Fig. 15), Quintianus Stoa's treatise *De Syllabarum quantitate* (Fig. 16), Lorenzo de' Medici's *Selve d'amore* (Fig. 17), and Pietro Aron's *Toscanello della musica* (Venice, 1523). On the back of a contemporary bronze plaquette (Pl. 30a) cast in honour of the Bolognese humanist Ercole Bottrigari, author of the treatise *Il Desiderio overo de concerti di varij strumenti musicali* (Venice, 1594), it appears among the traditional symbols of the *quadrivium*, and there are numerous other examples among treatises on astronomy, mathematics, and other subjects.

6 · Early Violins in Paintings by Gaudenzio Ferrari and his School

One of the great lacunae in the history of musical instruments is the question of the origin of the violin. This seems absurd, considering the increasing importance of this instrument for more than three hundred years. How different was the treatment accorded by musical historians to that other ruler among the tools of music, the pianoforte! We know almost everything about its origin and evolution, as it has been recorded in minute detail. True enough, the history of the pianoforte posed a much easier problem: one man, after a few years of experimentation, produced what the fashion of his time demanded — a keyboard instrument with a hammer action that enabled the player to perform crescendos and decrescendos, simply by modifying the pressure of his fingers on the keys. Thus a new keyboard style was at once made possible.

The violin, however, was not an 'invention.' Rather, it was the final product of a long and variegated process of development, a combination or fusion of many patterns and elements contributed by a number of different bowed instruments. Only when the great Lombard instrument-makers in Brescia and Cremona took over, after the middle of the 16th century, did something like a standard form emerge — standard, it is true, only in the sense of adherence to basic characteristics that still admitted countless variations of proportion, curvature, tonal quality, and so on. From that time on, we have something like a coherent history of the violin, told, if not in treatises, then by a considerable number of wonderful specimens that have survived to the present day.

A reliable account of the pre-history of the violin, and by that I mean the process of development mentioned above, has not yet been written, and a consultation of the modern books on the history of this instrument proves disappointing — they are vague or incorrect, or they simply avoid the problem.[1]

[1] a) George Hart, *The Violin*, London, 1884, pp. 24–25, refers to manuscript notes by Vincetto Lancetti that mention a three-stringed violin in the collection of Count Cozia di Salabue, in the form of the Italian viola, dated 1546 and attributed to Andrea Amati, but 'altered in the 19th century'! Then Hart continues: 'When or where the four-stringed Violin, tuned in fifths, first appeared in Italy is a question, the answer to which *must ever remain buried in the past.*'

b) Alexander Hajdecki, *Die italienische Lira da Braccio*, Mostar, 1892, p. 50, says: 'The Italian lira da braccio . . . is the mother of our violin. . . .'

So the origin of the violin is still obscure. Neither the alleged strict distinction between the families of the viola da gamba and the viola da braccio, nor the supposed direct evolution of the violin from the lira da braccio, conforms to its actual evolution,[1] and some attempts at condensation of its complex story have resulted in oversimplification. One cannot even blame the simplifiers, for the history of the violin is a process emanating from wide and wild experiments towards standardization, a standardization which is, in fact, almost unparalleled in the history of instruments. According to pictorial evidence, and contrary to the neat and departmentalized *Syntagma* of Praetorius, there were lire da braccio with 'violin' scrolls, violins with exuberant rebec sickles, violins with *C* holes, viols with bulging soundboards, and near-'violins' still with the flat peg leaf or peg box of the lira da braccio.

---

c) Laurent Grillet, *Les Ancêtres du violon* . . . , Paris, 1901, p. 9, refers to Lanfranco's *Scintille*, published in Brescia, 1533, and to an account from the same year of the 'dépenses secrètes' of Francis I, which mentions 'tous vyolons et joueurs d'instruments du Roy' and some later French sources (from after 1550), including Rabelais, that refer to 'joueurs de violon', but is silent about Italians before Andrea Amati, 1572.

d) The article in the *Encyclopaedia Britannica*, 11th ed., 1911, refers to a tenor viola 'bearing in general outline the typical features of the violin,' exhibited in 1872 in the Loan Exhibition of Musical Instruments at South Kensington, with the label 'Pietro Lanure, Brescia, 1509'.

e) W. Leo von Lütgendorff, *Die Geigen und Lautenmacher* . . . , Frankfurt-am-Main, 1922, cautiously credits Gasparo da Salò with 'the merit of having built the first violins and of having given them their definitive [*endgültige*] form' (Vol. I, p. 31).

f) Gerald R. Hayes, *Musical Instruments and their Music*, London, 1930, clearly reflects the embarrassing situation of the historian when he says (II, 160) that 'the violin is one of the very few important instruments of which it can be said that at a given date it was not at all, and that shortly afterwards it is found full-fledged in active life.' He very prudently refuses to decide whether Lanfranco's reference to the 'Violetta da Arco senza tasti' (*Scintille di Musica*, 1533) means rebecs or violins (II, 169).

g) Edmund van der Straeten, *The History of the Violin*, London, 1933, p. 35, refers to the well-known print showing a portrait of Gasparo Duiffoprugcar, dated 1562, which shows two early violins; and also to the description of a 'violin' in Philibert Jambe-de-Fer's *Epitome Musical*, Lyons, 1556, which mentions tuning in fifths, but does not say anything about the form of the instrument.

h) Francis Farga, *Violins and Violinists*, transl. Egon Larsen, London, 1950, regards Tieffenbrucker as the 'probable inventor of the violin' (Illus. XXVII) and says on p. 32: 'The violin is depicted in the paintings of some Bolognese masters towards the middle of the 16th century, for example, in a picture by Giulio Romano (*c.* 1550). There is also a picture by Pellegrino Tibaldi in the Vienna State Gallery which portrays St. Cecilia with two violin-playing angels. It is possible, therefore, that the violin originated in Bologna in the third or fourth decade of the 16th century.' He considers two violins by Andrea Amati with the year 1551 on the label as unquestionably authentic.

i) David D. Boyden, in his article on the violin in *Musical Instruments Through the Ages*, ed. Anthony Baines, London, 1961, carefully and prudently formulates the problem (pp. 110, 111): 'It is fruitless to try to attribute the "invention" of the violin to any one man or country. . . . The most impressive contributions were those of northern Italy where, shortly after the middle of the 16th century, the Italian school of violin-making dominated all others.'

[1] In Chapter 5 above, I have discussed these problems.

The situation is further complicated by the predilection of the curio collectors of the 15th and 16th centuries, who liked to commission unique and fantastic shapes as worthy additions to their *Kunst- und Wunder-kammern* or *Musikkammern*. The only straight and clear evolution in Renaissance string instruments, as far as I can see, was the gradual transformation of what pre-16th-century Italy called the 'viola' (a fiddle with a flat head and frontal pegs, with or without drones, such as was depicted, for instance, by the school of Giotto) into the full-fledged lira da braccio of about 1500, as shown in countless representations by Carpaccio, Giovanni Bellini, Cima da Conegliano, and others.

The veil that covers the origin of the violin may be lifted, at least a little if not wholly, by the evidence of pictures, and specifically by pictures that pre-date the time when the Cremonese masters created what appears in retrospect to be the first 'standardized' pattern of the violin. The first outstanding painter we have to consider in this connection is Gaudenzio Ferrari, whose creative years filled almost the whole first half of the 16th century. Very close in time and place to the great giants, Leonardo and Bramante, he achieved and maintained an astounding originality and independence. His frescoes and other paintings are characterized by vivacity and a great ease and variety of composition. His art is deeply rooted in his native soil, and many of the faces, figures, and gestures that he depicted can still be found today in Lombard and Piedmont villages.[1]

Apart from his glory as a painter, Ferrari was deeply interested in the other arts, including music. Several of his works contain representations of musical instruments, including violins: the frescoes and sculptures in and near Varallo; his altarpiece, *La Madonna degli aranci*, in the Church of San Cristoforo in Vercelli; the cupola fresco in the Santuario in Saronno; and others. A detailed study of these representations seems indispensable for the history of Renaissance instruments, and it is hardly too much to say that Gaudenzio's name is inseparable from the early history of the violin.

Now we turn to Ferrari's gigantic cupola fresco in the Santuario at Saronno,[2] one of his most important and original works. He received the commission for it in 1534 and worked on it throughout 1535. His idea of representing a large angel concert in a cupola had only one forerunner, Correggio's famous fresco of the *Assumption of the Virgin* in the cupola of the cathedral in Parma. We do not know

---

[1] This article is not the place for an evaluation of the importance to history of this great Lombard-Piedmontese painter, but I should like to refer here to one of the most lucid and concentrated studies of Ferrari's importance, recently written by Anna Maria Brizio as the introduction to her catalogue of the unforgettable exhibition in Vercelli, 1956, *Mostra di Gaudenzio Ferrari*, Milan, 1956.

[2] It was Karl Geiringer who first drew the attention of musical historians to this fresco, in 1927, in an excellent article, *Gaudenzio Ferrari's Engelkonzert im Dome von Saronno*, in the *Kongressbericht der Beethoven-Zentenarfeier*, Vienna, 1927.

whether Gaudenzio knew Correggio's fresco, which had been finished only a few years earlier, in 1530. In any case, Gaudenzio's composition is quite different and original; it represents the arrival of the Blessed Virgin in Heaven. Mary appears at the outer rim of the cupola, flanked by *puttini*; God the Father, in glory, is represented in stucco relief in the centre of the painting. The whole enormous, shallow, and circular vault between these two main figures is filled with angels, arranged in four concentric circles: the innermost circle next to God consists of thirty-one dancing *putti*; the other three circles are comprised of numerous large figures of angels, sumptuously clad in flowing robes. Some of them pray, some adore and exalt, but most of them play instruments. Of the eighty-six large angels, no less than sixty play or assist in playing instruments.[1]

There are, in all, fifty-six instruments. Among the bowed instruments we find several viols, several lire da braccio, rebecs, a Sicilian cane violin, a bizarre compound of fiddle with recorder, to be blown and bowed at the same time,[2] and, last but not least, a number of instruments that show most if not all of the basic characteristics of the violin.

But before concentrating on the violins, we should say something in general about the perspective in this fresco. The linear projection is far from being optically exact or — should we say? — pedantic. Even a quick glance convinces the beholder that most string instruments appear to be asymmetrical, with the bouts on either side not corresponding to each other. Also, the necks of instruments curve slightly upward so that their strings could not run parallel. Some of these irregularities are explained by the unevenness of the stucco surface in the cupola, and many spots are warped by fissures. But apart from that, Gaudenzio, with all his love for fancy detail, was not aiming here at photographic precision. He would, for instance, show the neck of an instrument with its sickle-head or scroll at a slightly different angle from that of the body, in order to insure identification of the instrument by its most characteristic feature. The scholar must be aware of this freedom in handling perspective 'con alcune licenze'; only then will he justly interpret the painted shapes, or rather 'reconstruct,' as it were, the actual instrument from its fanciful appearance in the painting. There is also another 'unrealistic' feature in the fresco: none of the stringed instruments, not even the lutes, citterns, harps, or psalteries, has its strings painted in.

---

[1] It was thanks to the late Fernanda Wittgens, the director of the Brera and the Soprainten-dente delle Gallerie di Lombardia, that numerous detailed photographs of my favourite angels were made. I had visited the Santuario of Saronno so often that I was called by the sacristan and his family 'questo Americano pazzo,' and when, soon after World War II, I noticed rain damage in the cupola, 'La Fernandissima' lost no time in effecting repair and restoration. It was on that occasion that the photographs were taken which accompany this chapter.

[2] On this and other 'fantastic' instruments and their interpretation, see Chapters 1 and 16.

The suggestive position of the stopping, plucking, and bowing hands was evidently sufficient for the onlooker far down below.

To the left of a beautiful positive organ are four angels with bowed instruments (Pl. 38a). The one on top, which certainly has nothing to do with the violin, we may in the main disregard here. The angel plays a bizarre three-stringed instrument of very complex shape. Its curves project and, again, cut in deeply toward the centre of the body; its back is strongly bulging; and its broad rim is profusely decorated with intarsias. Its heart-shaped head with frontal pegs is typical of the contemporary lira da braccio.

The three other instruments, however, different as they are from each other, all have some features that can be related to the violin. Closest to our present-day standard violin is the alto-sized instrument played by a feminine angel at the right (Pl. 38b). There are the typical upper, middle, and lower bouts, and a shallow body with a bulging soundboard and projecting edges. There is also the narrow neck and fingerboard, and an elegantly shaped scroll. Inside the peg box, four stems are clearly visible.[1] Beside all these typical violin traits, however, there are other features that would perhaps seem abnormal today: the sound-holes, although they correspond fairly well to standard f holes, are placed very high, at the height of the middle bouts, which are extremely short and deep; the lower part of the body is much wider than the upper; and there are no purflings.

The bass (or tenor) instrument nearby, played by the sitting angel at the lower rim of the cupola, shares some elements of the violin with the alto instrument to its right: the outline, consisting of three bouts; the strong moulding of the soundboard; the shallowness of the body in comparison with that of a regular viola da gamba; the projecting edges; the long thin neck; and the scroll. On the other hand, there are many differences: the proportions of the body; the much less marked angle at which the shoulders meet the neck; the position and reversed shape of the sound-holes; the leaf-shaped string holder; and the position of the bridge, between the sound-holes and therefore much higher up. In fact, the differences are so remarkable that one hesitates to regard this second instrument as belonging to the same whole consort. The pegs are not clearly visible in the deep shadow, and the strings, as usual, are not drawn. The narrow fingerboard would probably not allow more than four strings, a number not contradicted by the position of the stopping fingers.

---

[1] I am aware of the fact that Curt Sachs, who referred to Ferrari's depiction in his *History of Musical Instruments*, New York, 1940, p. 357, calls this violin three-stringed, and indeed only three peg heads are visible. A close scrutiny, however, reveals that these heads do not precisely coincide with the four visible stems and that the somewhat shoddy perspective, attributable to quick fresco painting, or perhaps to a careless assistant, was intended to suggest a fourth peg hidden behind the juncture of the fingerboard and the sickle-shaped peg box. Certainly the painter would hardly have depicted the four stems without a factual base.

The smallest of our three pre-violins is somewhat hidden between the lute player and the player of the richly curved string instrument with the lira da braccio head. We see only half of its body, in a three-quarter back view, and the sickle-shaped peg box, without scroll, is turned with some freedom of perspective so that we can look into it. The middle bouts are obscured by the peg leaf of the lira da braccio in front of it but, as far as we can see under these circumstances, the proportions have some similarity to those of the alto instrument. The head, however, is much more primitive than the elegant scrolls of the other two instruments; it resembles, in fact, that of a rebec (which, by the way, is twice represented in this fresco). Three pegs are indicated.

In short, our three instruments, although they have several common features, are so different in proportions and in other respects that one again hesitates to consider any of them as part of one set or consort.[1] Certainly, if Gaudenzio had wished to design three sizes for one homogeneous set he would have expressed his intention more clearly. He actually did so in a drawing of playing angels (now in the Staatliche Graphische Sammlung in Munich), which is probably a study for the Saronno fresco and which shows an actual set of three musical instruments that differ only in size, from treble to tenor (Pl. 40a).[2] They are instruments of fantastic shape, with extremely long necks terminating in flamboyant sickle heads. Their bodies are of such complex curvature that one does better to avoid the danger of verbalizing a description. Out of their shoulders grow projections in spiral shape, similar to those on many Renaissance citterns — projections that were, in fact, a last atrophic reminiscence of the arms of ancient and Carolingian lyres and kitharas.[3] And even these fantastic instruments are not the last word in Ferrari's exuberant fantasy of form: among his many beautiful sketches of musical *putti* and *amorini*, there is one that is even richer in curves, a veritable orgy in spirals (Pl. 40b). The body is spade-shaped — its tail decorated with sculptured leaves (a frequent ornament not only of Gaudenzio's instruments but also of real instruments of the Renaissance); and the long neck ends in a giant spiral. The shoulders not only continue in side spirals, but also carry double scrolls that imitate, in reverse shape, the form of the *f* holes.

Oddly enough, since Karl Geiringer's reference to the Saronno fresco and Curt Sachs's pointing out the three angels (as playing '*violette da braccio senza tasti* with three strings in the true shape of the present violin family'), there has been no analysis of these representations, but only passing remarks, by historians

---

[1] Cf. Curt Sachs, *op. cit.*, p. 357.

[2] I should like to express my thanks to Prof. Degenhart, the director of the Staatliche Graphische Sammlung, for kindly providing me with a photograph of this drawing.

[3] See Chapter 3.

of musical instruments. It is even more curious that attention has never been called to another violin in the same fresco (Pl. 41b). This violin is in a section quite remote from the instruments mentioned before and is also somewhat obscured there by the surrounding instruments, two psalteries, a harp, a plater-spiel, and a lira da braccio. Our violin is shown face forward, presenting a top view of the soundboard, whose bulge is strongly marked by shading. The middle bouts are precisely in the centre of the sides — a position quite different from that on the alto instrument above; the sound-holes correspond in shape to those of the 'bass violin' but are much more finely drawn, terminating in delicate spirals; and there is a three-pronged string holder. The bridge is placed between the lower parts of the sound-holes, just where their curve affords maximum width; this arrangement is different from that on the alto instrument, on which the sound-holes converge toward the bottom of the instrument, causing the bridge to be placed extremely low. The neck is narrow, and the head, to the dismay of the organologist, is covered by the arm of an angel playing the lira da braccio. But from the small width of the neck it is quite clear that no lira da braccio was intended here, since that instrument had to accommodate five melody strings on its fingerboard, to say nothing of the two bourdons running outside.[1] The bow may seem short at first glance, but part of it is actually covered by an angel wing. From the position of the stopping fingers it appears that the angel is not playing at the moment, but is awaiting his turn.

We now turn from these violins in the Saronno fresco to one appearing in an altarpiece painted by Gaudenzio for the Church of San Cristoforo in Vercelli, in oil on wood. It is called *La Madonna degli aranci* because of the beautiful orange grove that forms its background, and it is reliably dated 1529 — that is, six years before the Saronno fresco (Pl. 39a). But we have chosen to defer discussion of it until now, since the variety of shapes and the free style of drawing and perspective apparent in the Saronno fresco have sharpened our eyes for the appreciation of the 'Aranci violin.' This violin differs in many ways from the Saronno instruments. Most striking are the proportions: its body is compact, very wide, and its upper half is almost mirrored by its slightly wider lower half; also, the double curve of the shoulders is repeated at the bottom of the body. This is a shape as different from all the Saronno fresco violins as it is from the modern violin. The marked bulge of the soundboard does not begin near the edges, but is confined to a rather narrow middle section. The *f* holes diverge slightly towards the neck; they are cut precisely into the rims of the strong middle bulge of the soundboard. There is a heart-shaped string holder. The long fingerboard terminates in a long peg box with a scroll and three pegs. The

---

[1] This can be seen, for instance, in the lira da braccio to the right of our violin. Pl. 41b shows only the bowing hand and a small section of the contour of the body.

instrument is played with the head pointing downward, the bow is short, and the bowing and stopping hands, with the thumbs visible, are depicted most carefully and convincingly.

The execution of the whole painting reveals the master's hand. There is no question here of assistants. The two *putti*, and especially the violin player with his tender and meditative expression, are of exquisite workmanship. The instrument itself appears in perfect perspective in front view, and is turned just a little to make one side wall and the projecting edges visible.

That the shape of this instrument was not just a passing idea of Ferrari's appears from the repetition of the same shape in his sketch for an *Adoration of the Child*, in the Palazzo Reale in Turin (Pl. 41a), although there the contours appear rather sketchy and perfunctory. It seems also significant that this same shape was taken over by Gaudenzio's school, especially by his long-time pupil and assistant, Bernardino Lanini.

There is no doubt that Gaudenzio had more than a profound interest in musical instruments; he must have been an expert player and, I am convinced, also a builder of instruments. His paintings reveal not only a deep familiarity with the forms of instruments (although there are occasional slips, probably committed by assistants), but also with their function — that is, their practical use. The attitudes of the musicians' bodies, the positions of arms and shoulders, the embouchures and finger positions in the wind instruments, and the truthful, lively rendering of hands and fingers in bowing, stopping, or plucking on the string instruments, are based on sharp observation. Telling, also, is the great variety of instruments shown, unsurpassed in any other angel concert and approximated only, perhaps, in a Northern painting: Geertgen tot Sint Jans' *Virgin and Child*, which shows virtually all the instruments existing in his time.[1]

Still more strikingly, Gaudenzio's profound acquaintance with instruments reveals itself in his crossing of the borderline between reality — that is, the exact portrayal of existing instruments — and free imagination — creating shapes that are functional enough but divergent from tradition even in a period that was remarkably little restricted by standardization. But in these fantastic instruments, such as a double bagpipe and a fiddle that could be both blown and bowed at the same time, Gaudenzio was not merely making wild creations of the brush for the sake of visual beauty; his instruments are functional — they could have been constructed and perhaps even were, for the fun of it, in a playful mood. In this they differ fundamentally from the many fantastic and scurrilous instruments that were created with sinister fantasy — the bird monsters with oboe beaks, etc., which a northern contemporary of Gaudenzio's,

[1] See Chapter 11.

Hieronymus Bosch, used in his hell scenes. But, of course, hell admits more of the grotesque than does heaven!

There is, finally, another fact that makes it seem probable that Gaudenzio built instruments himself: he was not only a painter, but also a sculptor, as we know from his expressive life-size figures at Varallo peopling many scenes from the New Testament.

Vasari (*Vite*, ed. Milanesi, IV, 652, and VI, 518) mentions Gaudenzio in a few laudatory words without going into detail; he was evidently not directly acquainted with Gaudenzio's work. Strangely enough, then, in the evaluation of the musical subjects painted by Ferrari, the most important biographical source has been entirely neglected, although it exists in a book often quoted by art historians: Lomazzo's *Idea del tempio della pittura* (1590?). Lomazzo, a painter and poet, was a nephew of Gaudenzio's, and his superlatives, with which he was never thrifty, should perhaps be taken *cum grano salis*: in his account of Gaudenzio's works in the *Trattato dell'arte della pittura scultura ed architettura* (1584), he calls Gaudenzio (p. 185) 'my old master Gaudenzio, not only an expert painter . . . but a most profound philosopher and mathematician. . . .' But he is more precise, at least as far as Gaudenzio's musical activities are concerned, in his *Idea del tempio*. There, in Chapter IX, entitled 'Fabbrica del Tempio della Pittura, e dei suoi Governatori' (p. 37 ff.), he establishes an analogy, in his fanciful poetic way, between the seven planets and the seven governors in the Temple of Painting, whose statues are to be erected in the temple. The governors are to be Michelangelo, Gaudenzio, Caravaggio, Leonardo, Raphael, Mantegna, and Titian (in that order). Of Gaudenzio, second only to Michelangelo, Lomazzo says: 'He was born in Valdugia, and was a painter, sculptor, architect, master of perspective, natural philosopher, poet, and performer on the lira and the lute.' The 'lira' was no doubt the lira da braccio.[1] Thus, on the basis of this information, Gaudenzio played the most noble and difficult bowed instrument of his time, a fact quite significant in view of his inclusion of violins in his pictures.

The basic shape of Ferrari's violin in the altar painting of *La Madonna degli aranci* was retained by his followers, especially by Bernardino Lanini. Lanini, who lived from about 1510 to 1583, had joined Ferrari's workshop in 1530 and was probably still assisting the master in the work on the Saronno fresco. As we shall see, Lanini was not deeply interested in musical instruments. Yet, since his many altarpieces included numerous representations of the Adoration of the Infant, the *sacra conversazione*, and the Assumption of the Virgin, the

---

[1] In Chapter 5 above, I have investigated the various names applied to this instrument and the resulting confusion, especially with reference to Vincenzo Galilei's explanation that the viola da braccio had begun to be called 'lira' only in what for him were modern times.

musical angels traditionally connected with these themes had to be represented.

Lanini repeated the broad and short pattern of the 'Aranci violin' in his altarpiece of the *Assumption* in the Church of San Sebastiano at Biella, in 1543, and also in his *Madonna with Saints and Angels* in the church of San Paolo, Biella, and the *Adoration of the Infant* in San Magno, Legnano. A surprising difference appears, however, in another instrument painted by him in a *sacra conversazione* (from the Cook Collection in Richmond, which later came to the Kress Collection in New York and is today in the Raleigh Museum in North Carolina; Pl. 39b).[1] There, one single *putto* plays a fiddle before the throne of the Virgin. At his feet are lying a lute, a recorder, and a jingle drum. The fiddle, although unmistakably a violin, with four strings and a strongly marked bulge in the soundboard, does not repeat the broad pattern of Lanini's other violins mentioned above, nor of Ferrari's 'Aranci violin', but is of an extremely long and narrow shape and shows purflings which, to my knowledge, had not been represented before. The painting reveals that Lanini, for all his good intentions and neat drawing, was not a player or connoisseur. The representation of the bridge disregards perspective to such an extent that it appears to be upside down, and the positions of the stopping and bowing fingers are so lifeless and perfunctory that they could have been drawn only by a musical ignoramus. But for just this very reason we must assume that this violin did not spring from Lanini's imagination, but portrayed an existing instrument; and this makes the painting an important record, especially since it is dated. To the left of the bow handle we read 'B.nardinus Laninus . Ucellen . F . 1552' (that is, thirty-two years after Ferrari's *Madonna degli aranci*).

Most treatises on the violin have pointed to Brescia and Cremona as the cradles of this instrument. But the great Brescian master, Gasparo da Salò, was only born about 1540 and would not have been constructing violins before the 1560s. And Andrea Amati, the founder of the Cremonese dynasty of Amatis, was born about 1535 (according to Lütgendorff, *Die Geigen und Lautenmacher*); his earliest known violins are dated about 1564, according to *Grove's Dictionary of Music and Musicians*, although some instruments dated '1551' are listed as authentic by Francis Farga (in *Violins and Violinists*).

But the violins represented in the paintings of Gaudenzio Ferrari and Bernardino Lanini point to another and considerably earlier root west of Milan or even to the Piedmont. They also add another little bit of information to the complex and fascinating story of the early violin: they show such a bewildering

---

[1] I am grateful to the Kress Foundation and Dr. Alessandro Contini-Bonacossi, who have made photographs of this picture available to me and permitted me to use them.

variety of shapes and proportions that one almost directly senses the morphological fermentation of which they were a part and which had not yet reached
the point of crystallization into the more or less standardized patterns later
created in Brescia and Cremona.

7 · The Golden Harpsichord and Todini's *Galleria Armonica*

One of the outstanding examples of baroque decorative art in the collections of the Metropolitan Museum in New York is a musical instrument, a gilded harpsichord of fantastic form (Pl. 42a). The wing-shaped body of the instrument is supported by three fishtailed tritons (Pl. 44b), gliding on softly swelling waves. Between them rise two sea nymphs, and riding behind is a *putto* (Pl. 44c), perched high on a sea shell and driving two dolphins. All these fishy folk move through the water with bold and cheerful gestures. The water itself, silvery green and shimmering, is enclosed by a massive ledge that repeats on a larger scale the outline of the harpsichord proper. And this whole oceanic phantasmagoria rests on lions' feet.

The right side of the harpsichord is decorated with an elaborate gilded frieze representing the triumph of Galatea (Pl. 42b). Sitting in a wheeled shell car drawn by fishtailed horses, Galatea travels over the waves; trumpeting tritons herald her approach and follow her carriage. *Putti*, some of them winged, ride sea horses, and everywhere one can see a gay medley of fins, spiralling tails, and agitated horses (Pl. 44a). Even the clouds in the background participate in the interplay of moving curves. On the extreme left, next to a span of three wildly excited horses yet quite removed from all the watery commotion, sits the only tranquil figure in the frieze, an idyllic youthful musician on a rock. In contrast to the other creatures, who blow on trumpets, he plays a string instrument, the noble lute.

The harpsichord in its basin is flanked by two life-sized figures, each sitting on a rock (Pl. 42a). Both, like the harpsichord, are made of gilded wood. The one on the left represents Polyphemus, the right Galatea. Polyphemus plays a bagpipe. Galatea's instrument is missing, but to judge from the position of her arms and fingers she probably had a lute. Here Polyphemus is not the ferocious man-eating and rock-throwing giant of the *Odyssey*, who devoured Ulysses' companions and crushed Galatea's lover with a stone, but the longing, unhappy shepherd, saddened and dandified by his unrequited love of the nymph, as we find him in Alexandrian poetry and particularly in Ovid's *Metamorphoses*, Book XIII:

Behold, that savage creature, whom the very woods shudder to look upon, whom no stranger has ever seen save to his own hurt, who despises great Olympus and its gods; he feels the power of love and burns with mighty desire, forgetful of his flocks and of his caves. And now, Polyphemus, you become careful of your appearance, now anxious to please; now with a rake you comb your shaggy locks, and now it is your pleasure to cut your rough beard with a reaping-hook, gazing at your rude features in some clear pool and composing their expression.

The representations in art of this one-sided love affair would fill a museum. They range from Pompeian wall paintings to the grandiose Caracci frescoes in the Palazzo Farnese in Rome. In the east loggia of the Villa Farnesina Raphael painted his exuberant procession of Galatea (the frieze of the harpsichord is, as it were, a side view of the procession that Raphael depicted from the front). Immediately to its left is Sebastiano del Piombo's Polyphemus, sitting on a rock like our figure but holding a panpipe, or pastoral syrinx, in his right hand and gazing tenderly out to sea, that is, towards Raphael's Galatea.

The syrinx, made up of many small reed pipes, was the customary shepherd's instrument in classical times and was depicted as such in sculpture and painting. The bagpipe, known to antiquity as *tibia utricularis*, was not a pastoral but a sophisticated instrument. According to Suetonius it was, for example, played by Nero. It appears for the first time in the hands of shepherds in medieval miniatures, although in a more primitive form than that played by our Polyphemus (Pl. 46, left). What we see here is the elaborate *sordellina*, or musette, of the 17th century, equipped with one chanter and two drones. There is no blowpipe like that through which earlier pipers filled the bag with air; instead there are bellows attached by a leather belt to the right wrist. This was a technical improvement not found before the last quarter of the 16th century. One of the earliest examples of the improved form, an instrument mentioned as early as 1596 in the inventory of the Kunstkammer of Schloss Ambras in the Tyrol, is today in the Vienna collection of old instruments.

Such an impressive piece as our harpsichord, evidently designed by a first-rate artist, provokes curiosity. What was its origin and what is its history? The instrument entered the Metropolitan Museum in 1889 as part of the monumental Crosby Brown collection. It was known to have once been in the possession of Viscount Sartiges, who was the French ambassador to the Holy See in the 1860s, but here our information ended. However, two lucky discoveries have since provided answers to our questions.

In 1949 I heard various rumours about a very large private collection of musical instruments in Italy, brought together by Evan Gorga, the Rumanian tenor who performed the title role in the first performance of Mascagni's

L'Amico Fritz in 1891. I visited Mr. Gorga in Rome, and he told me enthusiastically about his collections of various objects. Before the Fascist period he had collected several thousand musical instruments and had later sold them to the Italian government. Much to his regret, they had never been exhibited, and he had only vague information about the places, mostly basements, where they were stored. He could, however, show me a mountain of photographs, all signed by Ottorino Respighi, who had taken part in the sale to the government, and also a small booklet that he had printed many years previously as a condensed description of the collection. Among its few illustrations there was one that, blurred and yellowed as it was, could be recognized at first glimpse as a model for our harpsichord. Mr. Gorga remembered that he had once owned such a model, made of clay, but had no idea what had become of it.

A little later, deeply saddened by the war damage in Subiaco and other old familiar hill towns, I revisited the Palazzo Venezia in Rome, whose director, Antonino Santangelo, kindly showed me storerooms where heaps of fragments salvaged from Genzano, Albano, and other bombed sites were temporarily stored. In one of these rooms was a wooden box filled with small reddish clay fragments. Among them I recognized a tiny bagpipe, about the length of a finger joint, closely resembling the sordellina of our Polyphemus. When the head of Polyphemus also emerged I was able to convince my slightly dubious host that this was a terracotta model closely related to our harpsichord. We quickly fitted the pieces together, and there was no doubt. A photograph taken at that time shows the half-assembled model (Pl. 43a). Soon afterwards, I sent photographs of our instrument to the Palazzo Venezia as a guide for the final reassembling of the fragments and received in turn pictures of the assembled model (Pl. 43b). Only minor details like fingers were missing, and still are today.

At first glimpse the little sculpture looks like a *bozzetto*, or model, made for the person who commissioned the instrument or as a guide for the woodcarvers who were to execute the real instrument. It is of the finest workmanship, elegant in its proportions and finished to the smallest detail. Yet, although it agrees with the instrument in the shapes of the figures and the relief, there are some puzzling divergencies. In the model the *putto* almost touches the end of the harpsichord, joining with the central mass of the body and its carriers, while the flanking figures sit so far away that the spaces between make symmetrical shapes. In the large sculpture these proportions are lost (Pl. 46).

There are even more subtle stylistic differences: the figures of the model have a soft roundness and a classical restraint lacking in the large sculpture, which shows more animation and 'baroque' exuberance. However, the problem of the relationship must be left open for the moment. One thing seems fairly certain: the large sculpture suggests the circle of Algardi, possibly his pupil Domenico

Guidi, or perhaps Ercole Ferrata.[1] Similar monumental wooden sculptures, designed as carriers, were not infrequent in Rome at the time. A pair of table supports in the form of winged tritons in the Palazzo dei Conservatori may be the work of the sculptor of our figures, or another of the same circle.

While the discovery of the model was a welcome surprise, it still left in darkness the history of the harpsichord. By good luck this has been clarified. In the library of the Palazzo Corsini I found one of the rare copies of the *Galleria armonica* by Michele Todini, published in Rome in 1676. The full title is *Dichiaratione della galleria armonica eretta in Roma de M. Todini Piemontese di Saluzzo, nella sua habitazione, posta all'Arco della Ciambella Roma 1676*. This amusing little book is the description of a museum of musical instruments by its enthusiastic founder and owner. The house that harboured this museum, in the Arco della Ciambella, a small street near the present Largo Argentina, does not exist anymore. But from the text of Todini's treatise we learn that it contained all sorts of music machines, which were extremely popular in the baroque period, not only in Italy but also in southern Germany and Austria. With understandable pride, Todini describes his treasures and his efforts to assemble them.

Todini, a Piedmontese, lived in Rome and made his living by playing the violone, the large bass fiddle of the time, in concerts and the trumpet in the wind band at the Castel Sant' Angelo. His real interest, however, was the construction of music machines. Some amusing details of his life are to be found in J. G. Walther's *Musicalisches Lexikon* (1732),[2] Filippo Buonanni's *Gabinetto armonico pieno d'istromenti indicati* (1722), and the first book of the *Phonurgia nova* (1673), by the versatile, learned Jesuit father Athanasius Kircher, who knew Todini.

For many years Todini designed and built musical clockworks, mechanical fiddles, novel types of organs, and harpsichords. He exhibited them in three large rooms of the Palazzo Verospi, probably to secure an income during his later life by charging admission. It was, as far as I can see, the first museum exclusively devoted to musical instruments. As he says in the preface of his book, he was urged by connoisseurs to publish a description of the objects in his collection and the difficulties he had to overcome in building his machines. Chapter 3 is called 'Descrittione della machina di Polifemo e Galatea' and is concerned with the second room of his museum, where the story of Galatea and Polyphemus was represented by a gilded harpsichord rich in carving and carried by

---

[1] After the first publication of this study, my colleague at the Metropolitan Museum, Dr. Olga Raggio, suggested very convincing reasons for an attribution to the circle of Filippo Parodi.

[2] Facsimile edition, Kassel, 1953.

life-sized Tritons, by large figures of Galatea and of Polyphemus 'in the act of playing a sordellina to please Galatea,' and by a *putto* driving two dolphins. He even mentions that the marine monsters in Galatea's procession carry *frutta di mare*, evidently referring to the fish, turtle, and large crab in the frieze of our instrument. He also states that Polyphemus was 'sitting on the slope of the mountain where he had his home.' Our figure has a flat back, which must have fitted against the background of the exhibition gallery. Thus it seems that our harpsichord was the central feature of a musical machine that, like each of the others, filled an entire room and that the whole decorative scheme was continued to the ceiling by means of stucco mountains and a painted landscape.

With these facts in mind we can now return to the clay model, in which the flanking figures are united to the instrument by the common base and by the harmonious design of the whole group. Why and when were the two figures separated from the central piece? If the little sculpture was a presentation or working model preceding the execution of the large group, we may assume that when the finished group came into Todini's possession he had it broken up to fit his scenic arrangement. Another possibility should perhaps also be considered: the model may have been commissioned by a visitor to the gallery who wanted a replica of the harpsichord and its figures for the music room of his palazzo or villa. Here we must leave the problem, trusting that future research may furnish more facts for its complete solution.

Todini's harpsichord group, like most of his machines, had a hidden mechanism that provided a surprise effect. Polyphemus's bagpipe played real music, sounding together with the harpsichord and thus achieving a combination of winds and strings. The one-man orchestra was an old dream of musicians that was realized over and over again in Renaissance and Baroque instruments, one example being the *claviorganum*. The sound of Polyphemus's bagpipe was actually produced by a set of pipes hidden in the mountain behind the figure and connected with a special keyboard concealed beneath that of the harpsichord. In his Chapter 20 Todini tells in amusing detail his troubles in building this mechanism and how difficult it was to get bagpipe experts to make metal pipes without cheating on the metal. Unfortunately, no illustration of the complete arrangement in the exhibition room has come to us.

However, another of Todini's tricky machines, described by him in Chapter 4, is also found in the *Appendix de mirifica phonurgia* to Kircher's book and is illustrated there as well as in Buonanni's *Gabinetto armonico*, Plate XXXIII. This was a group of no less than seven instruments, four with quills, two bowed, and one organ. The player of one of these instruments, the *archiclavicymbalum*, could make the other six sound from afar, or so it seemed to the listener. The engraving in Kircher's book (Pl. 45a) shows Todini playing the *archiclavicymbalum* at the left and three indefinite string instruments without keyboards standing freely in the middle before the organ. This schematic illustration was clearly not made on the spot but was done either from memory or hearsay. The engraving in Buonanni's book (Pl. 45b), however, seems to be a faithful portrait of the same machine, showing the three clavicymbals attached to the large organ case in the back. Still, Kircher complains in his awkward 17th-century Latin that Todini did not give his secret away, although we can say in retrospect that anyone familiar with late Baroque organs and their several compartments and complex tracker machinery would not have been puzzled. The baroque décor of the whole enormous structure reached to the ceiling, like the machine of Galatea and Polyphemus. On the organ case is the suggestion of a landscape, which according to Todini was painted by 'Gasparo Poussin,' evidently meaning Poussin's brother-in-law Gaspar Dughet, who was working in Rome at the time and who, by the way, also decorated a beautiful harpsichord in the Metropolitan Museum's collection.

Neither the artistic nor the musical aspect of Todini's machines exhausts our interest in them. For the historian of art they reflect a world passionately devoted to the theatrical effects inherited from the late Renaissance but vastly expanded through the new progress in the mathematical sciences. These are, however, only the artistic trappings, overlaying a deeper stratum of the mind. In a more profound sense, these musical machines were part and product of a world where — in theology and philosophy — the image of the automaton with its secret, hidden operator was often taken as the symbol of the Creator, mysteriously and incessantly imparting motion to the universe.

8 · The Importance of *Quattrocento* Intarsias for the History of Musical Instruments

As we have observed previously, music history for obvious reasons deals chiefly with music as it has survived in written form, and, for a long span, written music was prevailingly sacred vocal music. With this state of affairs, it is understandable that the wide realm of unwritten music remained for a long time a secondary field of interest for the historian of music. This area includes not only folk music in its narrower sense, but also some of the most subtle forms of instrumental music, such as the improvisations of the 15th and 16th centuries.

Where scores are lacking, it is the instruments themselves that are the main witnesses of this musical culture and its performance practice; and, where the instruments have not survived, we must rely on their representation in the visual arts. Georg Kinsky, Curt Sachs, Willibald Gurlitt, Hugo Leichtentritt, and others have pointed out the importance of these representations. Little noted, however, were the problems and difficulties inherent in the interpretation of these pictorial documents. Are the shapes of the instruments, the way they were played, and their combinations into ensembles reliably represented in paintings, frescoes, drawings, woodcuts, engravings, sculptures, embroideries, and the like? To what extent are these representations faithful portrayals of reality, and to what extent are they products of artistic imagination? And what are the reasons for which an artist would depart from accurate depiction? Any evaluation of the faithfulness of the representations presupposes intimate familiarity not only with musical matters, but also with the ever-changing aims and methods of expression through every period of the plastic arts.

I should like to draw attention to a still unmined treasure of pictorial sources: the Italian intarsias of the *quattrocento* and the first decades of the *cinquecento*. These sources are important for two reasons: first, the short-lived fashion of intarsias coincides with the famous improvisations, mentioned in numerous literary sources of the time, by the great virtuosos on the viola and the lira da braccio; and second, the instruments in the intarsias are rendered in life size or nearly so, and with such accuracy that they differ from real instruments only by their lack of a third dimension. The main aesthetic impulse for the intarsia fashion seems to have come from the refinement of theoretical perspective as a tool of the painter, above all through the treatises of Piero della Francesca and Luca Pacioli; the new technique of geometrical projection benefited, of course, the precision of representation.

There is no space here to discuss the dynasties of *intarsiatori*, the local characteristics of their style, the competition between the schools of Urbino, Monte Oliveto Maggiore, and Verona, or even to give a survey of the wealth of material; but I would like to give a few characteristic examples.

Some of the most interesting instruments in intarsias are to be found in the ducal palace of Urbino, the main residence of Federigo da Montefeltro. There, in the so-called *studiolo,* one of the great showpieces of the new technique of *quattrocento* linear perspective, we find a large clavichord (Pl. 51a) with no less than forty-seven keys — twenty-nine long and eighteen short ones, the former decorated with carved frontal slats of Gothic pattern. To these forty-seven keys there are twenty-two corresponding single strings; the instrument is, like all early clavichords, a 'fretted' one. The curvature of the keys and their tangents is drawn in precise perspective. A consistent application of foreshortening brings the strings so close to each other that the artist preferred to represent them not by wooden strips but by metal wires. An instrument of these remarkable dimensions and construction must have been the product of a long tradition. It is interesting that the earliest surviving clavichord, made in 1537 by Alexander Trasontinus and decorated with the complacent inscription 'Ut rosa flos florum ita hoc clavile clavilium'[1] (today in the collection of musical instruments in the Metropolitan Museum of Art in New York), has only thirty-six keys (twenty-one long and fifteen short ones) and an arrangement of bridges that is incomparably more primitive than that in the clavichord from the Urbino *studiolo.*

On the same wall of this *studiolo* we see a nine-string lute side by side with an early form of the lira da braccio, the latter with five strings: four stopped strings and one free bass string — equipment somewhat different from that which was customary later: five stopped strings and two free bass strings (Pl. 52a). Its peg box is still round and simple, its belly flat, and one can clearly observe how the side walls curve in between the strongly projecting edges of the belly and the back, a result of the fact that the side walls then were much thicker than those of the later violin; there were no blocks like those that help to hold the side walls of modern instruments to the belly and the back at the neck, bottom, and corners of the middle bouts. In the old instruments the broad upper and lower edges of the thick side walls were glued to the belly and back and then carefully hollowed out with a knife or chisel.

[1] 'Just as the rose is the flower of flowers, this is the clavichord of clavichords.'

Federigo da Montefeltro had, beside his gigantic palace in Urbino, a second residence in Gubbio.[1] The much smaller palace there also had a *studiolo* with wall intarsias; it is today one of the treasures of the Metropolitan Museum in New York. This *studiolo* is even richer in musical instruments than the one in Urbino. To mention one single example, there is a richly decorated positive organ with a double row of metal pipes: twenty-six in the first row, and a second row visible behind the feet of the pipes at the front (Pl. 47a). The keyboard consists of twenty-two long and thirteen short keys. Behind the organ, in one of the many cupboards of which the intarsias of these flat walls make believe to consist, we see a vielle with four stopped strings and one free drone string — thus an immediate predecessor of the lira da braccio in the *studiolo* of Urbino. During his years in Urbino, Raphael must have been familiar with these intarsias. In the upper section of the cupboard, a lute and two *cornetti curvi* of octagonal cross section are represented.

An interesting predecessor of the fully developed clavicembalo is found in the choir stalls of the cathedral of Genoa (Pl. 51b). The soundboard shows two sound-holes. Of special interest are the arrangement of the keys and the unusual form of the jacks, carrying quills cut from bird feathers.

A large lute of the high Renaissance, with eleven strings, is shown in daringly foreshortened perspective in a series of Bolognese intarsias, probably by Damian da Bergamo (*c.* 1545), also in the collection of the Metropolitan Museum (Pl. 47b). Nine strings are visible, but it would seem that there should be two more, since eleven pegs are indicated, of which some are of light and others of dark wood. Next to the lute on the complex tiled floor, of a type often seen in these intarsias, there is a music book: the open pages show a four-part and a seven-part canon which are both, curiously, without text.

The richest treasure of intarsias made for the decoration of churches is found in the choir stalls of the convent of Monte Oliveto Maggiore, not far from Siena. These intarsias come from the famous workshop of Fra Giovanni da Verona. Of particular interest is the bulky cittern seen in the upper section of one of the many half-open cupboards (Pl. 48a), with its characteristic hook behind the neck, its stair-shaped or terraced frets, and the peculiar ears protruding from its shoulders, atrophic rudiments of the arms of the late ancient and early medieval kithara.[2] The refinement of the whole composition attests to the elegant taste of the artist. The *trompe l'œil* effect (spatial illusion) is enhanced by the doors of the cupboards, which open at different angles, and by the way in which the neck of the lute protrudes out of the shelf towards the beholder. Exquisite also is the manner in which the geometrical and functional forms of the instruments themselves are accompanied by and contrasted to the spiral

[1] See Chapter 9 below.   [2] See Chapter 3 above.

curves of the music sheet, and the broken lute strings that also help to fill otherwise empty spaces in the composition.

Finally, there are several examples from the inlaid doors of the Stanza della Segnatura in the Vatican, which have, strangely, escaped the attention of art and musical historians — probably because these doors are always open with their inlaid fronts leaning against the wall. Here we encounter the most daring musical still-lifes in perspective ever created by the art of the *intarsiatori*. One panel shows two lutes (Pl. 48b) in unusual counterpoint, and again the undulations of the broken strings fill the empty spaces. There is a five-string viola da gamba, with sharp corners defining the middle bouts, quite unconventional sound-holes, and a massive bow (Pl. 50b); a set of five cromornes, together with a jingle drum (Pl. 49a); a harp, still of late Gothic shape, with a set of three recorders (Pl. 49b); and a spinettino of complex spherical contour, which floats so beautifully in space that, notwithstanding its precise rendering according to the *quattrocento* technique of geometrical projection, one is almost reminded of the spatial caprices of the Baroque (Pl. 50a).

These examples are a very small selection from the wealth of intarsias that have survived to our day, and that are not only of great interest for the history of musical instruments, but of immediate importance for the connoisseur of the improvisation practice of the *quattro-* and *cinquecento* and of the tools of the great virtuosos of the Renaissance.

They are objects of meditation and as such play a role in the early history of the still-life; they are reflections of actual musical activities at the Papal court, in palaces and churches of the time; they are remnants of the traditional allegories of the *quadrivium*; and, last but not least, they belong among the most fascinating showpieces demonstrating the new fashion of linear perspective.

9 · *Quattrocento* Science in the Gubbio Study

If any monument of art be an invitation to the past, an interior like the intarsia study of Federigo da Montefeltro now in the Metropolitan Museum of Art, has this appeal in an eminent degree. Sculptures have pedestals, paintings frames, leading from our everyday world to that of illusion; but here the illusion is complete, the visitor wholly enters the past. When we have accustomed ourselves to the spell of the warm, golden-brown dusk, the walls begin to speak. A graceful architectural setting becomes visible, its pillars framing cupboards with benches projecting beneath, all filled with books, musical and scientific instruments, armour, and library tools in pleasant order and variety. The illusion of depth is so great that we must make an effort to convince ourselves that we face two-dimensional pictures in inlay (Pl. 52b).

Was this little room a real study, a workroom for the learned Duke? Fill it in your imagination with the customary appliances of a private library of that time and you will see how the charm of the imagery upon the walls would be destroyed by any competition from actual objects. The Duke, we must suppose, had better taste. Besides, the balance of the decorative display, unbroken as it is, would only be disturbed by any outside intrusion. What then is the idea of this room? It is a witty play with the exciting new technique of strict linear perspective. It also pays homage to the Duke, with his various interests and activities. Finally, it is a mirror of the rich intellectual life at the court of which he was not merely the illustrious head but also the stirring heart.

Libraries have been written on Federigo da Montefeltro. His contemporaries called him the light of Italy. Statesman, warrior, scholar, and connoisseur in the arts, he stands out even against the background of his most versatile time as the embodiment of the practical, theoretical, and aesthetic gifts. In short, he approximated the ancient Greek ideal of harmony, well known to him from his beloved Aristotle. There was one trait of character, however, which distinguished this humanist *condottiere* from most of his fellows. This was his sense of justice and responsibility. That he, unlike most princes of the day, could dare to stroll unarmed among his subjects and be heartily greeted with 'Dio ti mantenga, Signore!' he owed above all to his celebrated system of taxation.

There is no image in the little study which does not celebrate the many interests of this universal man. The books, no less than fourteen, remind us of the library he built up in his main residence, Urbino. It was the greatest library of its time, containing in its wealth of items the catalogues of such libraries as the Vatican, San Marco, Florence, and Oxford. He preferred written to printed books and for many years employed thirty or forty writers, with an output of sometimes as many as two hundred books in twenty-two months.

Besides these compendia of the learned mind, we find the tools of the searching mind: a pair of dividers, a quadrant, a lever, a celestial globe. The latter particularly reminds us of the Netherlander, Paul von Middelburg, who was Federigo's court astrologist and mathematician.

The many arms depicted appear to be symbols of the art of war, in which the Duke was a learned and successful master. His authority in the rules of 'correct,' scientific warfare was undisputed, his victories famous, his new techniques, such as the use of heavy field artillery, epoch-making. He was a patron of all the sports of chivalry and loved to lead the evening contests of his young courtiers.

We next observe an amazing variety of musical instruments, fourteen in number, witnesses of the exquisite musical taste at Federigo's court. Besides percussion instruments, such as a tambourine and a tabor, we find plucked string instruments: two lutes, a cittern, a harp; bowed instruments: a rebec and a fiddle; wind instruments: two cornetti, a hunting horn, a pipe, and finally a magnificent portative organ. The cittern (Pl. 53a), similar to that of Fra Giovanni da Verona (Pl. 13c), shows some features lost afterwards, when the cittern became the fashionable instrument in the barbershops of Elizabethan England: namely, the characteristic hook at the neck and the sharp detachment of the neck from the body, which also occur in some fiddles of the same time (Pl. 53b). The pear-shaped rebec (Pl. 53c), leaning beside its bow, is clearly recognizable through the latticework of the cupboard door by its sickle-shaped peg box. Its box has not the usual cucumber or boat shape that is shown, for example, in the rebec played by an angel in a fresco by Pinturicchio in Santa Maria in Aracoeli, Rome (Pl. 54b), but rather a very long, thin fingerboard, tapering gradually into a broad sound box with a rounded profile. The almond-shaped fiddle (Pl. 53d) is depicted often in Renaissance painting, for instance by Signorelli in the Church of the Casa Santa at Loreto (Pl. 54a). The representation in our intarsias does not show its peg box, but it is easily recognized as a bowed instrument by its bridge, the form of its fingerboard, and the position and shape of the sound-holes. Besides its four melody strings, a drone is visible, foreshadowing the later transition into the lira da braccio, played in numerous Renaissance paintings by Orpheus, by Apollo, and by many angels. Characteristically, the string instruments, regarded as the nobler and favoured by Pallas and Apollo, outnumber the winds, the playing of which distorts the face, according to Plutarch (quoted in Book II of Castiglione's famous book on the courtier). What must have excited the inlay worker — the portrayal of wooden instruments in their natural substance but with their bulk reduced to two dimensions — is a sheer delight for the historian today. Old woodcuts of keyboard instruments caused many a headache to the connoisseurs before they discovered that the woodcuts had been reprinted in reverse. In our intarsias, the exact rendering of functional details, such as strings, frets, pegs, and so forth, in their natural dimensions, surpasses in exactness most other modes of illustration.

The multitude of the objects depicted, however, is not merely a reflection of the versatile personality of the Duke. There is a deeper bond between them. They are symbolic of the intimate connection among the arts at that time and between the arts and the sciences, and it is only of secondary importance to what extent this symbolism was intended by the maker of the study; he was a creature of his time. Both art and science in the *quattrocento* drew their inspiration from one strong impulse: the tendency toward rationalization, sweeping through all branches of natural science, aiming at calculation and control of nature by establishing its laws. The basic structure of nature was to be found in simple numerical formulas. This conception of natural science swept the artists along with it, but they were themselves pioneers in its development; in portraying nature 'correctly' they hoped to capture its secrets. Art was research into nature, the artist an experimental scientist, the canons of nature the canons or rules of 'correct' artistic creation.[1] Art was thus a sort of science, a body of knowledge dealing with the basic relations between phenomena, visible or audible. So, on the formula of the harmonic proportions were based, among other things, the standards for the human body and for architecture as well as the musical scale, and, as the most recent pearl on this string, the theory of linear perspective. The artist-scientists around Duke Federigo were among the most influential standard-bearers in this new adventure of the mind, and our study, looked at from this angle, is a monument and showpiece of the new achievements.

The main key to this interpretation of the study is found not so much in the objects depicted as in the manner in which they are depicted: it is a triumph of linear perspective. Problems of the utmost complexity are mastered here with playful joy and accuracy; no intricacies are avoided. To begin with trifles: the border patterns consist of strings of geometrical bodies, simulating three-dimensional forms (Pl. 56a & b). The turban ring (Pl. 56c) is only a slightly

---

[1] Leonardo: 'Those who are enamoured of practice without science are like a pilot who goes into a ship without rudder or compass and never has any certainty where he is going' (MS G, Institut de France, 8 r.). 'Perspective therefore is to be preferred to all the formularies and systems of the schoolman, for in its province the complex beam of light is made to show the stages of its development, wherein is found the glory not only of mathematical but also of physical science, adorned as it is with the flowers of both' (*Codice Atlantico*, 203 r.a.).

different version of one of the construction diagrams (Pl. 56d) described by Piero della Francesca in his famous treatise *De prospectiva pingendi*, dedicated in 1469 to Duke Federigo and most influential in the whole further development of theoretical and pictorial perspective, particularly on Luca Pacioli and Leonardo. The architectural details, such as the flutes of the pilasters and the mouldings of the architrave, burst forth with plastic life. The cupboard doors are open at all possible angles. Only a master of projective geometry could have designed the shadow of the lectern shaft, running over the complex mouldings of imaginary architecture (Pl. 54c). Particularly interesting is the border ornament around the cupboards which flank the window (Pl. 57c). It consists of little disks threaded on a small stick, a common frame pattern in *quattrocento* woodcuts, where it appears in cruder versions (Pl. 57a). But here what accuracy! If we sweep our eye upward along this string, we progress gradually from a top view to a bottom view of the disks. One disk shows its rim only and thus appears at eye level — it might have been the Duke's — and we remember Leonardo's advice to painters to take as the vanishing point the eye level of an average man. If, however, we run our eye along the horizontal ledge below the cupboard, no disk shows us only its rim; though these disks also appear in successive positions, it is clear that they are adjusted for an eye placed somewhat farther to the right than the disk at the extreme right corner. This requires an observer placed not in the window niche but more to the centre of the room. Thus the two rows of disks have a point of vision precisely determined as to its vertical and horizontal position.

Such a fixed position of the point of vision, as is possible for a single panel with its limited field, cannot be maintained for a whole interior: here the visitor turns around from wall to wall, continually shifting his point of vision. The complexity of this problem of a perspective interior may be shown by the following consideration: any three-dimensional object offers an infinite number of different two-dimensional aspects or images.[1] Only one of these images is chosen for a painting or any other two-dimensional representation, corresponding to one selected point of vision. Our intarsia room, however, is not a painting, or even a set of relatively independent images, but, like space itself, it continues and returns upon itself. Therefore, we might expect that, like any round object, it should offer to the observer, as he moves, a new aspect with every step, corresponding to his changing point of vision. But this it cannot do, being two-dimensional. Therefore, a sort of compromise is necessary to do justice to the observer in any possible position. How this compromise is approximated here without any loss in power of illusion constitutes an inexhaustible source of intellectual pleasure.

[1] Leonardo: 'Each body alone of itself fills the whole surrounding air with its images' (*Codice Atlantico*, 138 r.b.).

This problem of pictorial projection is made even more difficult by the further problem of the shadows. That the objects represented should throw shadows is obvious here where the highest degree of plastic illusion is aimed at. These shadows, particularly those of the balusters, are adjusted to two sources of light, the window and the door. Double shadows for one and the same object would have produced too confusing an effect. So in this too a compromise has been attempted. One has only to look at the corner formed by the small wall to the right of the door and the adjoining long wall to observe that the balusters at the small wall apparently receive their light and shadow from the window, while the long wall seems to be lighted through the door (Pl. 55a).

I am indebted to Cordray Simmons for an ingenious remark he made to me when I told him some observations made in the study. Being a painter and accustomed to constant shifting between one- and two-eye vision in his own painting, it occurred to him as he was helping to restore the study to wonder whether or not the one-eyedness of the Duke had anything to do with the particular character of the study as accomplished perspective illusion. The facts are that the Duke had lost his right eye in a jousting accident, and that the discrimination between a real object and its accurate portrait is much harder for one eye than for both. This defect in depth-sensation must have made the illusion even more perfect for the Duke.

The mastery of the visual reality by finding and formulating the numerical rules of space, that is, linear perspective, is only one aspect of the interfusion of creative art and science in the Renaissance. 'Practice,' in Leonardo's words, 'should always be based upon a sound knowledge of theory, of which perspective is the guide and gateway, and without it nothing can be done well in any kind of painting' (MS G, Institut de France, 8 r.). The first art to be founded on a grammar of this sort was not one of the visual arts but music. After the Pythagorean school discovered the precise dependence of the musical intervals upon certain arithmetical ratios of length of string, the search for a precise theoretical foundation of the arts and the conception of the scientist-artist never died out. Behind subjective beauty, an objective, rational grammar took shape, teachable and learnable, that of harmonic proportions. How amazing and at the same time reassuring — the chaos of sensations ruled by a simple and rigorous formula! Here a bridge was found, no less amazing, between the realms of the eye and the ear. From Vitruvius up to the last stragglers in the wake of Palladio, the theorists admonish the architects to borrow the rules of harmonic proportions from the musicians, who were the masters in this field. Leonardo, who, in his research on perspective, discovered the harmonic proportions in which a body withdrawing from the eye seems to diminish, regarded music as the 'sister of painting.'

It was for its strictly theoretical foundations that music was regarded as a science in antiquity and kept its place in the *universitas literarum*, beside rhetoric, geometry, arithmetic, dialectic, astronomy, and grammar, and that within the medieval classification of the arts into *artes liberales* and *artes mechanicae* it belonged to the first and nobler class, which imparted an elevated social position to its masters. This was by no means true of the visual artists; Plato ranked them with any other people exercising a skill, such as doctors, farmers, and sailors, and this was still the prevalent view in the *quattrocento*. No wonder the visual artists then, formulating the rules of their crafts, looked to music, where this formulation had been accomplished before. Besides, their social position could be improved by adding the same scientific rigour to their work as music enjoyed. Thus, after the model of music, the grammar of the visual arts was fashioned.

Viewed in this light the musical instruments in our study are of more than decorative importance; they are the tools of the most venerable 'science art.' The cittern mentioned above is flanked by a pair of dividers and an hourglass (Pl. 53a), the instruments for measuring space and time. True, they belong to the common paraphernalia of a Renaissance study, but the appearance of these metrical tools, side by side, and especially with a musical instrument, is perhaps more than accidental; and, indeed, these are the symbols by which, in the Renaissance theory, the mathematical foundations of music are indicated. A woodcut in Franchino Gaffurio's *Angelicum ac divinum opus musice*, Milan, 1496 (one of the standard musical treatises of that time), shows the author teaching, while to his left dividers and an hourglass remind us of the Pythagorean discovery that our scale, and hence harmony, is based on certain numerical relations, for instance, those of the lengths of strings or air columns producing sound (Fig. 18). These lengths are illustrated also by lines with their measurements added and pipes with the same proportion numbers. In woodcuts from Gaffurio's *Theorica musice*, Milan, 1492, it is old Pythagoras himself who works on chimes and glasses, strings and flutes, all with their proportion numbers added (Pl. 57b).

From here we do not have to pass far to other tools which we find in the cupboards, a celestial globe and a quadrant (Pl. 54d). There is no military leader from Alexander to Napoleon, and even beyond, who did not consult the stars. But the Pythagorean heritage, so vital in Federigo's time, points rather to the nobler sister of astrology, astronomy. The Pythagoreans had found the harmony of tones in the proportions of the planets and their orbits. This leading motif sounds throughout the history of astronomy from ancient Greek speculation to the famous title of Kepler's *De harmonice mundi* and the *Harmonie universelle* by the great musicologist and friend of Descartes, Father Mersenne. How unfor-

Fig. 18. Gaffurio teaching the theory of music. Woodcut from Gaffurio's *Angelicum ac divinum opus musice*, 1496. Compare the dividers and hourglass with those in Pl. 53a.

tunate that we cannot open the books above which the celestial globe is hanging, perhaps among them a treatise of the court astronomer, Paul von Middelburg!

There remains a last group of objects, the arms, evidence of a world apparently remote from the realm of science. But even warring, that exercise of sheer force, was carried on as an art in Federigo's time, art meaning skill based on science. War became a topic of scientific speculation and was subjected to conventional and technical rules, the rules of correct warfare. Federigo, the Gonfaloniere of the Church, was a celebrated master of the 'scienza militare.' His adviser in this matter, who built his castles and constructed his bombards and mortars, was the greatest military expert of the time, Francesco di Giorgio Martini,[1] whose *Trattato d'architettura civile e militare*, written in Urbino and dedicated to the Duke, had its influence as late as the time of Prince Eugene of Savoy and even Napoleon. The revolution in the technique of war of that time is marked chiefly by the use of heavy artillery and the adaptation of fortification plans to this new

[1] On the importance of Francesco di Giorgio Martini as theorist of military technique, see Leonardo Olschki's very instructive *Geschichte der neusprachlichen wissenschaftlichen Literatur*, Vol. II, Leipzig, 1922, p. 119.

Fig. 19. Title page of the first English edition of Euclid's *Elements* (London, 1570), illustrating the Pythagorean union between the sciences. In 1569 Urbino was visited by the English mathematician John Dee, who wrote the preface to the edition shown here.

weapon of attack. These arms, as well as the proper defences against them, demanded a more systematic control of space. Shooting with heavy cannon actually means practical mastery of space; levelling a gun implies thinking in terms of levels of space; scientific gunnery, or ballistics, as well as the technique of fortification against artillery fire, is nothing else but applied perspective, and it may very well be that the practical needs of the new gunnery contributed more to the 'rationalization of sight'[1] than is commonly supposed. Francesco di Giorgio, in a drawing for the treatise mentioned, illustrates one of his heavy guns levelled at a fortress by means of sights, which are also depicted in enlarged form (Pl. 55b). A glance at one of Dürer's woodcuts (Pl. 55c) shows that the aiming device for the gunner is basically akin to that used by the artist working on linear perspective. Although both contrivances serve quite different practical ends, they both assist in that calculation of which the factors are object, distance, image, the gunner starting from the image given and searching for the distance, the draughtsman defining the shape of the image with respect to a given distance. Both those operations are founded on the same mathematical principle, the precise proportions between the increasing distance of an object from the eye and its apparent diminution. Though the theoretical formulation of this principle is found first in Leonardo's writings, there seems to be no doubt that it had been practised before as a rule of thumb.

Thus, even the arms in the panels stand for a 'science art,' the theoretical conquest of space, brought about by the geometers, the portrayers of nature, and the military geniuses. This rational conception of space is based on numerical rules, the same divine harmony of proportions that is realized by the musical instruments and observed by the planetary orbits (Fig. 19). This is the great, the peremptory credo of the time: only by investigation into the blueprint of creation can one dare to portray it truly, to re-create it. In Leonardo's words, 'in Art we are grandsons unto God.' This belief, this search for the one in the many, the order in the chaos, the simple in the entangled is written not only in the treatises of the *quattrocento*, but, with considerable eloquence, on the walls of the study from Gubbio.

[1] To quote the title of Mr. Ivins' very original treatise on Renaissance perspective (*Metropolitan Museum Papers*, No. 8, 1938).

10 · Bagpipes for the Lord

The art of the drolleries in the Hours of Jeanne d'Évreux, acquired in 1958 by the Metropolitan Museum of Art, New York, belongs to those puzzling branches of medieval imagination where the sacred and the unholy are in close proximity. This is not the only branch of medieval art where these incongruous realms meet. In medieval church plays as well as in the architectural decorations of cathedrals, the untamed ocean of life, full of wild and fantastic creatures, pipes and drums, satyrs and nymphs, jugglers and beggars, foaming with sin and sex, surges, if not to the altar, at least to the portals of the house of God. The sacred and the profane, even the vulgar, meet as close neighbours. And while art in the Middle Ages — the visual arts almost completely and music to a large extent — means sacred art, the business of everyday life with its dreams and nightmares, its obsessions and fears, its games and amusements, was by no means banned from the sacred world. It is admitted in outspoken illustrations or in various allegorical guises and personifications as an integral part of this world. This is not to say that the devil is given free play, but his existence is more than acknowledged. He receives a limited concession for his business, and the demons of hell, together with other fantastic creatures, are permitted to perform their lusty games even under the watchtowers of the cathedrals.

Thus the pages of the Jeanne d'Évreux Hours, illustrated by Jean Pucelle, *c.*1325, admit a crowd of whimsical and funny creatures, laymen and clerics and dream-born compound animals such as lion-reptiles and snake-goats, dragons with monk heads and friars with the hind legs of beasts of prey, mingling with the innocent beasts of the woods and fields, hares and deer, birds and monkeys. There are also peasants, shepherds, knights, jugglers, and acrobats.

The wide margin beneath the text is peopled usually not by single figures but by whole ensembles performing little burlesque stage plays or buffooneries: dog-trainers, for example, with their audience astonished or pleased as the case may be.

Sometimes these scenes even ascend to fill the upper margins. And some form of fantastic life appears unfailingly in the space to the right of the text. Wherever the written sentence of the text leaves part of the line empty, monsters creep in to continue the black of the line up to the margin, and then widen out and expand in broader design on the border of the page. This, in a way, is a reversal of the position of gargoyles, which, for static reasons that are quite evident, adhere to the church walls with a broad, compact *derrière* and then thin out to reach far into the air with their long, slender necks. This high proportion of reptilian anatomy and long-tailed monsters is the only stereotyped aspect of Pucelle's otherwise boundless fancy, for the line left unfilled by the sacred text only leaves space for something long and thin — tails, if it is to be a living creature, and it inevitably is. Sometimes, however, these tails assume plantlike patterns and on occasion even the form of Gothic architectural decoration. Occasionally the artist must have become bored by all this monotony, for he frequently tries to wedge the body of a monster into an empty line space, with the tail then curving out unhampered into open space (Pl. 58b).

The effect, as I said before, is absurd and almost sacrilegious. An *averte iram tuam nobis* may end in a long-tailed goat, a *Deo gratias* in a reptile-man, or a *Gloria patri et filio et spiritu sancto* in a lion's tail with the top-heavy body of a hooded monk attached to it. Thus we have here a mingling of the most venerable words of the liturgy with the amusing, if not ridiculous and eery, creatures that are figments of the artist's imagination.

This specific irruption of the bizarre and farcical into the sacred, as happens in the Hours of Jeanne d'Évreux, is a Northern phenomenon confined chiefly to Flanders, France, and England. Yet one is tempted to look for a moment across a span of two centuries to a Southern fashion, the Italian grotesques of the *cinquecento*, beginning with Pinturicchio's famous vault decorations in the library of the cathedral of Siena, which, if not strictly parallel, still afford similar aspects from more than one point of view. Their habitat, of course, is walls rather than paper. Their immediate source is the ancient stucco and fresco decorations in the Thermae of Trajan and other buildings rediscovered at the time. Like the drolleries they spin a frivolous web of playful creatures around a centre of totally different significance, this time not a text of the Scriptures, however, but frescoes with sacred, mythological, or historical content. One recalls here combinations such as the rich fungus of grotesques sprouting all over the walls of Raphael's loggias in the Vatican, accompanying and crowding in the Biblical stories in the middle of the vaults. Here in the very centre of Western Christendom the satyrs and nymphs play their jolly games around the Deluge, the Birth of Christ, or the Last Supper.

To be sure, the single figures in the Italian grotesques, for all their fun and variety, are a rather domesticated brand of fantasy, and their symmetrical arrangement on the walls is largely dominated by their decorative function within the architectural frame. There is never any doubt that they are imitations — however free — of ancient models, while the medieval drolleries bear all the stamp of immediate, original, and inexhaustible imagination. If one were to look for a *cinquecento* parallel to our drolleries one would rather find it in Dürer's marginal drawings for the Emperor Maximilian's prayer book, which has that very same fusion of Northern exuberance and Latin clarity.

In the Hours of Jeanne d'Évreux a surprising number of the creatures, human or beastlike or compound, are engaged in playing musical instruments. Surprising, that is, to the spectator who is not familiar with the teeming, colourful musical life of the Middle Ages, and especially with the number and variety of musical instruments as compared with the standardized specimens which make up our modern symphony orchestra.

Illustrations of this kind are a true gold mine of information for the student of medieval musical instruments. They are an indispensable supplement to the occasional descriptions appearing in musical treatises and poetry, which necessarily lack the accuracy provided by illustrations as to the variety of types of instruments, of playing techniques, and their use in ensembles. Modern history of music has, with few exceptions, exploited these visual sources little — understandably so, for historians have concentrated above all on the music itself and thus on written music, which was chiefly sacred music. Therefore the music never confided to paper, that is, a large part of secular music, such as dances and the improvisations of solo performers, has remained somewhat outside the focus of musical history.

It is for this reason that the visual representations of instrumental performances assume great importance, providing an open window on secular music of the past. How important a role secular music played about 1325, when Pucelle decorated the Hours of Jeanne d'Évreux, may be hinted at here by one fact only. In 1321 there was established in Paris the Confrérie of Saint-Julien-des-Ménestriers, a guild — or, as we would call it today, 'union' — of French instrumentalists under a *roy des ménestriers*. This was the time of the *Ars nova*, when secular instrumental music in dances and arrangements of songs reached such heights that it in its turn began to influence the style of sacred music with its new inventions.

If we examine the various instruments depicted in the Jeanne d'Évreux Hours, we will find that some are playful caricatures while others are realistic depictions of actual instruments of the time, often portrayed with amazing precision considering the miniature size of these drawings.

We turn first to the wind instruments, which were prevalent from the Middle Ages until well into the Renaissance. Let us look first at the bagpipes, which appear in various forms on our pages. The bagpipe is one of the oldest instruments shown here; its history reaches back to antiquity. According to Suetonius and Dio Chrysostom, Nero played the bagpipe, though it is not reported whether he did this while Rome burned.

Some bagpipes on the margins of our pages are precise drawings of actual specimens, while others are burlesque versions. A large bagpipe is played by a musician perched cross-legged on a ferocious long-tailed beast (Pl. 62b). His thin legs and forearms form a strange pattern with the abnormally long chanter of the bagpipe, which ends in a carved animal head similar to that of the long-tailed monster. The bagpipe has an enormous drone reaching over the player's shoulder.

A smaller bagpipe is held — but not played — by a hooded reptile-monk who extends, as it were, the line of the text *spiritu sancto* (Pl. 62d). Here the drone is hardly longer than the chanter. The point where the chanter leaves the bag is decorated by a little crowned head. Such little wooden sculptures were quite common decorations on bagpipes of that time. This usage was retained for centuries, and the carved heads are still found in the powerful bagpipes played at the drinking parties painted by Jordaens, for example in the various versions of *Le Roi boît* in the museums at Brussels, Leningrad, and Antwerp.

On another page a bagpipe, this time without a drone, is the focal point of a little comedy scene (Pl. 62e). The small instrument is being trained as a dog. The little decorative dog head is that of a real bagpipe, but little dog feet appear under the bag. Two rustic characters are so overcome by the spectacle that they cavort with gestures of surprise. Even funnier is a canine bagpipe which decorates the page showing Christ before Pilate (Pl. 62f). Here two monstrous musicians compete in the production of noise. Both are half animal, with long, intertwining tails that sprout oak leaves. The right one, with puffed cheeks, blows a reed pipe that terminates in a large bell, possibly of cowhorn. This is a realistic picture. The other musician, however, employs a dog as a bagpipe, using its tail as a blowpipe and one of its hind legs as the chanter. One can imagine the sound.

While these three bagpipes have no inner relation to the spiritual content of the page, we find quite a different situation on the page illustrating the Annunciation to the Shepherds (Pl. 58a). The central scene overflows into the margin, where we see shepherds with all their attributes — sheep and crook and a dog — looking up in wonder. One of them plays the typical shepherd instrument, a small reed pipe (shawm or *chalumeau*). The reedy, bleating, guttural tone of the shawm, associated with the pastoral realm since time immemorial, has become symbolic in Christian iconology of the Nativity scene, one of the many strange ways in which musical and visual symbolism often mingle. Later the piffero and zampogna with their heavy drones appear for many centuries and still today as the inevitable attribute of the shepherds surrounding the Child in Italian *presepi*. The symbolic union between the sound of reed pipes and the crèche in the stable, or, in other words, of pastoral music with its characteristic drone and Christmas, pervades more than five hundred years of music up to the *Christmas*

Oratorio of Johann Sebastian Bach, and to Handel's *Messiah*, and still further. If, with this in mind, we look at the initial D of *Deus*, it does not seem altogether accidental that it is formed by a bagpipe player, for the bagpipe has the same reedy timbre as the simple pipe beneath. The only difference is the bag, a mere mechanical convenience that makes the player less dependent on the rhythm of his breathing.

Of other wind instruments in our Book of Hours we may mention in passing a transverse flute (Pl. 58b), several realistically drawn trumpets, and many specimens of the one-hand fife played together with a drum, according to age-old custom (Pl. 63g).

Turning now to string instruments, we find these represented in the Pucelle Hours by harps, psalteries, mandolas, and vielles, the first three instruments plucked, the last bowed. The harps are all small and have the characteristic rounded Gothic form. In Romanesque harps the three elements of the frame, that is, soundbox, neck, and pillar, were distinctly set off against each other, as they are in modern orchestral harps. The Gothic harp fuses the three elements into one curved design, as we see in the specimen plucked by the claws of a feathered monk-dragon in Pl. 60a.

The psalteries represented in our book all have the typical shape of a trapezoid with the two slanting side walls curving inwards (Pl. 61a). We find psalteries of this form in many angel concerts, both Northern and Italian, and they appear still in many illuminated manuscripts of the high Renaissance, in the hands of King David. In spite of the minute size of these illustrations, the hitch pins and the decorations of the sound hole have been indicated with great care.

The mandola, of Near Eastern origin like the psaltery, appears three times in our manuscript. All three forms have a lute-like body with a round sound-hole in the centre, and a characteristic long, thin neck passing into a widely curved sickle and terminating in a carved animal head. But our specimens differ in the shape of the soundbox. The smallest one has an almost circular corpus to which the neck is joined at a sharp angle (Pl. 61b). The larger one has a corpus of oval outline (Pl. 60a), and a third one of medium size shows the corpus gradually passing into the neck (Pl. 62c). Two of the mandolas are clearly plucked with a plectrum, with the plucking arm in a rather mannered, uncomfortable position.

The last of the string instruments — and the only bowed one — is the vielle, the typical fiddle of the time, depicted in countless Italian and Flemish paintings in the hands of angels and also in some secular manuscripts such as the Manesse Codex. One vielle appears on the lower margin of the page showing the education and chastisement of Saint Louis (Pl. 59b). It is played by a youth comfortably seated on the back of a monster. Since the youth resembles somewhat the young Saint Louis in the main scene, vielle-playing may have been shown here as part of his education. The instrument has the typical flat, leaf-shaped head so different from the scroll of the later violin; it has an elegant, shallow body with the side walls curving in slightly, already bordering on the shape of the Italian lira da braccio, a refined improvisation instrument which developed from the vielle and which we find, for instance, in the hands of Apollo playing to the Muses in Raphael's *Parnassus* in the Segnatura. The other vielle, played by a monster in an initial, is bulkier and is played in droll fashion, the right hand stopping the strings — or does it? — the left drawing the bow over the strings on the wrong side of the bridge (Pl. 61c).

Up to now we have observed only pictures of real instruments or caricatures of them, but the variety of existing instruments was apparently not sufficient for the imagination of our draughtsman; his comic sense supplied as instruments objects that are not instruments at all but other tools employed by his creatures for blowing or plucking or bowing. Among these, bellows play a large role. Now bellows are indispensable tools known to civilization ever since the technique of melting metal was invented. They even served as auxiliary gadgets for musical instruments; from antiquity, for example, they have provided air pressure for the wind chest of pipe organs. And they were added for a similar purpose to bagpipes when these instruments were transformed into the neat little musettes played by court ladies in the *fêtes champêtres* of Versailles, relieving these make-believe shepherdesses of the unbecoming act of blowing. But in the Évreux Hours the bellows themselves are exalted into tools of music. They are played as heraldic trumpets (Pl. 63c & d), or plucked with a plectrum by a monstrous monk, a sinister Orpheus who by his singing and playing entrances the creatures of the fields and woodlands (Pl. 61a). Another comic pseudo-instrument is, of all things, the jawbone. It appears twice in our drolleries. Once it is plucked by a lion-footed king, to the amazement of a dog, which may perhaps be more interested in the bone than in the music (Pl. 59a). Another time the jawbone is bowed with a rake by a billy goat, which is deterred somewhat from its perform-ance by a ferocious, weasel-like creature attacking its tail (Pl. 63i). This brings to mind the Biblical jawbone of an ass, but one must be an obdurate iconologist to credit Pucelle with scriptural intentions here.

Besides wind and string instruments we find in the Hours of Jeanne d'Évreux a variety of percussion instruments, or, to use the scientific terms, sonorous substances and membranophones such as drums. The cymbals, an instrument going back to the ancient Orient and Rome, appears in our pages played by a monster in an initial (Pl. 62a). Its appearance in 14th-century illustrations is rather rare, but it is frequent in angel concerts of the 15th century, especially in Italy. Here each of the two disks has a simple form, curving gradually from the centre towards the rim, while later cymbals usually consist of a flat rim sharply set off from a central boss. Cymbals of the later type are shown in one of the reliefs by Luca della Robbia for the Singing Gallery, formerly in the cathedral at Florence, which illustrates a line from Psalm 150: *Laudate eum in cymbalis jubilationis*; they also appear in the angel orchestra surrounding the Madonna in the painting by Giovanni Boccati in the Pinacoteca Vannucci at Perugia.

Another noisemaker of metal is the triangle. It is played by a snake-tailed youth who suspends it with one hand while the other strikes it with a stick (Pl. 63e). The triangle in this illustration has several jingling rings that add a clattering noise to the sharp tones of the metal frame.

Bells — *tintinnabula* or *cymbala* — play a large role in the medieval instrumentarium. Our manuscript shows several forms: a youth perched on the shoulder of a monster plays a set of three bells with clappers; a hairy musician swings a set of bells with clappers while playing a small shawm with the other hand (Pl. 63f); and a bearded man strikes a large suspended bell with a stick (Pl. 63h). Chimes, so frequent in medieval illuminations, are for some reason absent from this book.

Of special interest is a rattle appearing in our pages, for rattles, especially of the form we have here, are rarely shown (Pl. 63b). We can clearly see a hammer attached to a horizontal bar. When this crossbar is shaken it is hit by the hammer. Rattles of this and other types played a large role in religious and folk customs of the Middle Ages and even of later times; they were used by night watchmen or by beaters in hunting, or to 'break the bones of Judas' on Good Friday. The Metropolitan Museum's collection of musical instruments also contains a medieval *crécelle*, a rattle of slightly different construction which according to custom was used to replace the sound of the church bells while they 'travelled to Rome' during the week before Easter.

Of single drums only one type is represented, a snare drum attached to the shoulders of the players (Pl. 63a & g). It has two drumheads, evident from the bracing cords that connect the two skins. In one case the player hits the drum with a large stick, playing at the same time, as usual, the one-hand fife. In the other case the player blows a larger pipe, stopping its holes with both hands, while the drum is behind his shoulders, possibly waiting to be pounded with the elbows. Such playing methods were by no means unusual. When I was a child in Vienna there were still musical beggars, veritable one-man orchestras, who played their many instruments at the same time with mouth and hands, knees and feet, head and elbows.

While up to now we have observed single instruments individually played, we also have two ensembles in our Book of Hours. The smaller one appears in the scene of the Nativity over the monumental cradle of the Child (Pl. 59a). One angel plays the cymbals, the other a large vielle.

The other and larger ensemble is an angel concert that significantly accompanies the page showing the Adoration of the Magi (Pl. 60b). The lower margin illustrates as fitting counterpoint the Massacre of the Innocents supervised by Herod himself. Musical angels invaded sacred imagery relatively late, during the second half of the 13th century, and most probably under the influence of Jacobus de Voragine's *Golden Legend*. The combination of loud instruments such as trumpets and drums with the fine silvery sound of small stringed instruments is by no means uncommon. In this heavenly orchestra we see a large psaltery in the centre similar to the one shown in Pl. 61a. The angel immediately right of it plays the vielle, while the one on the left side holds in each hand a set of bells with clappers. The flanking instruments, a trumpet and a pair of kettledrums, are old, inseparable companions throughout the Middle Ages and ever since. They have always been the attributes of high nobility since the Middle Ages, providing the musical equivalent to heraldic pomp and announcing with fanfares and flourishes the coming of princes and peers. And just as the shawm and the bagpipe accompanied the Annunciation to the Shepherds (Pl. 58a), trumpets and kettledrums here lend their majestic sound to the entrance of the three oriental kings.

It is here in the last-mentioned two pages from the Hours of Jeanne d'Évreux that the musical instruments make a deeply meaningful contribution to the spiritual content of the main illustrations. In this role they exceed their function elsewhere in the manuscript, where they merely provide an amusing and sometimes bizarre counterpoint to the scriptural text.

11 · On Angel Concerts in the 15th Century: A Critical Approach to Realism and Symbolism in Sacred Painting*

The historian of musical performance, especially that of early instrumental music, often has occasion to regret the sparseness of his sources of information. He draws on contemporary reports, but they are often vague and technically inaccurate. He draws on musical treatises, but they are usually devoted to pedagogical ideals rather than to descriptions of contemporary usage; understandably they take everyday routine for granted and thus leave untold what would interest him most.

There exists, however, another important and not yet systematically exploited reservoir of information in the form of representations of musical scenes in painting, sculpture, and the graphic arts. Such pictures are often likely to be more complete and detailed, and therefore presumably more reliable, than verbal descriptions. They too, however, present difficulties of interpretation. The farther back we go in the history of art — European or any other — the larger looms the role played by religious imagery. Apart from the twenty-four elders of Revelation and the well-known patrons of music, King David and St. Cecilia,[1] it is chiefly the angels who sing and play in sacred painting.

But in the heavens depicted in paintings, how much reliable information can we expect to find about secular music? Did the painters simply transfer earthly

---

* The principal ideas set forth in this study are the results of my preoccupation with the subject of angel concerts and of the lectures I have given on various aspects of this topic for many years at numerous universities and museums. Originally the present essay included an account of the history of angel concerts, tracing their iconology in doctrine, poetry, and the visual arts, as a prelude to the systematic examination of their value for the historian of musical performance. After completing my script, however, I saw the excellent book recently published by Reinhold Hammerstein, *Die Musik der Engel, Untersuchungen zur Musikanschauung des Mittelalters*, Munich, 1962, in which the author concurs independently with many of my own findings. To avoid duplication, I have restricted this study to problems that were approached differently or not at all in Hammerstein's book.

[1] A 'musical patron' only because of the misinterpretation of the phrase 'organis sonantibus,' describing her wedding.

ensembles, profane or ecclesiastical, into the celestial spheres? If so, were they not implying restrictions on the supernatural abilities of angels, restrictions based on the poorer range of human instrument-building and performance? Or were the painters straining their imaginations to compete with the mystic and poetic interpreters of the Scriptures, filling the heavens with fantastic shapes and other objects never seen on earth?[1] If the verbal interpretation of the Scriptures struggles with the corporeality of *pneumata*, what should the painter do?

The complex situation may be envisaged as a double process of symbolization, striving to make the invisible visible: first the text of the Scriptures themselves, creating verbal images of spiritual (i.e. incorporeal) creatures, such as the angels; second, the painter's translation of these verbal symbols into visual shapes. Actually the situation appears further complicated by the existence of exegesis which enriches the symbols found in the Scriptures by trying to reconcile evident contradictions or by filling lacunae through the establishment, for instance, of a systematic angelology.[2]

Paradoxically, the painter of sacred subjects for the Church is, at the same time, less free and freer than the mystic poet or exegete facing the same subjects. He is far less free inasmuch as he is usually not permitted to apply his full imagination to his subject. The interpretation of the Scriptures and other ecclesiastical texts is provided for him by the Church. He is in fact depending on the guidance and often on the strict instruction of the ecclesiastical authorities.[3]

Yet within these limits he enjoys the freedom inherent in his role as a painter. Where the poet or theologian uses words, the painter is privileged — and of course compelled — to specify and to detail, or to create a concrete sensuous appearance. Or, in Goethe's words:[4] 'Language cannot express the individuality

---

[1] Many examples of this are found in the paintings of Gaudenzio Ferrari, and especially in his fresco in the cupola of the Santuario in Saronno; see Chapter 6 above. On imaginary and fantastic musical instruments in sacred and profane art, see Chapter 10.

[2] I may point here only to Dionysius the pseudo-Areopagite, to whom a large part of early angel doctrine is due. It is remarkable and quite surprising to find that the same Dionysius who in grandiose mystic and poetic vision described for the first time the complete organization of the angelic hosts, uttered a warning against too beautiful and too sensuous images and pleaded for imperfect images since their imperfection would remind the worshipper of the spiritual essence behind the physical appearance. Thus the worshipper would never forget that the images are only symbols pointing at something beyond themselves.

[3] One of the most original and perceptive examinations of the relation between religious art and church doctrine is found in Rudolf Berliner, *The Freedom of Medieval Art*, in *Gazette des beaux-arts*, XXVIII (1945), 264–88. He discusses the question of how art could presume to represent certain themes in such a way that verbal descriptions of them are historically or dogmatically or intellectually acceptable, and comes to the conclusion that the freedom of art resulted from theological concepts of its role in the realm of religion.

[4] To Riemer, 1804.

of the phenomenon [*das Individuelle der Erscheinung*], the specific. Our words for the species are always general.'

Throughout nearly two thousand years of Christian art, methods of representing the supernatural did not remain unchanged. The invisible was made visible in many ways and forms, ranging in persistence from firmly ingrained and long-standing traditions, and even clichés, to the passing flight of fancy of an individual imagination. Familiarity with these iconographical traditions is often helpful and sometimes indispensable to the historian of music who turns to works of sacred art as documents of early styles of vocal and instrumental performance. Some problems implied in a critical interpretation of sacred painting may be illustrated by the following investigation, which will concentrate on a limited span of time in the late *quattrocento*. In that century, progress in the study of anatomy and the technique of linear perspective based on a strict mathematical method had brought about a new 'scientific' pictorial conquest of the visible universe centred around a new mundane concept of man. Consequently, even the heavens were then depicted in terms of the human world; angels were represented in the image of humans;[1] and — important to the historian of music — celestial musicians and ensembles appeared in the shapes of those familiar on earth. Heavenly liturgy was depicted not by dreams and visions, however standardized, but by a portrayal of the everyday routine on earth.

Naturally, this artistic interpretation went through many phases and did not conquer the North at the same time as it did Italy. Individual artists, moreover, still adhered to visionary representations. The paintings chosen here as examples are from this Janus-headed period of transition. They are approximately contemporary, yet remarkably different in their visualization of celestial music. Hence the difficulties for the historian searching for authentic records of *Aufführungspraxis*.

The first of our examples is a small picture of the Virgin and Child painted near the end of the 15th century by Geertgen tot Sint Jans, which only recently came to light in America and is today in the van Beuningen Museum in Rotterdam (Pl. 65b). Geertgen, not more than a dozen of whose works are known, was probably born in Leiden and died at the age of twenty-eight. According to Carel von Mander's famous biographical work on Northern

---

[1] The problem of depicting supernatural creatures and the gradual 'humanization' of angels in Renaissance painting is discussed by Jakob Burckhardt in his famous article *Das Altarbild*, in *Beiträge zur Kunstgeschichte von Italien*, 2nd ed., 1911, pp. 3–161. Some of his judgements have to be taken *cum grano salis*. His absorption in the Renaissance canon of anatomical proportions made him critical of 'unrealistic angels' in earlier and later periods of art. To indicate his bias we shall cite only his disapproval of Rembrandt's angel leaving the threshold of Tobit as anatomically so deficient that he is fortunate to be able to fly because he would not be able to walk — 'He departs in the most ridiculous manner, a real Flying Dutchman.'

painters, published in 1604, Geertgen lived and worked in Haarlem. His whole known *œuvre* dates from the decade between 1485 and 1495.

Geertgen's painting of the Virgin and Child is a visionary work of great originality, unforgettable to anyone who has ever seen it, because of its poetry and its miraculous luminosity. The bulky shape of the Virgin seems to be suspended in the centre of an oval of blinding light.[1] A closer look discloses beneath the heavy folds of her garment the two attributes of the apocalyptic Woman of the Sun, the crescent and the dragon (Revelation 12). At one and the same time, she is the idyllic young mother with the infant and the crowned queen of heaven in glory. The Child shakes two large jingle bells and is in excited motion, almost dancing, with His right leg up in the air and both large toes turned up.

The Virgin is surrounded by an enormous number of angels neatly grouped into several distinct concentric ovals. The innermost of these, which has the greatest luminosity, consists of fourteen adoring, many-winged cherubim and seraphim. In the next, somewhat darker oval, twelve angels carry the instruments of the Passion; and four angels around the head of the Virgin hold pennants inscribed with the abbreviated form of the word 'Sanctus.'[2] The outermost oval and the corners of the panel are filled with the largest group, consisting of twenty-three angels playing musical instruments. The instruments are: from the top, counter-clockwise — a lute, large shawm (without protective cylinder), vielle, flat handbell struck with beater, long pipe with snare drum, hurdy-gurdy, jingle-bells, small clapper, coiled trumpet, pair of handbells, another coiled trumpet, large clappers, curved trumpet, bagpipe, set of seven small jingles strung on a rope; left upper corner — positive organ played by one angel and held by another; left lower corner — clavichord played by one angel, while another holds music; below centre — cromorne; right lower corner — dulcimer, double shawm, pot; right upper corner — clavicytherium (?) played by one angel and held by another. This is a very rich and nearly complete instrumentarium of the time, including even the three contemporary keyboard instruments — organ, clavicytherium, and clavichord. Only the tromba marina, so frequent in Flemish paintings of the period, is absent. There is hardly any

[1] Geertgen's Virgin and Child preserves the basic form of the mandorla, but the hard linear shape is resolved in luminous concentric ellipses. The broad outline of the mandorla of Byzantine heritage had by this time been gradually softened by surrounding it and finally replacing it with rows of angels. Perhaps the most important landmark in this evolution is Orcagna's famous relief of the Death and Ascension of the Virgin, dating from before 1360, on the tabernacle in Or San Michele, Florence.

[2] The range of colours from the almost blinding yellow glare around the Virgin through the pink circle of cherubim to the darker red of the angels with the instruments of the Passion and the purplish black of the musical angels is strongly reminiscent of the moon-halo, very appropriate, of course, for the Virgin on the crescent.

need to state that Geertgen was not thinking of any actual ensemble. By depicting nearly all the instruments he knew, he gave an allegory of the loudest and richest possible sound.

The crowned Virgin, enshrined by dense crowds of angels, is the visual embodiment of a very old theme — the lauding and adoring angel choirs in heaven. Much has been written on the iconology of angel choirs. Here, it suffices to recall Dionysius the pseudo-Areopagite, St. Thomas Aquinas, and Dante. To determine to what degree Geertgen partakes in this pictorial tradition (not to say cliché), one has only to look at one of the many contemporary paintings of the same subject, for instance that by the Master of the Glorification of the Virgin (Pl. 65a; Worms, Collection of Baron Heyl). There too, the crowned Virgin rests on the crescent, surrounded by a multitude of angels. And there we even find angels with lute and vielle close to her and to the Infant, and in the lower corners there are two elaborate groups of musicians and instruments — on the left a portative organ and a psaltery, and on the right a little shawm and singers. Yet, what a difference from Geertgen's picture! In the Glorification of the Virgin, the angels crowd around her like a thick cluster of swarming bees, organized only by the application of a device as terrestrial as the gradual foreshortening from the nearer to the farther angels. All seem as heavy as any earthly creatures, and their earthliness is even more marked in the lower-corner groups, which are set firmly into the landscape.

Geertgen's painting is more ethereal; it seems to hark back to traditional notions which, during the Middle Ages, became curiously intermingled with the Christian doctrine of the angelic host, specifically the even more ancient idea of the celestial spheres developed in the writings of the Babylonians and the Pythagoreans, in Plato's *Timaeus* and *Politeia* and Cicero's *Dream of Scipio*, and still continued in the treatises of Kepler and Athanasius Kircher. Geertgen organized the angels into concentric rings or ovals, sharply distinct in their function, evidently alluding to the revolving spheres. One need only focus on the lower part of the ovals to see how the angels there, floating in nearly horizontal position, partake of the rotation.

This observation might help us still further to detect a deeper meaning, imparted to the picture by one striking and unique detail. As pointed out above, the Child shakes a pair of jingle bells with great animation. He looks down to the side and, in the line of His gaze, one of the musical angels in the outer ring is intently returning His glance (Pl. 64). It is the only angel whose eyes, notwithstanding the minuteness of the whole representation, are so distinctly rendered as to make their direction unmistakable. And it is this very angel who shakes a smaller pair of jingle bells towards the Child. An amusing little genre detail?[1]

[1] Such genre details occur later in the Venetian *sacre conversazioni*.

Perhaps so, although the unique mystic character of our picture and the thoughtfulness of the painter as manifested in other works may suggest a deeper interpretation, which is submitted here with the caution proper in the intricate field of pictorial symbolism: The *concentus* between the two pairs of bells reveals Christ as the leader or generator of the heavenly orchestra.[1]

Since Geertgen seems to have been familiar with the Areopagitic and Thomistic doctrine, one may assume also that the consonance of musical instruments — that is, the rapport between the two pairs of bells — is meant to represent God as prime mover of the universe, imparting the first impulse to the harmony of the spheres whose rotation is so vividly depicted here. This would be in line with Thomas Aquinas, *Summa Theologiae* I, *Questio* 105, discussing the problem whether God, as spiritual substance, can directly move a body, that is, corporeal matter; he states in Reply Obj. 1:

> There are two kinds of contact: corporeal contact (when two bodies touch each other) and virtual contact (as the cause of sadness is said to touch the one made sad). According to the first kind of contact, God, as being incorporeal, neither touches nor is touched. But according to virtual contact, He touches creatures by moving them but He is not touched. . . .[2]

So much for the Geertgen picture, which, rich as it is in theological and poetic symbolism, offers little to the historian of *Aufführungspraxis*.

Turning now to our second main example, we find a basically different attitude towards the representation of music and musicians, which stems from a different tradition and environment. This picture (Pl. 68), signed and dated 1474 and now in the Museum of Dijon, is a work of the Tuscan painter Zanobi

[1] Pseudo-Dionysius, in his *De divinis nominibus*, IV, 5, calls God 'the cause of consonance and clarity,' a statement commented on by St. Thomas Aquinas in *In Dionysii de divinis nominibus*, IV, lect. 5, nos. 340, 346, and 349. I am delighted to find in Reinhold Hammerstein's *Die Musik der Engel*, p. 118, two pertinent quotations: 1) According to Gregory of Nyssa, God generates the music of the universe; 2) Maximus Confessor defines the universe as music performed by God.— I may add that this notion is still alive in Athanasius Kircher's *Musurgia mirifica*, in which an engraving, Bk. VIII, p. 366, shows a big pipe organ, the instrument of the Creator, with several compartments, of which each is related to one of the days of creation according to Genesis.

[2] The existence of two similar pairs of bells and of the gaze exchanged between the infant Jesus and the angel has been pointed out by Daphne M. Hoffman in her article *A Little Known Masterpiece*, in *Liturgical Arts*, XVIII (1950), 44. There, this detail is explained by reference to the customary ringing of little hand bells during the Sanctus of the Mass. It is true that this custom originated before Geertgen's picture, in fact before 1400 according to J. A. Jungmann's *Missarum sollemnia, Eine genetische Erklärung der römischen Messe*, 1948, II, 160. Miss Hoffman's interpretation would seem convincing if only the angel were playing the bells. To have Christ Himself participating in the act of glorifying, which is the duty and function of the angels (according to Isaiah 6: 14; Ezekiel 3: 12, 13; later, Ambrose; and at the time of Geertgen, Tinctoris's *Complexus effectuum musices*, c. 1480), seems awkward and not consistent with the character of a painter as thoughtful and as familiar with doctrine as Geertgen. In any case, Miss Hoffman's interpretation would not necessarily exclude the presence of a deeper symbolism.

Machiavelli, one of the minor disciples of Benozzo Gozzoli. Zanobi was a provincial painter, but his work is no less interesting in composition and no less valuable for iconographical study than that of any of the 'great' masters.

The painting does not represent the Virgin with the Infant, but the Coronation, and it shows not the multitude of musician angels depicted by Geertgen, but rather a comparatively small number, in fact two ensembles of unequal size. This is by no means the rule within the Tuscan tradition, for the Coronation pictures of this school normally include — apart from earlier paintings of the Last Judgment — the largest aggregation of musical angels in all sacred painting.

Although we are in heaven, this heaven is not conceived in visionary free imagination, but is shaped after earthly models. The throne of Christ and Mary is solid, massive, strongly shaded, and firmly planted on a platform whose steps again solidly rest on a floor decorated with tiles shown in almost exaggerated linear perspective. The two central figures sit heavily; the four saints, John the Baptist, Francis, Mary Magdalene, and Peter, plant their feet firmly on the tiles, and the four angels in the foreground kneel weightily. All this heaviness is very 'realistic,' a characteristic of our everyday world, and different from the weightlessness and ecstatic floating in the Geertgen picture. No doubt our Tuscan painter felt all this as an achievement, as progress in the pictorial conquest of perceptible space through the increasingly refined technique of linear perspective. The size of the figures, too, is well planned according to the technique of foreshortening.

If all this implies a secularization or humanization through the use of new pictorial methods, we may consider whether this realistic attitude extends to the kind of music represented here. There are two ensembles depicted, one in the remote background, the other in front of the throne close to the spectator or rather the worshipper. The far group is large, consisting of nine musicians with their instruments: one bagpipe, one hand pipe with drum, two trumpets, a jingle drum, a pair of cymbals, and three more trumpets. Four of these five trumpets are arranged in pairs in strict symmetry on the left and right sides behind the pillars of the throne.[1]

This is indeed a noisy ensemble, consisting of winds and percussion only, and it would be difficult to select a louder or more shrieking group from the instruments available at that time. It could not have been a random choice of

---

[1] In paintings showing ensembles of musical instruments, the requirements of pictorial composition often led to a symmetrical duplication of instruments very much at variance with actual practice. Trumpets and organettos, especially, are often duplicated in this way, particularly in Italian 14th- and 15th-century angel concerts celebrating the Assumption and Coronation of the Virgin. Striking examples are found in the Coronations by Beato Angelico. For more examples, see Chapter 1 above.

instruments or a painter's whim. Pictorially it would have been more rewarding to show fewer and less-crowded players. The congestion in fact is such that the painter scarcely had space to hint at the angel wings, and he had to omit the haloes altogether. Yet this large ensemble could hardly be an imaginary or allegorical group such as the one in Geertgen. It seems in fact to be a very deliberate choice of timbres, particularly since some instruments such as organettos, psaltery, and dulcimer, regularly appearing in contemporary Italian angel orchestras to accompany the Coronation scene,[1] are absent. One is led therefore to look for parallels in actual orchestral ensembles of the time and to think of the typical outdoor wind bands that accompanied processions, dances, and out-of-doors festival occasions.

At the time of Zanobi's picture Tinctoris, in his *De inventione et usu musicae, Liber* III,[2] describes an ensemble similar to the one in this painting as typically producing 'loud music'; it consists of trombones and shawms, while in our picture the double-reed timbre is represented not by shawms but by a bagpipe. ('But as far as the lowest contra-tenor parts are concerned, and often also the other contra-tenor parts, one has to add to the shawm players: players of brass instruments and especially players of that kind of tuba which, as pointed out above, was called *trompone* in Italy and *sacque-boute* in France. The combination of all these instruments together is usually called "the loud music." ') In all probability the painter portrayed the band that had accompanied the Virgin in procession style on her rise towards the centre of heaven, to lend pomp to the act of coronation, as it would have been appropriate to do in representing any earthly ceremony.

To this wind and percussion band, the small group of four angels in the foreground presents the greatest possible contrast. The angel in the rear is clearly singing. The other three play a lute, a flauto dolce of treble size, and the six-stringed bowed instrument that the contemporaries of Zanobi called a viola and that, in retrospect, can be classified as an early form of the lira da braccio — its characteristic leaf-shaped peg box showing the rear ends of six pegs. The softness of the lute is proverbial, and that of the flauto dolce is revealed by its very name. Likewise, the lira da braccio produces a very soft tone; the very lax tension of the hairs of its bow is required by its polyphonic technique.[3] This little ensemble is of the softest possible silvery timbre, even if we assume that the players of the lute and the lira da braccio also join their voices with the instru-

[1] See Paolo Veneziano's Coronation, in the Accademia, Venice; Fra Angelico's coronation pictures in the Louvre and the Uffizi.

[2] Quoted by Anthony Baines in *Galpin Society Journal*, March 1950, p. 20 ff.

[3] On the technique of the lira da braccio and the use of this instrument in Italian angel concerts, especially in Coronations of the Virgin and in the *sacre conversazioni*, see Chapter 5 above.

ments. This group, then, distinguished by haloes and its central position, must be of nobler quality, devoted to the performance of pieces in three- or four-part polyphony. Here we find an anticipation of the small polyphonic instrumental ensemble in the foreground of many of the *sacre conversazioni* or the Madonnas of Gian Bellini, Carpaccio, Cima da Conegliano, Signorelli, and many others.

The simultaneous playing of both groups would make little sense, but each could well be thought of as an actual ensemble of the time; the big one for large court dances, banquets, or processions; the small one for more subtle music of polyphonic character, performed at intimate occasions permitting and requiring concentration on the intricacies of text and texture.

According to church doctrine, liturgical music is but an imitation of celestial liturgy. But in fact the painter, depicting the music of the heavens, has recourse to his own everyday environment. Thus his representation is often of great interest to the historian of musical practice. And his picture shows clearly the confrontation of two typical, standardized groups of the time — loud and shrill music versus soft and low (*haut* vs. *bas* or *douce*).[1]

Our third example is again a Marian subject. It is the Ascension and Coronation of the Virgin by the Master of the St. Lucy Legend, now in the National Gallery, Washington, D.C. (Pl. 66). The painter was Flemish,[2] and his dated works are from between 1480 and 1489. This picture was formerly in a convent near Burgos, Spain.[3]

The painting is of unique and highly complex composition in strict bilateral symmetry and of almost miraculously fine and accurate detail — even to the minute representation of the smallest feathers in the angels' wings, the brocade of the garments, the jewellery, and the decoration of the musical instruments, the playing hands, and the books and music sheets in the hands of the angels.

The tall and slender body of the Virgin, rising to heaven, forms the vertical axis of the picture. Beneath her in the human realm, a landscape rendered in finest detail with castles, trees, water, and bridges, showing even the small conch shell at the water's edge. The Virgin's feet rest on the crescent, just as they do in the paintings of Geertgen and the Master of the Glorification. Eight angels, four

---

[1] Edmund A. Bowles, in his *Haut and Bas: The Grouping of Musical Instruments in the Middle Ages*, in *Musica Disciplina*, VIII (1954), 115 ff., has accumulated many quotations from medieval poems and chronicles, mostly French, that attest to the standardization of ensembles of different sizes and their social functions. It might be wished that he would expand his collection to include the Renaissance and the Italian and Flemish orbit.

[2] The work has also been called Portuguese-Flemish, or said to be by a Flemish artist working in Portugal. The influence of Enguerrands Clarenton's famous Coronation of the Virgin at Villeneuve-lès-Avignon has also been suggested.

[3] I had the pleasure of seeing the painting before and during restoration in 1949, while it was still in the Samuel H. Kress Collection, when I was called upon to give some advice concerning the musical instruments represented in it.

large and four small, seem to carry her upward, although a slight touch of the graceful hands appears to suffice for the purpose. Two pairs of angels immediately above her head are singing, the two nearest her each holding a sheet of music and the other two peering over their shoulders to read also. The sheets in alto and tenor clef contain the beginning of an *Ave Regina* (Pl. 67). All along the left and right margins of the picture there are eight angels, four on each side: left, from bottom to top — organetto with two ranks of eighteen pipes each; a trumpet, of which only the mouthcup and the upper end of the coil are visible; a large (tenor?) shawm; a harp of typical Gothic shape. On the right side from top to bottom there are a medium-sized (alto?) shawm; a five-stringed vielle; a small (treble?) shawm; and a small nine-stringed lute.

We have an instrumental ensemble composed of loud instruments (one trumpet, three shawms) and soft ones (lute, vielle, harp, organetto) — that is, eight instruments against the small vocal body of four voices. The area occupied by Mary, the four singing, eight playing, and eight carrying angels, covers by far the greater portion of the painting. We may call it the middle region, or that of the outer heaven, in contrast to the landscape of the human realm below it.

But there is still another region. At the top of the painting the clouds have opened and, through the sharply defined circular rim that they form, the inner heaven becomes visible — the throne of the Trinity surrounded by another multitude of angels (Pl. 7). God the Father, crowned and sceptered, and God the Son hold between them a crown ready to place upon the head of the Blessed Virgin; above it hovers the Dove. Three blue-robed angels, following an old pictorial tradition, are holding the hanging behind the throne. Flanking it are two groups of angels. On the left are the singers, eleven in number, again divided into two groups, one of six angels and the other of five, each group singing from a book with music. It is curious that the singers of the foreground group are not winged; they appear to be older, and possibly they are entrusted with the lower voices. At the right of the throne are the instrumentalists, six in number, playing three recorders, a small lute, a dulcimer, and a harp — all 'soft' instruments. Like the eight instrumentalists in the outer heaven — and, of course, like 15th-century instrumentalists on earth — they have no need of written music.

So much for the visible facts. To what extent is the depiction of these ensembles, vocal as well as instrumental, 'realistic'; i.e. how does it correspond to Flemish practices at the painter's time? The music in the outer heaven presents questions regarding two subjects: the nature of the orchestra, and the possible relationship between it and the four singers. The first can only be answered with extreme caution. The five loud winds, including a trumpet, three shawms, and an organetto equipped with a double rank of metal pipes (not the considerably softer wooden pipes), would certainly overpower the three string instruments, a harp, a tiny vielle, and a small lute. This orchestra then, as in the Geertgen painting, may merely symbolize a great volume of sound. On the other hand, so many contemporary reports and pictures[1] tell us of medium-sized and even larger instrumental ensembles combining trumpets, trombones, and shawms with soft string instruments, that the effect of the orchestra shown here in the outer heaven would certainly have been less bewildering to 15th-century ears than it is to us today.

The second question, that concerning the relation between orchestra and singers, is again not easy to answer. The four singers would be drowned out by the eight instruments unless one may impute supernatural power to angel voices. However, in pictures of the Coronation of the Virgin, a combination of singers and instruments reflecting contemporary practice rarely occurs.[2]

In the inner heaven, the 'reality' of the instrumental group in terms of earthly practice is beyond any doubt. Numerous parallels are to be found in 15th-century paintings. And likewise, the composition of the vocal group corresponds to the usage of that period. Of the two books used by the singers in the Coronation by the Master of the St. Lucy Legend, the one in which the notation is visible cannot, unfortunately, be deciphered. But whatever the angels are singing, we have no secular evidence that would speak against the simultaneous performance of the vocal and instrumental groups. Significant, of course, is the superiority in numbers of the singers.

A simultaneous performance of the same music by the angels of the outer and inner heavens seems to be utterly beyond the intention of the painter. He could not have made the separation of the two realms more clear, and it may have been more than a mere whim on his part to show the singers of the outer heaven holding single sheets, perhaps needed only once for the singular event of the Ascension. The larger vocal groups in the inner heaven are using thick music books, possibly implying a rich and lasting repertory near the Lord.

A brief summary of the organological conclusions may be warranted here.

---

[1] For a small ensemble, see for instance the charming illustration of the authors of the psalms, in the Psalter of King René II of Lorraine (Paris, Arsenal Library) showing these instruments: dulcimer, harp, vielle, recorder, trumpet, organetto, and tabor (frame drum). Also along this line, if such a late example is permissible, is the title woodcut for the Orlando di Lasso *Patrocinium musices* (Munich, 1573), depicting a tenor viol, fiddle, lute, spinet, two transverse flutes, two cornetti, and two trombones. For a larger ensemble of this type, combining loud and soft, a miniature from the Mielich Codex showing Orlando di Lasso and his ensemble at the Munich court includes spinet, three viols, tenor fiddle, bass viol, lute, three boy singers, transverse flute, bassoon, bass trombone, straight cornetto, ranket, and curved cornetto.

[2] Among my collection of several hundred photographs of angel concerts in painting and sculpture, I have found only two altarpieces with a clear opposition of singers to a large orchestral group, and in each case the singers were also playing organettos.

Concerning the question of celestial musical practice, we are in the same plight as was the aged Gluck, who once told an Italian composer, seeking information as to whether the Redeemer would be singing tenor or baritone, that he did not yet have authentic information. None of the great connoisseurs of celestial ceremonial — Dionysius the pseudo-Areopagite and Thomas Aquinas, Jacques de Liège, Dante, and Jacobus de Voragine — informs us of the size and composition of the heavenly orchestra. A comparison with the human condition seems therefore inevitable. In each of the three pictures I have analysed, the instruments are depicted faithfully; there is not a single fantastic or imaginary instrument, such as those which Gaudenzio Ferrari invented a little later for some of his angels.

More complex is the question of the grouping of the angels in the ensembles shown in our paintings, and whether or not these correspond to contemporary usage. Here Geertgen provides no information; symbolizing a maximum of sound, he accumulates virtually all the instruments available. Zanobi represents two actually existing ensembles of different sizes, instruments, and purposes. The Master of the St Lucy Legend, like Zanobi, depicts the playing of loud, festive music with one group, the processional band in the outer heaven, although the inclusion of singers and softer instruments in this band may or may not reflect actual practice; and also, parallel to the small group in Zanobi's painting, his singers and players in the inner heaven correspond closely to the practice in intimate house music of the time.

There remains the delicate problem of the comparative distinction imputed to the ensembles. Zanobi, in accordance with similar representations of the time, clearly emphasizes the small and soft group as the superior one by placing it in front of the throne. But the larger and louder ensemble in the Zanobi painting is still so close to the throne that one might expect it to compete and alternate with the chamber group. In the painting by the Master of the St. Lucy Legend, however, the larger group seems to be only the transitory accompaniment to the Ascension of the Virgin, while the small and soft ensemble is the one worthy to perform perpetually in the presence of the Lord.

Two conclusions suggest themselves: the superior rank assigned to vocal music, evidently in keeping with the liturgical tradition followed by painters of the period, and the preference for soft instruments in the presence of the Lord.[1]

---

[1] In Hans Memling's triptych (1480) decorating the organ of the church of the Benedictines in Najera, the arrangement of the instruments seems to imply a graduation from loud to soft, with the loudest being nearest to the singers surrounding the Lord, as follows: left panel — shawm, trumpet, lute, tromba marina, psaltery; right panel — two trumpets, organetto, harp, vielle. Hammerstein (p. 242) sees in the relative distance from the central figure a difference in rank among the groups in this order: singers, *instruments hauts, instruments bas*. If Memling really had it in mind to represent a sort of celestial musical precedence, the symbolism implied would

Here we are reminded, and possibly the painters or their ecclesiastical advisers were too, of Elijah's experience as recorded in I Kings 19: 11, 12, and 13:

> And a great and strong wind rent the mountains, and brake in pieces the rocks before the Lord; but the Lord was not in the wind: and after the wind an earthquake; but the Lord was not in the earthquake: And after the earthquake a fire; but the Lord was not in the fire: and after the fire a still small voice: And it was so when Elijah heard it. . . .

---

be the reverse of that expressed in the inner heaven of the painting by the Master of the St. Lucy Legend except, of course, for the singers, who in both cases have the privileged place near the Lord.

12 · The Curse of Pallas Athena

The ancients had two legends about musical contests, one comical, the other deeply tragic. The comical one is the story of the contest between Apollo and Pan. Apollo's kithara easily triumphed over the syrinx of the goat-footed god, and the judge Tmolos had no trouble in according the victory to Phoebus. Pan was not punished, for he had not really irritated Apollo's pride or vanity. But the real joke is that a bystander was punished, the music critic King Midas. In spite of Tmolos' verdict, he had dared to consider Pan the better performer, whereupon Apollo transformed his insensitive ears into those of an ass.

More serious is the other contest, in which Apollo defeated Marsyas. Already the physiognomical appearance of Marsyas shows this; he is not a half-goat, but a satyr, quite human[1] except for a horse tail and slightly pointed ears (as we see him in countless Greek vase paintings and in sculpture). His *hybris* was incomparably more threatening to Apollo than that of Pan. He snatched the pipes that Pallas Athena, their inventor, had thrown away. The pipes,[2] still animated by the magic sparkle of the goddess, played as though by themselves, and the divine music so pleased Marsyas' compatriots, the Phrygians, that they considered it better than that of Apollo. Marsyas would not have been a professional musician if he had contradicted them. This was his undoing. Apollo insisted upon a contest, this time with the Muses as jury. Marsyas agreed and even accepted Apollo's condition that the winner could do as he pleased with the loser. All this seemed fair enough. For some time the Muses were inclined to favour Marsyas. Only then did Apollo resort to tricks. He played his instrument upside down[3] and challenged Marsyas to do the same, knowing well that the pipes could only be played from one end. He also sang, accompanying himself on the strings, and again the pipes could not match this feat. Finally, approaching

---

[1] Alkibiades in the *Symposium* (215) compares Socrates' appearance to that of Marsyas. The portrait busts of Socrates in comparison with the heads of Marsyas such as the one in the Museo Barracco, Rome, are an even more telling evidence.

[2] For generations archaeologists have chosen to call the aulos — and its Roman counterpart, the tibia — a 'flute,' that is, a pipe without reeds, whereas the aulos according to overwhelming literary and visual evidence is a reed pipe, or more precisely an oboe, that is, a tube fitted with a double reed.

[3] See the so-called Sarcophagus of the Via della Garbatella, Rome, Antiquarium del Governatorato; and Apollodorus, I, Vol. 4, p. 2.

sheer bribery he sang the praise of Olympus and Helicon, and the Muses did not fail to respond to this flattery.[1]

This then leads to the fatal conclusion. Marsyas is bound to a tree and flayed. Here the several versions of the myth diverge sharply: some authors, such as Apollodorus (I, 4, 2), Ovid (*Metamorphoses* VI), and Plutarch (*Alcib.* II), tell that Apollo himself did the flaying. Others such as Philostratus min. (*Imag.* 2) have the murderous act performed by a Scythian executioner, or describe the preparations such as the sharpening of the knife. There are also different versions about the transformation of Marsyas into a river: many hold that the river originated from the blood of Marsyas; in Ovid's *Metamorphoses*,[2] however, there is a more subtly poetical version relating that a river was formed out of the tears of the satyrs, nymphs, shepherds, and of Marsyas' pupil Olympus.

In their art the ancients significantly refrained from the portrayal of the flaying. The knife, however, often appears in the hands of the standing executioner[3] or of a squatting knife sharpener, who later became such an important motif for sculpture and painting, from the famous *Arrotino*, today in the Uffizi, up to Peruzzi's little monochrome on the ceiling of the Stanza delle Nozze in the Villa Farnesina. Even Philostratus the Younger did not go further in his description of the Marsyas painting than to describe the savage grin and glaring eyes of the barbarian whetting the knife.

In Hellenistic art the representation of Marsyas acquires a new dimension: the impertinent satyr rightfully punished for daring the god turns now into the outstanding image of tragic suffering. The face of a man hanging from a tree has now lost any traces of the satyr. Though furrowed and convulsed by pain, it is deeply human and pensive. Marsyas has become an image of the silently suffering creature, clearly the prototype of the crucified.

Numerous Greek myths, such as those of Prometheus, Pentheus, and Niobe, deal with *hybris* and its punishment, the merciless revenge of the offended god on the offender. Through the Middle Ages the Marsyas story remained familiar mainly as an allegory of temerity punished. But we also recall Dante's famous reinterpretation of the flaying in the first canto of the *Paradiso* as

---

[1] Lucian's irony in the *Dialogues of the Gods* formulates this sharply. 'Hera: "Isn't Apollo admirably clever? He, whom Marsyas would have skinned! If only the Muses had not been biased judges, since no doubt Marsyas was the better musician! But as it happened the poor, cheated fool became the victim of a rigged verdict. . . ." '

[2] Loeb ed., VI, 382; also *Fasti*, Loeb ed., VI, 703.

[3] See the wall painting showing Olympus begging clememcy for Marsyas from Apollo, repr. in J. A. Overbeck, *Atlas der Griechischen Kunstmythologie*, Leipzig, 1871–89, xxv, III, 13; and the ancient stucco decoration in the basilica of Porta Maggiore, reproduced in Ludwig Curtius, *Das antike Rom*, Vienna, 1944, p. 67. Raphael borrowed the motif of the standing executioner for his condensed representation of the contest on the ceiling of the Segnatura.

purification of the soul for the sake of its mystic union with God-Apollo.[1]

But the Marsyas story not only shows *hybris* punished but has a special flavour and message. It is a poetic condensation of an eternal conflict, the antagonism between two musical realms, between string and wind instruments. This means not only the difference between the serene and silvery sound of plucked gut strings and the bleating, shrill, guttural, exciting sound of a reed pipe, though this alone is sufficiently charged with symbolic meaning in primitive civilizations from the earliest times. It means in the rationalized form of the Greek myths the realm of inhibition, of reason, of measure — in the literal Pythagorean sense of measuring strings and intervals, and in the metaphorical sense of *mesure* — as opposed to the realm of blind passion: in short, the antagonism between Apollo and Dionysus.

This is not the place to give an elaborate picture of a problem as complex as the symbolism of musical sounds and of the instruments that produce them. A few quotations may suffice to show how strongly these feelings still run in later post-mythical Greek aesthetics and — significantly — in Greek education. Plato (*Gorgias* 501) considers 'aulos-playing an art which only pursues pleasure,' and declares (*Republic* III, 399) the instruments of Apollo 'preferable to those of Marsyas,' a statement that is much more than an aesthetic preference if we view it in the light of his suggestion that the traditional command of the Delphian god to his worshippers, 'Know thyself!,' be interpreted as 'Be temperate!' (*Charmides* 164). Aristotle denies moral standing to the aulos — it is too exciting and too emotional (*Pol.* VIII, 1341a, 20; 1342 6, 1) — but rationalizes the old myth of Athena's rejection of her invention, the aulos, by bending the myth into an educational precept: 'If the goddess threw the aulos away, it was not only because it made her face ugly, but because aulos-playing does not contribute anything to the mind' (*Pol.* 1341, 65).

Although the old orthodox antinomy between Apollo and Dionysus and their musical monopolies, Paean and Dithyrambus, has by now been blurred and undergone a gradual process of rationalization and reinterpretation in Aristotelian didactic philosophy, nevertheless within this process of rationalization the older and deeper-lying antinomy between the orgiastic, intoxicating 'low' music and temperate 'ethical' music has been preserved, and with it the differing symbolic characters of the kithara and the aulos, of the stringed and the wind instruments. Their symbolic and emotional function was too deeply rooted in mythical tradition — too much a part of immemorial usage to be diluted by such surface phenomena as the succession of philosophical systems

---

[1] Ghiberti (*Commentarii*, Book II) still misinterpreted the ancient carnelian with the three figures of Apollo, the bearded Marsyas, and the kneeling boy Olympus as an allegory of the three ages of man.

and educational doctrines. And their symbolic connotation has in fact not only outlived the ancient gods but persisted down through the ages. It is still firmly embedded in the undercurrents, for instance in the folk music of contemporary civilizations. And this is true especially of the orgiastic instruments, the reed pipes, which have preserved their exciting timbre and symbolic character from the Greek aulos through the Roman tibia, the medieval bagpipe and platerspiel, the shawm of the Renaissance, and the cornemuse and musette of the Baroque and Rococo, to the saxophone of our day.

However, it was not until the close of the *quattrocento*, with the vogue of great solo performers and improvisers, that the Marsyas myth as a musical contest recaptured the artistic imagination. The sudden crop of pictorial representations is enormous. And it is from this moment that these pictures become — or should become — of interest to the historian of music and especially of instrumental performance, because now in these pictures a variety of instruments appear in the hands of Apollo and Marsyas. They are frequently the ancient ones, aulos and kithara, borrowed from gems and sarcophagi in more or less stylized versions. But often they are replaced by their contemporary equivalents, by the lira da braccio or the viola for Apollo, and shawms or other pipes for Marsyas,[1] sometimes naively, but often also because a familiar instrument from daily life reveals its symbolism more directly to the beholder. Sometimes, too, contemporary instruments such as the lira da braccio and other bowed instruments were chosen because they were considered to be ancient ones; the invention of the bow, the viola, and the violin was attributed to Sappho even in *cinquecento* literature.[2]

One unusually rich and thoughtful representation of the Marsyas story appears on an Italian panel exhibited in the National Gallery, Washington, D.C. (Kress Foundation 433)[3] (Pl. 70a) and it certainly deserves more attention than has been bestowed upon it up to now, for it is one of the most original versions of the often depicted Marsyas story. It shows in narrative sequence several phases of the myth in an elaborate and variegated landscape. Of the five

[1] I know of only one painting where the challenger of Apollo has a string instrument: Cima da Conegliano's *tondo* with the contest between Apollo and Pan. While Apollo holds a stylized form of the lira da braccio, Pan has not his usual syrinx but a small rustic version of the rebec, evidently appropriate to the man from the woods.

[2] As for the Renaissance treatises on music attributing the invention of contemporary musical instruments to antiquity, see Chapter 14 below.

[3] The painting is labelled in the National Gallery 'unknown Florentine, sixteenth century.' As a historian of music I should leave dating and attribution to connoisseurs better qualified, but cannot refrain from suggesting an earlier and more northern origin — perhaps Brescian. The humid landscape, rich in water and mossy rocks, strongly suggests the foothills of the Alps rather than a Tuscan *ambiente*, and the whole composition, still breathing a spirit of the late *quattrocento*, may be placed not later than the first quarter of the *cinquecento*.

large figures, the central and dominating one is that of Apollo. With slightly opened lips, perhaps singing, and a serious expression in his languid, dreamy eyes, he bows his large fiddle. The other bow, his weapon, lies beneath his feet, discarded in favour of the musical bow. The quiver with the arrows is visible behind his right shoulder. Marsyas listens to him with an anxious, preoccupied, and worried face. He is a rustic character, with bare feet and thick, bushy hair, and holds a bagpipe in his lap.

We may just as well pause here to devote a few words to his musical instrument and that of Apollo, which after all are the real contestants and in a way the protagonists of the whole story. The bagpipe — or, as the *quattro-* and *cinquecento* would have called it, 'zampogna' or 'zamparella' — is in timbre the counterpart of the ancient Greek aulos or Roman tibia, for its sounding pipes, the chanter and the drone, are fitted with reeds like the aulos and produce a similar bleating 'reedy' timbre (these reeds are inside the bag). Yet bagpipes are extremely rare in Renaissance illustrations of the Marsyas story; we usually find simple reed pipes without a bag, like those in Perugino's drawing in the Accademia, Venice, or in the beautiful painting in the Hermitage attributed to Bronzino and Correggio, executed for the decoration of a harpsichord lid. In fact I know of only three artists who show bagpipes in the Marsyas story; one is the author of the woodcuts for the *Ovidio volgare* 1497; a second is Benedetto Montagna in his engraving (Arthur M. Hind, *Early Italian Engraving*, London, 1938–48, V, 186, No. 41); the last is Andrea Schiavone in his drawing of the flaying of Marsyas (Louvre), with a bagpipe in the foreground strangely paired with the ancient lyre. In his *cassone* painting of the contest in the Accademia, Venice, Schiavone again uses the bagpipe, played not by Marsyas, however, but by a small female figure near the margin.

The syrinx, composed ordinarily of seven pipes of different length, is usually the instrument of Pan in Renaissance painting,[1] as well as in ancient Roman sculpture,[2] but occasionally it also accompanies Marsyas.[3] In single cases the wind instrument is even replaced by a string instrument, as in Cima da Conegliano's *tondo*, in which Pan holds a rustic form of the rebec while Apollo bows a beautifully stylized and highly decorated string instrument, a version of the lira da braccio.[4]

[1] For instance, Tintoretto, *The Judgement of Midas*, National Gallery of Art, Washington, D.C.

[2] See the group *Pan and Daphnis* in the Museo Nazionale, Naples.

[3] See for instance the medallion with the flaying of Marsyas in Annibale Carracci's ceiling in the Galleria Farnese. In the sketch of Marsyas in the Louvre (No. 5923), attributed to Correggio, reproduced in A. E. Popham, *Correggio's Drawings*, London, 1957, Plate X, Marsyas plays an ancient syrinx; the same figure in the painting of the contest on the harpsichord lid in the Hermitage referred to previously shows the syrinx replaced by a large 16th-century shawm.

[4] Further about the lira da braccio, see Chapter 5 above.

The lira da braccio in our painting has four melody strings and one clearly visible drone string passing next to the thumb of the player's left hand (Pl. 69a). Its form is typical of the beginning of the *cinquecento*. This form is characterized by side walls consisting of two curves separated by a projecting point — as opposed to the later forms, which already approach the violin, with two projecting points resulting in a division of the side walls into upper, middle and lower bouts. Good examples of this type are to be seen in Lorenzo Liombruno's *Judgement of Midas*, before its destruction in the Berlin Museum; Perugino's *Coronation of the Virgin* in the Vatican; the Apollo in Raphael's *Parnassus* (Pl. 84a); Signorelli's Virgin in the Pinacoteca in Arezzo; and above all, the most beautiful depiction, in Carpaccio's *Presentation of Jesus in the Temple* in the Venice Accademia (Pl. 33b).

In the Italian literature of the *quattro-* and *cinquecento*, 'lira' means sometimes the ancient lyre, sometimes the contemporary lira da braccio. The numerous Renaissance treatises dealing with the music of the ancients and its relation to contemporary music make it quite clear that the name 'lira' was given at the time not only to the ancient lyre but also to the modern bowed stringed instrument, which sometimes is also called 'lira moderna,' as for instance, to mention only one source, in Vincenzo Galilei's *Dialogo della musica antica e moderna*, 1581, fn. pp. 136, 147.[1]

The left section of the painting shows the flaying (Pl. 69b). Marsyas is nude, his cloak and bagpipe at his feet, his right arm tied to the bare tree. His face is filled with horror and pain as he turns his head toward Apollo, who performs the cruel punishment himself, with a brutal gleam in his eye. This is quite rare. As I have mentioned, the Greeks in their innumerable representations have never shown the actual skinning.[2] It was in the Baroque, when art revelled in torture and martyrdom, that the act of flaying, frequently carried out by Apollo himself, became a generally accepted subject.[3]

[1] Vincenzo Galilei, the father of Galileo Galilei, was a famous composer, theoretician, and historian of music, and was deeply interested in ancient Greek music and the possibilities of reconstructing it.

[2] The preparation for the flaying is frequently symbolized by the standing or squatting figure of the Scythian executioner. The squatting figure was retained by Peruzzi in his frieze with the stories from Ovid's *Metamorphoses* in the third floor of the Villa Farnesina.

[3] Among the earliest scenes showing the flaying are Correggio's (Bronzino's?) painting on the lid of a harpsichord in the Hermitage, and Andrea Schiavone's painting, once in Andrea Vendramin's collection (Tancred Borenius, *The Picture Gallery of Andrea Vendramin*, London, 1923, pl. 59, fol. 71), and his drawing in the Louvre mentioned above. In all these representations, Apollo himself wields the knife. In Domenichino's fresco for the Villa Aldobrandini, later in the collection Lanckoronski, Apollo again does the flaying. The most elaborate vivisection, of almost Vesalian flavour, occurs in the painstaking engraving by Melchior Meier (after Martin Rota), Adam Bartsch, *Le Peintre graveur*, Leipzig, 1876, Vol. XVI, p. 246. There Marsyas under Apollo's knife appears as an anatomical showpiece, similar to Marco Agrate's statue of the

This brings us to the last of the five figures, a roundish and pretty young woman also playing the bagpipe at the edge of a pond (Pl. 69c). It is precisely the same kind of bagpipe which is held by Marsyas and lies at his feet in the flaying group. Who would guess at first glance that this bareshouldered and barefooted girl engaged in pastoral music is none other than Pallas Athena herself? But her attributes, the helmet, shield, and lance beside her foot, are clearly depicted; and, if there were still doubt, her pose would explain her function in the Marsyas story, for she takes no delight at all in her music, but bends forward anxiously to observe her reflection in the water. In short, we have here the representation of another myth, closely related to the Marsyas story. It is the story of the invention of the reed pipe by Athena. She invents the aulos and plays it at an Olympian banquet. Most of the gods are delighted, but Hera and Aphrodite smile at the distorted face and the puffed cheeks of Athena. The embarrassed Athena rushes into a Phrygian wood to look at her image in a pond, and, agreeing that her appearance is hardly improved by performing on the pipes,[1] she throws them away and curses them. When Marsyas snatches at them, she tries to prevent him,[2] but he takes them anyway and falls victim to the curse.[3]

---

skinned San Bartolomeo in the cathedral of Milan near the side entrance. In Titian's painting in the archiepiscopal castle of Kremsier, Apollo plays the lira da braccio while Marsyas, hanging down like one of the carcasses in Rembrandt's and Daumier's paintings, is butchered by the Scythian executioner and his assistant.

[1] See for instance, Athenaeus, Bk. 14, quoted in Natalis Comes, *Mythologia*, 1596 and 1616, Bk. VI, Ch. XV, 'De Marsya.'

[2] Illustrated in Myron's famous group (see Pausanias, I, 24, No. 1). The invention of the aulos itself by Athena — and, by the way, Hermes' creation of the lyre — was not illustrated, as far as I know, in Greek art.

[3] It is remarkable how this short myth reflects in a condensed form the ambivalent attitude of the Greeks towards the wind instrument (described above), and how attitudes common to primitive civilizations are rationalized in Greek myths, and parallel with this, in their arts. In primitive cultures the pipe is usually an initiation instrument and therefore under a taboo for women. In Greek writers the aulos is the instrument of passion, urges, instincts — in short, of what orthodox psychoanalysts would call the Id. Thus we find it in the entourage of Dionysus, in the hands of satyrs, and it is also the customary instrument in the hands of music-making girls in numerous scenes of drinking parties. But apart from this a woman would not ordinarily be shown with the aulos.— The Dionysiac connotation of the wind instrument is obvious in countless representations in Renaissance art, of which I mention here only a few characteristic examples from the late *quattro-* and early *cinquecento*: an engraving by Zoan Andrea, *Youth and Girl Embracing* (c. 1475) (Hind, *op. cit.*, V, 68, No. 18); engraving by Marcantonio, *Satyr and Nymph* (Henri Delaborde, *Marc-Antoine Raimondi*, Paris, 1888, No. 140), and its reinterpretation in the bronze *tondo* by pseudo-Antonio da Brescia, *Pan and Abundance* (A 395, 118 B., National Gallery of Art, Washington, D.C.); *The Sacrifice to Priapus* in the *Hypnerotomachia Polyphili*, with many wind instruments; the engraving by Girolamo Mocetto, *Metamorphosis of Amymone* (c. 1514) (Hind, *op. cit.*, II, 166), and the related drawing by Benedetto Montagna (Uffizi, Gabinetto dei Disegni 14589F); Luca Signorelli's famous *Pan and Attendants*, in the Berlin Museum until its destruction, with a syrinx and several pipes; Francesco Cossa's *Triumph of Venus* in the

As the patroness of crafts, Pallas Athena was credited with the invention of a tool as complex and delicate as the full-fledged aulos. Yet as a goddess revered as the embodiment of reason she could not favour an object charged with the connotation of passion, sex, and inebriation. But being the inventor of the instrument and the initiator of the whole chain of events she remains an important element of the story, and it is evidently for this reason that she is included in many of the larger representations of the contest between Apollo and Marsyas in Greek vase painting as well as on Roman sarcophagi. But she never acts; she is just present, just a bystander, and she does not hold an instrument.[1] It is in this passive function that she has been retained in most Renaissance and Baroque representations of the contest, that of Marsyas as well as that of Pan,[2] as for instance in the painting on the harpsichord lid in the Hermitage, mentioned before.[3] Athena's appearance in a musical contest as a main figure and even holding a musical instrument is of the utmost rarity, and if she does so in our painting it seems a poetic idea to round out the contest scene not only with its later tragic consequences but also by alluding to the origins of it all, the unlucky invention of the ill-fated pipes.

---

frescoes in the Palazzo Schifanoia, Ferrara (see Chapter 2 above); about the many pastoral girls with flutes in Titian, see Chapter 2 above.

While some of these scenes evidently pay lip service to ancient art, especially gems and sarcophagi, it is quite clear that the symbolic function of the wind instrument is contemporary in feeling. This tradition is continued in the numerous flute lessons (e.g., the drawing by Lodovico Caracci, Uffizi, Gabinetto dei Disegni 787E) and other genre scenes of the Baroque and even later. The clearest self-explanatory subject from antiquity is perhaps the combination of aulos-playing satyrs with the Dionysiac serpent baskets, for instance on the right side wall of the famous sarcophagus with Bacchus and Ariadne in the Louvre, and on the left side wall of the sarcophagus with the triumph of Dionysus in the Lyon Museum.

[1] I know of only one ancient representation of Athena playing the aulos: a first-century Roman sarcophagus in the Palazzo Barberini, once part of the famous collection Valle Capranica (Karl Roberts, *Die Antiken Sarkophag-Reliefs*, Berlin, 1890–1952, Vol. 3/2, p. 244, and Pl. lxiii), depicts, in three sections framed by *putti* that carry a garland, three phases of the Marsyas story, including in the first section Athena playing the aulos and watching her badly distorted face in the water. Also interesting in this connection is the myth of Athena as the inventor of aulos music as told by Pindar in his poem for Midas of Acragas, the winner in an aulos-playing contest (Pythian xii), a tale, by the way, of profound bearing on Greek aesthetics of instrumental music. According to this tale, Athena invented the aulos in order to imitate on this instrument the death cry of Euryale, the one of the three Gorgons who was beheaded by Perseus.

[2] The large canvas with the *Contest between Apollo and Pan* by H. de Clerck in the Rijksmuseum is an exception; there Pallas, in obvious ignorance of her traditional role in the ancient myths, counsels the playing Apollo.

[3] Mentioned in Vasari, *Vite*, ed. Milanesi, VI, 276; and in Raffaello Borghini, *Il Riposo*, Florence, 1584, Bk. IV. See also H. Voss in *Jahrbuch der Königlichen Preussischen Kunstsammlungen*, XXXIV (1913), 314 ff., and in *Die Malerei der Spätrenaissance in Rom und Florenz*, Berlin, 1920, p. 209 ff.; Hans Tietze and E. Tietze-Conrat, *Tizian-Studien*, in *Jahrbuch der kunsthistorischen Sammlungen in Wien*, Neue Folge, X (1936), 144 ff.; and A. E. Popham, *Correggio's Drawings*, London, 1957, p. 21 ff.

Fig. 20. *Contest between Apollo and Marsyas.* Woodcut from *Ovidio metamorphoseos volgare*, 1501, fol. 49v.

As the immediate source and inspiration for the master of our picture I should like to suggest the two woodcuts in the first edition of the *Ovidio volgare*.[1] The first of these illustrations (Fig. 20) shows in reverse all the five figures of our painting, all with the same instruments, the lira da braccio and the bagpipe. Here, as there, Athena looks at her reflection in the water, Apollo himself performs the flaying, and the musical instruments appear in the same number and order: the lira da braccio twice, in the hands of Apollo and discarded on the ground; the bagpipe three times, played by Athena[2] and by Marsyas, and again

---

[1] *Ovidio metamorphoseos volgare*, Venice, 1497 and 1501; leaf xlix verso in the 1501 edition with the contest between Apollo and Marsyas; and leaf cxxxxiii recto in the 1501 edition with the contest between Apollo and Pan.

[2] I know of only one other *cinquecento* representation in which Pallas Athena plays the bagpipe to study her appearance. It is in a *Judgement of Midas*, one of the two *cassone* paintings by Andrea Schiavone (Meldolla) in the Accademia, Venice (Pl. 71a). There the two contestants sit in the middle, Marsyas playing and Apollo listening. On the left are King Midas and Pan with his syrinx, and on the right margin in the middle ground is a small figure, Athena with a pipe in front of a pond. Marsyas, the 'villano' in the *Ovidio volgare*, wears a peasant straw hat. It is not without interest that Schiavone does not give the contemporary lira da braccio and bagpipe to the contestants but manifestly aims at archaeological accuracy: Marsyas plays the *diaulos* (double pipe), Apollo holds a stylized version of the ancient lyre — thus, instruments apparently

Fig. 21. *Contest between Apollo and Pan.* Woodcut from *Ovidio metamorphoseos volgare,*
1501, fol. 143r.

on the ground. The woodcut, however, shows two important additions necessary
to do full justice to the text: Athena playing the pipe at the banquet of the gods,
and the temple of Apollo where the skin of Marsyas is displayed.[1]

derived from ancient sarcophagi. This is the more curious since Athena retains the bagpipe, but
evidently this is again a reminiscence of the *Ovidio volgare* illustration. Lili Fröhlich Bum in her
description of this painting [*Andrea Meldolla, genannt Schiavone,* in *Jahrbuch der kunsthistorischen
Sammlungen des Allerhöchsten Kaiserhauses,* XXXI (1913–14), 112] does not recognize Athena,
but calls this figure 'eine fliehende Frauengestalt.' The arm which at a quick glance may indicate the resolute gesture of a fleeing woman is in fact reaching to hold the instrument. The
larger canvas by Andrea Schiavone at Hampton Court, showing the contest between Apollo
and Midas, includes Athena only as a witness of the contest.

[1] It is worth noting how much the Olympic scene and the little temple in the upper corners
of this page differ from the main scenes below. The latter must have been drawn by a great
master: a few sure economical strokes delineate Athena's absoption in her playing, and Marsyas'
zeal as he plays eagerly like a puffed-up frog, and likewise his pain and horror in the flaying
scene, and again the light and graceful posture of Apollo with the lira. And how sure and
convincingly these five figures are placed in the wide landscape, intersecting the many horizon-
tals enlivened rhythmically by tufts of grass. On the other hand, the Olympian banquet is stiff,
almost childishly rough, the cloud rims hard, and the figures wooden and misproportioned.
Similarly, Apollo's temple lacks any perspective. All this strongly suggests that the upper two
scenes have been added by another hand, possibly to complete literally the references in the
text to the banquet and the temple. The temple sketchily indicated in the woodcut has been

The display of the skin of Marsyas in Phoebus' temple is a crude popularization of the original versions of the myth, which were more subtle. Herodotus (VII, 26) quotes the Phrygians as saying that Apollo hung the skin of Marsyas near the source of the river Marsyas at the market place of the Phrygian town Kelainai, but Xenophon (*Anabasis*, I, 2.8) relates that the skin was hung in the cave whence the source of the river Marsyas springs, and Pliny (n.h.V, 106) adds that the river Marsyas disappeared into the ground and reappeared at the market place of Kelainai. There the hide moved when Phrygian tunes were played on the aulos. There is no evidence to suggest which of the ancient writers were directly known to the painter of our picture; we can only tentatively suggest that in his intentions the brook near the flayed man is connected with the river in the middle ground, and that the town far down in the deep plain is Kelainai.

There is, however, one notable discrepancy between this woodcut and our painting. In the painting Apollo actually plays and turns toward his rival who listens, while in the woodcut Apollo listens, holding bow and instrument in waiting position while turning away from his adversary, who eagerly plays the bagpipe. It seems more than likely therefore that the figure of the performing Apollo is borrowed from the second woodcut (Fig. 21), where Apollo bows the lira da braccio while Pan listens. The bearded Tmolus seated between Pan and Midas may also have lent his posture and preoccupied expression to the Marsyas of our painting.

The two woodcuts from the *Ovidio volgare* were also models for two engravings by Benedetto Montagna, one showing Apollo's contest with Marsyas (Hind, V, 186, No. 41) (Pl. 70b), the other with Pan (Hind, V, 185, No. 40) (Pl. 70c). Montagna in each of his engravings borrows only the central figures. Many details, such as the tunic of Apollo, twice girdled at the waist and at the hips, are repeated with great precision. This poses the question of whether the author of our painting also knew one or both of the Montagna prints. It is not improbable. In Montagna's representation of the contest with Pan, Apollo holds his lira against his left cheek, as in our painting, in a pose quite different from the one in the *Ovidio* woodcut. And in Montagna's representation of the Marsyas

retained — understood or not — in the Washington painting as the round tower above the flaying scene, and also in the Schiavone *Judgment of Midas* (Pl. 71a), where it appears behind the figure of Athena. In the latter case the significance of the temple has obviously not been understood, one of the innumerable examples of the persistence of elements after they have lost their original meaning.

On the subject of archaeological tendencies in the choice of musical instruments in Renaissance painting, see Chapter 14 below. Ulocrino, in his square plaquette with Apollo and Marsyas (C. L. M. E. Molinier, *Les Bronzes de la renaissance*, Paris, 1886, n. 252; examples in the British Museum, Victoria and Albert Museum, National Gallery of Art, Washington D.C., and other museums), is unusually cautious: he gives Apollo two instruments, a beautiful large specimen of the ancient lira, and a modern viola.

contest, Marsyas, characterized, by the way, as *villano* with the typical peasant straw hat, holds a bagpipe decorated with a checkered design precisely like that of Pallas and Marsyas in our painting.

The five figures are harmoniously spaced in the landscape, with Athena a little back toward the middle ground to suggest the origin of the events. The landscape, organized in near and far hills, is an admirable counterpoint to the chain of protagonists. Rocks, trees, and masses of foliage of varying densities form the background for the figures. Only the tree to which Marsyas is tied — though the rope is not visible — is bare. Between the hills of the middle ground far vistas open towards towns, one deep down in the plains, the other crowned

Fig. 22. *The Flaying of Marsyas*. Initial from Nicola Vicentino, *L'Antica musica ridotta alla moderna practica*, 1605.

by a castle on the rocks. Satyrs and humans are scattered over the paths, a pair of satyrs on the extreme left under the round tower run away, evidently terrified by the flaying.

There is also a rhythmical chain of significant objects scattered across the panel from the right middle ground to the left foreground, telling as it were the story in terms of instruments: passing from Athena's bagpipe over her divine attributes to the bagpipe played by Marsyas, rising to Apollo's lira da braccio, and falling to his shooting bow beneath his feet, the lira da braccio and the quiver laid aside by the god engaged in the flaying, and finally, sadly abandoned, Marsyas's bagpipe once more on the ground. Furthermore, in addition to this string of meaningful objects tying the picture together into a fateful sequence, there is also another symbolic device that frames the narrative: water as prologue and epilogue, the surface of the pond that by reflecting Athena's face led to the curse; and the brook trickling at the feet of the flayed one, indicating the river created by his blood. And when all is said it is perhaps not

L   W.M.I.

too far-fetched to consider also the two tufts of reeds in our painting as related to the symbolism of the whole scene. It is reeds that furnish the material for pipes, not only for the tubes,[1] but also for the small thin blades that make the air vibrate in 'reed pipes,' in the aulos as well as the shawms, oboes, and bagpipes of later times. One cluster of reeds is shown near the pond near which Athena placed the bagpipe, her recent invention. The other cluster appears near the water that trickles at the roots of the tree to which Marsyas is bound.

Thus Marsyas survives as a living stream, and the stream grows reeds, and the reeds turn into pipes again. Strabo (XII, 578) reports of his travels in Asia that the folk living on the banks of the Marsyas River were induced to make pipes by the growth of reeds there. The mighty stream of folk music flows on, hardly rippled by the quick vogues of art music; the reedy tunes are still heard in the shepherd pipes in the mountain valleys of Greece and the Near East, and in the *zampogne* and *pifferi* of the Apennines, and in the many forms of bagpipes in the British Isles. Marsyas's music, though cursed by Pallas, never dies.

APPENDIX

It seems appropriate to quote literally the account of Apollo's contest with Marsyas in the *Ovidio volgare*, together with the 'Alegoria' which there follows the narration. Not only is the retelling of the myth in folksy Boccaccio style extremely amusing, it is also interesting to observe how the illustrator of the *Ovidio* adheres with great precision to the story.

The following 'Alegoria' stemming from medieval moralizations is of course quite beyond pictorial illustration, at least in the late *quattrocento*. There is hardly an element of the story which is not invested with allegorical meaning: the two contestants are the images of the true and the false philosopher, the sophist. The reddish, swollen cheeks produced by aulos-playing signifies how the preachers of false philosophies appear swollen and blushing. The resonance of Apollo's kithara signifies the truthful resonance of arguments. In the flaying Apollo deprives the false philosopher of his false arguments, and by revealing his entrails shows 'how little brains he had in him.' And so on, not neglecting a particle of the story.

Sapiate disse colui che vuol contare e dire di Apollo: che Iove uno dì convitò tutti gli dei a mangiare: la dea Pallas per compiacere al padre tolse la zaramella e comincio a sonare: et cussi sonando gli sgonfiaron le guanze oltra modo et tanto si gli arosavano gli ochi che tuti gli dei cominciorono a ridere per forma

[1] See, for instance, Pliny, n.h. xvi, pp. 164–72, who explains the making of pipes out of cane.

che tuti gli denti gli sariano sta trati: che non haveriano sentito. Alhora Pallas si vergognò e partisse: et discese de cielo e venne sopra le palude de Tritone: et riguardando nelaqua cominciò a sonar: et alhora vide che le guanze gli se gonfiavano et pensò che gli dei avevano per questo riso: per la qual cosa gito via quella zaramella: e non volse più suonare. A poco tempo poi quello strumento fo trovato da uno villano el qual lo prese e cominciò a sonar. Intanto che per la longa consuetudine esso diventò uno buon sonatore: si che era tenuto famoso homo. Intanto che fo ardimento di chiamare Apollo ala prova del sono et contendea con Apollo dicendo: che meglio soneria con la sua zaramella chègli non faria con la sua citara: et cussi dicendo elesero uno iudice che giudicasse fra loro. Apollo disse 'io voglio che tra noi sia alcuna pena': disse lo villano 'a me piace'. Disse Apollo 'faciamo cussi: che quello che sarà vinto porta quella pena che piacerà al vincitore': et cussi fo fermato tra loro et cominciò Marsia a sonare con la sua zaramella tanto solennemente quanto più potè. Onde Apollo udendo tanto bon sono che feva Marsia: temete di non esser perditore: et perciò nel suono interpose la divinità. Et alhora Marsia fo vento: et fo data contra lui la sententia. Alhora Apollo havendo cussi vento chiamò Marsia e disse 'vien qui'. Disse Marsia 'che vuoi tu fare?' Disse Apollo 'io ti voglio scorticare'. Et cominciolo a scorticare. Marsia cominciò a gridare ma non potè tanto gridar che gli giovasse: onde Apollo lo scortico: e lo sangue andò in terra e tuto se convertì in aqua tanto che gli si vedeano le budelle et si cominciò uno fiume: el qual per lo nome di costui fo chiamato Marsia: el qual fiume va per la regione di Frigia dove è la città di Troia. Da poi che Apollo hebe scorticato Marsia empì lo corio over la pelle e apicola ad alto nel tempio: a ciò che fosse exemplo a chi la vedea che niuna persona mai si ponesse per niuna cagione contra agli dei.   Cap. LX

Alegoria: Pallas dice Ovidio che sonava la zaramella: per questo dovemo intender tute le cagione: le quali sono sofistiche: et perchè sonava dinanci agli dei. Intendo questa sola sofistica perciò che quella arte sola per se opando vale e non amaestra. Che gli se sgonfiassero le guanze: tanto vien a dire: questo che quando gli sofistici operano cotale cientia: si fano rossi e infiati. Che gli dei se credesero:[1] questo vuol dire che li savii homini se rideno e fano beffe di tale scienciati. Dice che Pallas discese del cielo: e andò a l'aqua dove conobe perchè gli dei havevano riso: questo non vuol altro dire: se non che poi che il sofistico torna in sua mente viene a la terra e a l'aqua; cioè ale scientie formate dali homini terreni e naturali: et cognoscendo lo suo errore gitta a terra quello istrumento: cioè quella intentione: e per Marsia che la trovò: intendo uno el quale sempre se regie e defendese in falacie. Et tanto è a dire Marsia in greco

[1] Probably should read 'ridessero.'

quanto che Ironio in latino: et questi cotali voglino disputar con Apollo: cioè con gli savii: ma Apollo gli vince con la cithara: cioè con gli veri argumenti resonanti: a corde e non a voce: & cio vuol dire p che la scientia viene da gli organi del cor(e): et ciò dimostra la cithara: La quale sonando se tiene dal lato manco apogiata al core: et cio dimostra che la vera scientia viene da li organi del core. Vento che fo Marsia dice che Apollo lo scorticò: cioè che gli spogliò le sue falacie e si gli assignò le vere ragione: et fece manifesto a la gente el poco seno ch'elli havia dentro da se, dove dice che gli se vedea le budelle: et dice che diventò uno fiume: per ciò che si come el fiume va palese per la terra: e sono perpetui cussi e palesato lo error dela lor scientia et divulgata e fermata la scientia de Apollo: cioè di savii: per la quale e soto la quale el mondo se regie e governa.

[TRANSLATION]

You must know this, says he who wishes to tell the story of Apollo. One day Jupiter invited all the gods for dinner. The goddess Pallas, to please her father, took her pipes and began to play; and while she thus played, her cheeks became greatly puffed up and her eyes became so red that all the gods began to laugh so hard that, if all their teeth had come out, they would not have felt it. There-upon Pallas grew embarrassed and left; and she went down from heaven to the swamp of the Triton and, watching herself in the water, began to play. Then she saw that her cheeks became puffed up and she realized it was this that had made the gods laugh. For this reason she threw away her pipes and did not want to play any more. After a little while, this instrument was found by a rustic who took it and began to play; and by long practice he became such a good player that he was regarded as a famous man. So good was he that he dared challenge Apollo to judge the sound, and he competed with Apollo, saying that he would play better with his pipes than Apollo could with his kithara. Discussing this, they chose a judge who should decide between them. Apollo said, 'I want one of us to be punished,' and the rustic said, 'All right'; and Apollo said, 'Let's do it this way: the one who is defeated will suffer the punishment pronounced by the winner.' And so it was agreed between them, and Marsyas began to play his pipes as solemnly as he possibly could. Therefore Apollo, hearing the fine sound made by Marsyas, was afraid of being the loser, and imparted his divine power to his own sound. And so Marsyas was defeated and the judgement went against him. Now, since Apollo had won, he called Marsyas and said, 'Come here.' Marsyas said, 'What will you do?' Apollo said, 'I want to flay you.' And he began to flay him. Marsyas began to cry out, but all his screaming was to no avail. Therefore Apollo flayed him, and the blood ran into the ground and was all changed into water — one could see his entrails — and the water began to form a river. This river, after the name of the defeated man, was called Marsyas. The river goes through the region of Phrygia wherein is the city of Troy. After Apollo had flayed Marsyas, he cleaned the hide — or rather the skin — and hung it up high in the temple, to make an example for anyone who saw it there, so that no one, for any reason whatever, should put himself up against the gods.

ALLEGORY: Pallas, as Ovid tells, played the pipes. We must therefore try to understand the reasons for it, which are very subtle, and also why she played before the gods. The reason why the goddess played is that music is valuable for its own sake and does not teach anything. That her cheeks were puffed up: this means that when the learned employ such an art, they become red and inflated. That the gods laughed about it: this is to say that the wise people laugh and make fun of such scholars. Ovid says that Pallas went down from heaven and approached the water to find out why the gods laughed: this means nothing else than that the scholar turns to his own mind and arrives at earth and water, that is, the [positive] sciences made by earthly and natural man. Becoming aware of his error, he throws the instrument to the ground, thus abandoning his original intention. And Marsyas means: a man who always lives in error. And it is the same to say Marsyas in Greek and Ironius in Latin, since both of them wish to argue with Apollo — that is, the wise one. But Apollo defeats them with the kithara — that is, with real resounding arguments — with the strings and not with the voice. And this means that knowledge comes from the heart. This is proven by the kithara, which is played by being held against the heart; this shows that the true knowledge comes from the heart. That Marsyas was defeated and Apollo flayed him: this means he stripped him of his errors and assigned to him the truth, and made it clear to the people how little brains he had in him — at the place where Ovid says one could see the entrails. And Ovid says Marsyas became a river: this is because, as the river flows openly over the ground, the mistake of people like Marsyas is revealed, as is also the science of Apollo, that is to say, the wise people — the science by which the world is governed and ruled.

13 · Muses and Music in a Burial Chapel: An Interpretation of Filippino Lippi's Window Wall in the Cappella Strozzi

A wealth of musical symbols and allegories depicted in a burial chapel poses certain questions. These questions we shall try to answer in the following essay on one of the most interesting and profound creations of Filippino Lippi — the window wall of the Strozzi Chapel in Santa Maria Novella, Florence. In it there are several musicians and a number of ancient — or, rather, pseudo-antique — wind and string instruments; bone plectra draw sound from strings, but not a single singer appears. It seems almost absurd that the musical symbolism of the chapel, and the relation between death and music which it presents, has never been investigated in the literature on Filippino Lippi.[1] A study of it may, we hope, also throw some new light on the ancient models of some of the musicians depicted and complete our understanding of the numerous inscriptions scattered over the fresco, which have hitherto resisted coherent interpretation.

The design of the Strozzi Chapel's wall has been described repeatedly and therefore our description of it can be brief. As a muralist, Lippi had to take three immutable facts into account: the high Gothic shape of the chapel (Pl. 72); Benedetto da Majano's sarcophagus crowned by a massive semi-circular arch (Pl. 69d); and a high, narrow window. Lippi subdivided the available space by providing the strongest possible counterpoint to the Gothic elements, incorporating in his composition the powerful columns from the front of the Arch of Constantine. But only the two inner columns appear to project far out from the wall, as they do in the Arch. Lippi made them flank and frame the window in the chapel, as they do the middle door at the Arch, and here, as there, they rise from massive pedestals and support large figures above their high entablature.

[1] Some short but admirably precise and substantial comments on the Cappella Strozzi are found in Peter Halm, *Das unvollendete Fresko des Filippino Lippi in Poggio a Cajano*, in *Mitteilungen des Kunsthistorischen Institutes in Florenz*, III/7 (July 1931), 393. Neither Alfred Scharf, *Filippino Lippi*, Vienna, 1935, nor Katherine B. Neilson, *Filippino Lippi*, Cambridge, Mass., 1938, has focused on the problems of symbolism.

In the Arch of Constantine the pedestals were decorated with winged victories; Filippino adorned those in his fresco with the figures of Caritas and Fides (Pls. 74a & 75a). The entablature projecting over the columns of the Arch carried large statues of captive Dacian princes; in the fresco, giant angels carrying shields emblazoned with the Strozzi crescents decorate the frieze (Pl. 71b & c). The outer columns of the Arch have here become pilasters, scarcely projecting from the wall since now they form the transition to the side walls of the chapel, which are decorated with the miracles wrought by St. John the Evangelist and St. Philip.

If Lippi's composition is highly original, so also is his colour scheme. The only area with glowing colours is the stained-glass window, which seems to rise like a burning flame from the dark sarcophagus. It shows the Madonna (Pl. 73b) in its upper, and two saints, John the Evangelist and Philip (Pl. 73c), in its lower part. Jakob Burckhardt has called it the best Florentine window. Its intense luminosity almost suppresses the near-monochrome mural — so much so that one is reminded of the young Burckhardt's warning against concentration on stained glass: that the eye may not be weakened for the observation of murals.[1] But after readapting itself to the colour of the mural painting, the eye finds the fresco by no means monotonous or pale. Brown and blue tones are used — the wings of the figure of Parthenice (Pl. 74b) are dark blue; her large musical instrument, as well as the plectrum, is deep reddish-brown; some of the human figures show faint flesh tones which hold them in the twilight between sculpture and actual life. The gilding, used as highlights on certain small objects, chiefly those of symbolic importance, accentuates them in the design — a golden guide, as it were, for modern iconologists. Among these objects are the chalice, cross, and crown of Fides; the flaming crown of Caritas and the eternal flame at her feet; the large palm tree behind Parthenice; and most of the musical instruments depicted in the lower corners of the wall.

The gilding stimulates interpretation by inviting the eye to focus on points of symbolic interest, but there is a more direct attraction in the distribution all over the fresco of verbal allusions to the spiritual message of the window wall and perhaps of the whole chapel. Four of the inscriptions are connected by an elaborate system of ribbons on either side, which run from the top and go far down towards the allegorical figures. These ribbons or cords begin, garland-like, at the top of the Gothic window, continue to the large round plaques (Pl. 73a), and go from there through elaborate knots to the large angels standing on the entablatures of the Corinthian columns. Thence again, the ribbons continue diagonally towards two angels crouching on the entablature and from there, now divided into two thinner strands, go on down over the entablatures to hold

[1] *Cicerone*, Leipzig, 1925, p. 809.

the bulky oblong stone tablets (Pl. 75c) bearing Latin inscriptions. Yet even this is not the end of this suspension. Out of the sides of the tablet frames project harpies or woman-faced birds, holding other cords from which hang decorative objects. Weighty pieces of architecture suspended in mid-air, even if supported by angels, border on the burlesque, and Filippino makes it still more fantastic by counteracting the suspended fall with the figure of a grotesque little woman on either side, who seems to support the tablets easily with her outstretched hands while she herself blossoms out of weightless tendrils. The cords are not mere visual fancy, however; they connect (another easy guide for the 20th-century iconologist) the pieces of verbal revelation with the allegorical imagery in the lower part of the grisaille. The play of the floating ribbons, too jocular and airy perhaps for a chapel, clearly reflects Filippino's experience and participation in those magnificent though impermanent architectural displays fashionable in his time as important parts of *feste*: hanging tablets with inscriptions are, for instance, reported for the *Possesso* of Alexander VI in 1492 in Rome. I have not pursued the question of how far Filippino participated in its decor, but since he was working in Rome between 1488 and 1493 in the Caraffa Chapel, it would seem logical to assume that he was familiar with the *Possesso* and must have drawn on his knowledge of it when he helped to prepare the *feste* given in 1494 in Florence to welcome Charles VIII.[1]

As mentioned before, there are four inscriptions strung on the ribbons in the Chapel. High up, flanking the top of the window, we read inside circular tablets: SI SCIRES — DONUM DEI (Pl. 73a). These four words, being the largest in the fresco and so conspicuously displayed, might be expected to have profound bearing on immortality or another topic suitable for a memorial chapel, but they have never before been explained. The solution, however, is not difficult if we recall the conversation between Jesus and the woman of Samaria as recorded in Chapter 4 of the Gospel of St. John. Jesus asks the woman for water from the well and she at first questions him, wondering how a Jew could ask for a drink from a Samaritan ('for the Jews have no dealings with the Samaritans'); then (verse 10):

> Respondit Jesus, et dixit ei: *Si scires donum Dei*, et quis est, qui dicit tibi: *Da mihi* bibere, tu forsitan petiisses ab eo, et dedisset tibi aquam vivam.

The gift of God is the water of Life, or, as it is explained soon after, Eternal Life. This highly poetic metaphor of immortality becomes even clearer from the verses which follow:

---

[1] For an analysis of these *fêtes* and Filippino's participation in them, see the excellent study by Eve Borsook, *Decor in Florence for the Entry of Charles VIII of France*, in *Mitteilungen des Kunsthistorischen Institutes in Florenz*, X/2 (Dec. 1961), 106. On musical instruments in the *fêtes*, see Chapter 16 below.

Dicit ei mulier: Domine, neque in quo haurias habes, et puteus altus est: unde ergo habes aquam vivam?

Numquid tu major es patre nostro Jacob, qui dedit nobis puteum, et ipse ex eo bibet, et filii ejus, et pecora ejus?

Respondit Jesus, et dixit ei: Omnis qui bibit ex aqua hac, sitiet iterum, qui autem biberit ex aqua, quam ego dabo ei, non sitiet in aeternum:

Sed aqua, quam ego dabo ei, fiet in eo fons aquae salientis in vitam aeternam.

Dicit ad eum mulier: Domine, *da mihi hanc aquam*, ut non sitiam, neque veniam huc haurire.

Certainly no briefer or more pregnant motto than the four words 'Si scires donum Dei,' could be found for a burial place. In fact, Lippi himself used a longer quotation from these verses of the Gospel for an inscription on the tablet held by angels beneath his painting, *Christ and the Samaritan Woman*,[1] which is in the Seminary Museum, Venice (Pl. 76b). This inscription combines selections from verses 10 and 15: SI SCIRES DONUM DEI DA MIHI HANC AQUAM (a combination which seems a little strange since the first words, 'Si scires donum Dei,' are spoken by Jesus, and the following, 'Da mihi hanc aquam,' by the woman) Lippi or his learned advisers must have found the condensation into four words in the Strozzi Chapel clear enough for the 'initiati,' and of course this is not the only Renaissance example of an aristocratic preference for addressing the selected few.

Of the lower square stone tablets, that on the left is fully legible: SACRIS — SUPERIS — INITIATI — CANUNT. The one on the right is partially damaged and does not permit complete deciphering.[2] Here a happy coincidence helps to restore the complete text. An anonymous drawing in the Gabinetto dei Disegni of the Uffizi (No. 14587F), which is a fairly accurate copy of the two female figures in the lower right corner of Lippi's fresco, shows an elaborate inscription engraved on the broad base on which they are standing (Pl. 75b). On the fresco there appears only DEO — MAX. The copyist, however, found it appropriate to use a longer inscription: D. M. — QUONDAM . NUNC . DEO . OP . MAX . CANIMUS. There can be no doubt that he borrowed the inscription from the upper stone tablet of the Strozzi chapel mural, which in his time must still have been completely legible. It goes without saying that 'canere' (i.e. 'making music') also implies the playing of instruments.

Before turning to the lower part of the fresco with its allegorical figures, we must mention the two verbal messages in the stained-glass window. One is again on a stone tablet, which is suspended with cords and held by angels over the

---

[1] Painted about 1500, according to Alfred Scharf, *op. cit.*, p. 107.

[2] Halm, *op. cit.*, p. 416, reads it D. M. QUONDAM NVH . . . CANIMUS, and considers the last two words illegible.

head of the Blessed Virgin; it reads: MITIS ESTO (Pl. 73b), perhaps best translated as 'Be peaceful,' or 'Be without suffering.' The other inscription is on the pages of the book held open, toward the chapel, by St. Philip. It is not the only book there; St. John the Evangelist holds another, of which we can see only the back, and St. Philip reaches over with one hand towards St. John's book. The writing in St. Philip's book is today partly obliterated (Pl. 76a). Yet it clearly shows lines from the Apocryphal book of Ecclesiasticus,[1] or The Wisdom of Jesus the Son of Sirach. Actually, these lines are a free pasticcio from Ecclesiasticus with interpolations as well as omissions. The reader may compare the left page with Ecclesiasticus 44: 25, 26, and 27; and the right page with Ecclesiasticus 45: 3, 4, 6, and 9. Here is the text as far as I can decipher it:

(from *Ecclesiasticus* 44: 25, 26, 27)

BEN(EDICTIONEM) — — —
DOM(INUS) — — — — — —
(SUP)ER — — — — — —
— USTI. IDEO DEDIT
DOMINUS HERE(DI)
TATEM, DIVISIT ILLAM
PARTEM IN TRIBUB(US)
DUODECIM: ET INV(E)
NIT GRATIAM IN
COSPECTU REGU(M)
ET JUSSIT ILLI C(O)
(*RAM POPULO*) SU(O)
ET OST(ENDIT) — — —

(from *Ecclesiasticus* 45: 3, 4, 6, 9)

— — — — — — — (SU)AM
IN FIDE ET (LE)NIT(A)
TEM (IP)SIUS SAN(C)
TUM (F)ECIT ILLUM,
(E)T DE — — EUM EX OM
NI CARNE. ET DEDIT
(ILLI CORAM PRAECEPTA)
(E)T LEGEM VITAE ET DI
(SCIPL)INAE (ET) EXCEL
SUM (FE)CIT ILLUM — —
— — — — — (TEST)AMENTUM
— — — — — — — (CIRCU)MCI
— — — — — — — — (ZON)A

It is obvious that these pages have nothing to do with death and resurrection, but simply show a selection of phrases that seemed appropriate for the glorification of Filippo Strozzi, perhaps alluding to the beginning of Chapter 44: *Laudemus viros gloriosos, et parentes nostros in generatione sua. . . .*

We turn now to the allegorical figures in the lower section of the mural. The area next to the wide marble arch of the tomb represents the mortality of the flesh and its conquest by the Christian virtues. In the inscription over the centre of the arch, NI HANC DESPEXERIS VIVES (Pl. 74a), the mysterious 'Hanc' is not as enigmatic as it first appears if we relate it to the DONUM DEI in the right upper circular tablet, or rather to the latter's equivalent, HANC AQUAM.

[1] Halm, *loc. cit.*, mentions 'Eccl. 44: 25–27 und 45: 3–9 mit einigen Auslassungen.' The abbreviation 'Eccl.' is a little misleading since it points to the book of Ecclesiastes, whose sceptical text would hardly have been considered appropriate in a Dominican church.

The inscription thus implies a conditional promise: 'If you do not shun the water, you will live.' It is actually a paraphrase of 'Spes,' completing the three Christian virtues of which Caritas is shown at the left and Fides at the right. The tablet with this inscription partially covers a wall niche filled with human skulls. Other skulls are displayed by two winged angels: the right one holding a single skull aloft while stepping on another skull and a human bone; the left one holding up a skull and human bone while stepping on a single skull (Pls. 74a & 75a). The beautiful figures of Caritas and Fides, with their conspicuously gilded attributes, form the counterpoint — death overcome by charity and faith.

However beautiful the personifications of the virtues, and however striking their contrast to the hard, merciless angels, the iconology of this portion of the window wall does not transcend traditional imagery. But how different and how original is the symbolic role of the figures in its extreme corners — all musicians, as we shall see.

The group at the left is engaged in playing different instruments. Parthenice (Pl. 74b), a young woman[1] conceived *all'antica*, holds a string instrument. Two winged *putti* at her knees try their luck with wind instruments. The instruments represented here are a veritable gold mine for the collector of Renaissance misinterpretations of antiquity. Parthenice's instrument is, in today's terminology, a lyre-guitar, although Filippino himself certainly would have called it a 'lira' or 'cetra' (the Italian name for the ancient kithara).

In order to understand this instrument and its role in Italy around 1500, we must go a little deeper into organology, especially since connoisseurs of art are not always familiar with the radical metamorphoses of musical instruments, their changes of form, function, and name since late antiquity, and the puzzling renascences and pseudo-renascences to which they were subjected. One of the salient facts in the history of string instruments was the introduction of the fingerboard for the purpose of stopping strings, thus shortening their length and raising the pitch. Every musician or musical amateur is familiar with this device through knowledge of the violin and its family, or from the lute, guitar, or similar instruments. One of the great advantages of the fingerboard is that each string can be made to produce several tones. Yet in Greek and Roman antiquity the fingerboard technique did not exist or, at any rate, was exceedingly rare (confined largely to some long-necked instruments we find occasionally represented on sarcophagi, which are anachronistically called lutes by archaeologists). The string instruments that were most common by far, the kithara and the lira, had no fingerboards (Pl. 77b). They had sound boxes — a

---

[1] André Chastel, *Art et humanisme au temps de Laurent le Magnifique*, Paris, 1959, p. 391, fn. 2, was the first to point out, in relation to Filippino's Parthenice, that this name had been used as the title of one of the poems of G. B. Mantovano, celebrating the Mother of Christ (1488).

turtle shell or wooden bowl, or a box artfully constructed — from which sprang two arms carrying a yoke. The lower ends of the strings were fastened to the sound box and their upper ends to the yoke. Thus they ran freely through the air and could not be stopped against any surface.

Not before the Utrecht Psalter, written in the 9th century but based on models of the 6th or possibly even the 5th century, do we find string instruments with fingerboards firmly established; they have the shape of kitharas but their arms are non-functional, they have no yoke, and all their strings run over a long fingerboard and are fastened to its head. Significantly, these pseudo-kitharas with fingerboards are frequently depicted side by side with real kitharas (Pl. 16b). In 1960, through a fortunate accident, I became acquainted with a Roman mosaic from Qasr el-Lebia that includes a representation of a fingerboard instrument with rudimentary lyre arms (Pl. 17c). It is played by a youth among animals, probably a representation of Orpheus. We may call such pseudo-lyres (with a fingerboard) 'lyre-guitars,' not for want of a better name or in ignorance of their ancient one, but because of the French *lyre-guitares* of the late 18th and early 19th centuries, which became fashionable as ladies' instruments in the French Empire and throughout the Biedermeier period; they posed as ancient because of their lyre shape but were actually played like guitars.[1]

Between this Napoleonic Renaissance and the Carolingian Renaissance which produced the Utrecht Psalter had occurred the Renaissance of the *quattro-* and *cinquecento*, with its intense and immediate concern with the artifacts of Greco-Roman civilization. Absurdly enough, precisely this sincere archaeological concern, not to say passion, also produced a 'lyre-guitar.' It occurs frequently in paintings, prints, and sculpture with mythological and religious topics. One may ask why the ancient models, abundantly available in statues, reliefs and frescoes, were not strictly copied; strict adherence to the ancient models seems to have been the exception (one of the rare cases is the beautiful ancient kithara in the hands of Erato in Raphael's *Parnassus* — an instrument taken over, with admirable accuracy in every detail, from the Sarcophagus of the Muses that was once in the Mattei Collection and is now in the Museo Nazionale in Rome).[2]

The misinterpretation of ancient instruments by Renaissance artists was favoured by several circumstances, and their modification in pictures was hardly intentional. The ancient sculptures and reliefs could not, for obvious technical reasons, represent in marble the free-running strings of lyres, and thus the artist often resorted to making bands in which the strings were marked by incised lines. No wonder then that the *cinquecento* artists, in their drawings of statues or reliefs from sarcophagi, interpreted these bands as the solid fingerboards which

[1] See Chapter 3 above.   [2] See Chapter 14 below.

were familiar to them from contemporary instruments, and in line with the predominant playing technique of their time. Thus the lyres, copied with archaeological intention from ancient works of art, became 'lyre-guitars' by inevitable misunderstanding.

The wind instruments of the two *putti* are both *all'antica*. The syrinx, so big for the little musician that Parthenice must help him to hold it, is represented faithfully according to ancient models, with its seven pipes whose sacred number alludes to the planets and the harmony of the universe.

More problematic is the instrument of the other *putto*. It is a fantastic blending of various models, evidently influenced by ancient representations of the aulos (tibia). The two tubes with flaring bells vaguely recall the diaulos which, contrary to the terminology still common in archaeological literature, is not a double flute but a double oboe — that is, an instrument with double reeds. The unequal length of the two pipes, and the curving of one of them, recalls the Phrygian aulos. Also interesting to note are the little projections on the upper side of the main tube, which are seemingly operated by the left hand of the *putto*. The type of aulos usually represented on Roman sarcophagi, the tibia, had a special mechanism for adjusting the instrument to play in different modes: the fingerholes on the tube were covered by adjustable rings, which also had holes. By turning the rings, one could close the fingerholes either partially or entirely. In many tibias there were small cup-shaped projections attached to the ring-holes, which could enlarge the vibrating air column in the instrument by a small fraction and thereby lower the tone. One can see such cups in all well-preserved tibias in Roman sarcophagi. Raphael copied this device for the instrument of Euterpe in his *Parnassus*.

Unlike Raphael, Filippino — for all his archaeological penchant — could not have been a practising musician, for his pseudo-aulos is entirely non-functional. The *putto* blows into the tube between the fingerholes and the lower end of the pipes. It is curious that an analogous misunderstanding occurs in another contemporary Florentine representation of a fantastic instrument, the plucked and blown instrument in Pietro di Cosimo's *Liberation of Andromeda* (Pl. 92).

Finally, one notices another wind instrument at the foot of the *putto* on the right. Only a small part of the tube and the bell are visible, but the strong shadow on the stone base makes it conspicuous. It was probably meant to be another tibia.[1]

[1] Although we cannot be sure whether or not Filippino knew it, wind music, especially as represented by tibias, was a fitting accompaniment to funerals; see, for instance, Ovid, *Fasti*, VI, 659: 'cantabit sanis, cantabit tibia ludis cantabit moestis tibia funeribus' ('the flute played in temples, it played at games, it played at mournful funerals'; tr. by Sir James George Frazer, London, 1931).

One could profitably compare the instruments in the Parthenice group with Filippino's so-called *Allegory of Music*, now in the Berlin Museum (Pl. 96b). Here we again find the seven-pipe syrinx and, beneath it, what must have been intended to be a tibia. Here, with greater archaeological fidelity than in the Strozzi Chapel, two of the rings that close the side holes are shown, and each ring carries the little cup-shaped projections explained above. There is also a lyre, one of the numerous stag-head lyres of the *cinquecento*. Here we find the mixture of elements borrowed from ancient models with pseudo-archaeological elements. Archaeologically faithful are both the shape of the crossbars (although only one crossbar was employed in ancient lyres and kitharas) and the sacred number seven of the strings. But of course ancient lyres had — for acoustical reasons — sound boxes. In Filippino's lyre the strings never reach the stag head, which, in any case, could not have functioned to reinforce the sound. The *raison d'être* of the stag head is a symbolic one; as a symbol of the velocity of sound, the stag appears commonly with the Allegory of Music.

Coming back to the Strozzi Chapel fresco, we find that Parthenice, whose left hand assists one of the *putti* to blow the syrinx, holds with her right hand the lyre-guitar and a plectrum. This plectrum is quite different from those seen in the hands of Muses on Roman sarcophagi. It is made of bone, specifically the bone of a goat or deer foot; the hoof is clearly visible. Bone plectra occur occasionally in mythological paintings of the Renaissance. In one mentioned before, Filippino's *Allegory of Music*, a bone plectrum lies beneath the stag-head lyre.[1]

An interesting Florentine comment on this plectrum and on Filippino's faithfulness to the decorative language of the ancients is found, perhaps surprisingly, in a musical treatise of the 16th century — Vincenzo Galilei's *Dialogo della musica antica e della moderna* (Florence, 1581). Vincenzo, the father of Galileo Galilei, was a fertile, brilliant, and witty writer, and was steeped in the ancient authorities on music. His *Dialogo* is full of quotations from Aristoxenos, Aristides Quintilianus, Polibios, Pliny, Plutarch, and others. The book includes a detailed discussion of the difference between the modern bow and the ancient plectrum (p. 130 ff.); he illustrates the regular form of the plectrum by a woodcut, and explains the use of the deer-foot plectrum and the way it is fashioned, and then he reminds the reader of a good opportunity to see one (this entire passage is reprinted as an Appendix to the present chapter).

Of this account we must say that Vincenzo, in spite of his Florentine local

---

[1] On this and other attributes of Musica, see Chapter 16 below. A deer-foot plectrum can also be seen in a Florentine engraving of about 1470, showing a fat, vine-leaf-crowned player with a large deer-foot plectrum (Arthur Hind, *Early Italian Engravings*, London, 1938–48, A.IV.22, Vol. 2, Plate 150).

pride, must have neglected to refresh his memory by a visit to the chapel — the 'two women' are on the right side, and neither of them sings — but he obviously did mean that the figure on the left holds the *plettro alla zampetta*, described so vividly by him. The reference to Poliziano, as an expert in the musical practice of the ancient world, is not badly taken. Poliziano's *Fabula d'Orfeo* is full of stage directions as to the music to be sung and played during the performance, especially with reference to Orpheus playing the lira (although the latter, in the famous performances at Mantua, was without doubt a lira da braccio — that is, a bowed instrument).[1] The plectrum in Poliziano's *Fabula* acquires symbolic power when it rivals Pluto's sceptre. In the words of Pluto:

> *I' son contento che a si dolce plettro*
> *S'inchini la potenzia del mio scettro.*[2]

> (I am pleased that the power of my sceptre
> yields to so sweet a plectrum).

The two figures in the right lower corner of the chapel wall (Pl. 74c) are no doubt patterned after Muses from Roman sarcophagi, but no concrete model has ever been suggested.[3] The general type of these figures occurs, in slightly different versions, in numerous sarcophagi.[4] However, there is in my belief only one sarcophagus that offers an exact correspondence to our two figures. It is the sarcophagus with Muses, Apollo, and Minerva, from the Collection Giustiniani,[5] now in the Vienna Kunsthistorisches Museum (Pl. 77a & c; it was once in Rome, where it was drawn by the draughtsman of the Codex Coburgensis).

On its long side, this sarcophagus shows the nine Muses, Minerva, and Apollo. Minerva, in profile, is the central figure; on her left are five Muses, on her right four, and at the extreme right Apollo. The Muses that interest us are the first and third from the left. The third one has been directly taken over by

[1] See Chapter 5 above.

[2] On musical symbolism in Poliziano's *Fabula*, see Emanuel Winternitz, *Orpheus als Musikallegorie in Renaissance und Frühbarock*, in *Die Musik in Geschichte und Gegenwart*, X, Cassel, 1962, col. 412.

[3] If one considers how long and zealously historians of Renaissance art have searched for instances in which artists have borrowed literally from ancient models, it seems astonishing how little exact 'imitation' has been found in the works of the great *antichizzanti* such as Mantegna, Filippino Lippi, or Raphael. Fischel's *Raphaels Zeichnungen*, Berlin, 1913–41, for instance, does not establish any clear case. As for the Muses, I discovered one such case, which is discussed in Chapter 14 below.

[4] For instance, two sarcophagi in the Palazzo Mattei (Figs. I and II, *Monumenta Matthaeiana*); and one each in the Palazzo Farnese, the Louvre, the Berlin Museum, the British Museum (Cat. 2305), and the Museo Nazionale in Rome — the last two of the Sidamara type.

[5] Reproduced in an engraving in Vincenzo Giustiniani, *Galleria del Marchese V. Giustiniani*, Rome, 1631, II, Tav. 40, the sarcophagus has also been described and illustrated by Eduard Freiherr v. Sacken, *Die antiken Skulpturen des k.k. Münz- und Antiken-Cabinets in Wien*, Vienna, 1873, and (p. 41) 'the artistic value of the relief' judged as 'not considerable (*nicht erheblich*).'

Filippino Lippi. He has repeated her pose, with the elegant turn of the upper body towards her left and the gracefully turned left leg. Lippi's figure bends the head lower, towards the instrument, and her hair and robes flow in the wind. The plectrum in her right hand, which has the conventional Roman form on the sarcophagus, here becomes a bone. On the sarcophagus, her lyre rests in symmetrical position on a base,[1] which is only suggested in flat relief. The muse farthest to the left on the sarcophagus, with crossed legs and chin in hand — pensively listening — again is taken over by Filippino in precisely the same pose, except that the figure is reversed; hair and robes, as in the other figure, are dramatized. The *rotulus* in the left hand of the muse on the sarcophagus is turned by Filippino into a bone plectrum, so that in the fresco both figures become musicians with plectra.

An enormous transformation, however, takes place from the sarcophagus to the fresco in the representation of the musical instrument. In the relief it is the traditional kithara of the time, less than one-third the height of the player. In the fresco, between the two Muses, we find a magnificent lyre of gigantic dimensions on a high marble pedestal. It is strange that no attention has even been paid to this conspicuous instrument in the literature on Filippino, and that it has not even been recognized as a musical instrument.[2] This is even more curious in view of the fact that this lyre is distinguished, more than any other section of the fresco, by extensive gilding. Two high round columns carry a fantastic superstructure[3] crowned by a flaming lamp, which has perhaps given cause for misinterpreting the whole instrument as an altar. Only six strings are represented, not the sacred seven, and again Filippino reveals himself as uninterested in the acoustical and functional construction of instruments: the

---

[1] Of the other sarcophagi listed in fn. 4, p. 175, only one — that in the Berlin Museum — shows a base for the lyre of a Muse which resembles the one copied by Lippi. The second Muse on the Berlin sarcophagus, with chin in hand, is much less similar to the corresponding Lippi Muse than the one on the Vienna sarcophagus.

[2] Peter Halm, *op. cit.*, p. 414, and Alfred Scharf, *op. cit.*, p. 65, both speak of an altar.

[3] A similar superstructure on a fantastic lyre is shown in a drawing in the sketchbook of Amico Aspertini, in the British Museum. It is illustrated in Phyllis Pray Bober's invaluable book, *Drawings after the Antique by Amico Aspertini*, London, 1957, Pl. XLVIII, fig. 111 (Mrs. Bober speaks tentatively of a *putto* 'sitting on a skull before a fountain [?]'). The object and superstructure appear behind a *putto* sitting on a skull, opposite another mourning *putto* and beneath three Muses. The combination of mourning, skulls, Muses, and an instrument is too significant not to be compared with our fresco. The identification of the object with a fantastic lyre becomes even clearer if one compares it with an almost identical instrument held by one of the musicians surrounding King David in the Bible of Charles the Bald, Paris, Bibliothèque Nationale, MS Lat. I, fol. 215v (Pl. 15a). Without at all stressing a historical connection, this shows that non-functional elements in instruments easily become an opportunity for fanciful decoration. One should at least mention here Robetta's free fantastic version of Filippino's two musicians with the lyre, Robetta's lyre having a superstructure ornamented by grotesque half-moon faces and gryphons.

sound box, necessary of course for a string instrument, is suggested only by the sweeping curve on which the left column rests, and no real yoke holds the upper ends of the strings. In short, the whole thing is non-functional. But apart from these whimsical decorative details, the general design is solidly based on ancient models. Large lyres or kitharas on pedestals were frequent, and are often found represented on sarcophagi.[1] The famous 6th-century ivory diptych in Monza (Pl. 89b), with the poet and the Muse, shows the Muse with a large kithara on a base. And, at about the same time, Ammianus Marcellinus tells of lyres as large as horse carriages (*lyrae ad speciem carpentorum ingentes*).[2]

But examining the single inscriptions and allegorical figures is one thing; searching for a comprehensive and unified interpretation of the whole window wall is another. And thus we have to take up the question posed at the beginning of this study, and face the most unconventional aspect of the fresco — the proximity of death and music, the presence of Muses and instruments in the face of death. The appropriation by Renaissance artists of ancient images and mythological figures such as the Muses requires no comment here.[3] Libraries have been written about it. But was this absorption of ancient works of art always accompanied by a clear awareness of their ancient symbolism and of the spiritual atmosphere which had produced them? To what extent were the borrowings from ancient art paralleled by investigations into ancient literature? Our fresco here seems to present a good test case; for only a knowledge of ancient thought connecting death and music could vindicate a juxtaposition that otherwise must have been shocking to the visitors to the Capella Strozzi. Dirges and other sacred vocal music in church were not only acceptable but common; likewise, angels with instruments surrounding the dying or ascending Madonna (as in Carpaccio's *Death of the Virgin*, Accademia, Venice). But in a memorial chapel, inviting one to meditation, near to the tomb and the skull-bearing angels and the Christian virtues, what message could be conveyed by musicians and instruments?

[1] For instance: in the Villa Medici (M. Cagiano de Azevedo, *Le Antichità di Villa Medici*, Rome, 1951, Pl. XXIX, 45 [57]); in the Palazzo Mattei, two sarcophagi, one with the Muses and Pallas, and another with the Muses and a poet (both represented in the *Monumenta Matthaeiana*, Tav. XLIV); the sarcophagus with Muses in the Berlin Museum, which shows two pedestal lyres, one of them played by the third figure from the left (a Muse) and the other by the Muse on the extreme right. Pedestal lyres also occur in such representations as the statue of a Muse (Uffizi, No. 209) drawn by Dosio (cf. Christian Karl Friedrich Hülsen, *I Lavori archeologici di Giovannantonio Dosio*, in *Ausonia: Rivista della Soc. Ital. di Archeologia*, VII (1912), 41; and *Das Skizzenbuch des Giovannantonio Dosio*, Berlin, 1933, p. 28, Taf. LXXVIII); and, shown with an Apollo, in one of the medallions of the Arch of Constantine, so well known to Filippino.

[2] Ammianus Marcellinus, *Rerum gestarum libri XIX*, 6, 18.

[3] On Filippino as an imaginative heir of ancient imagery, see Chastel's excellent and comprehensive observations in his chapter 'Filippino Lippi: Les "singularités" du paganisme' (*op. cit.*, pp. 386–92).

These Muses certainly provide no dirge, nor would the instruments be suitable for consoling the bereaved. The meaning of the Muses here is on another plane and, we surmise, intimately connected with the topic of immortality.[1] It seems quite significant that behind Parthenice stands one of the symbols of eternity, the palm tree.[2] We can safely assume that Filippino and his advisers, in the Florence of Ficino and his Platonic academy, were familiar with the Platonic and neo-Platonic doctrine of the survival of the soul.[3] Immortality, according to Platonic doctrine, was not granted to every soul, but only to a certain selection. Plato's choice was the philosopher.[4] He had, by virtue of his profession, an intimate relation with death; in fact he pursued dying (*Phaedo*, 64). His desire to disengage himself from the body would make him rejoice in death (*Phaedo*, 68). His soul 'departs to the invisible world — to the divine and immortal and *rational* (φρόνιμος) — and forever dwells, as they say of the *initiated* (μεμνημένων), in company with the Gods.' I should like to point to the emphasis on the words 'rational'[5] and 'initiated' — to the latter in view of the 'initiati' in our fresco; to the former because it clarifies the principle according to which the choice is made. If the knowing ones, an intellectual élite, are chosen for eternal life, the

---

[1] For musical symbolism in Greek and Roman sarcophagi, see M. Henri Marrou, *MOΥCIKOC ANHP*, Diss. Univ. de Paris, Grenoble, 1937; and Franz Cumont's standard work, *Recherches sur le symbolisme funéraire des romains*, Paris, 1942.

[2] Pierius Valerianus, in his *Hieroglyphica*, Basel, 1567, p. 369, devotes a whole section, 'Temporis Diuturnitas,' based on Hesiod and Quintilian, to this topic. Also, the palm tree, no doubt as a symbol of resurrection, is frequently found on sepulchral urns, especially *kantharoi*, of which there are several examples in the British Museum.

[3] '. . . Is it likely that the soul, which is invisible, in passing the place of the true Hades which like her is invisible, and pure, and noble, and on her way to the good and wise God . . . will be blown away and destroyed immediately on quitting the body. . .? This can never be . . .' (*Phaedo*, 80).

[4] 'The soul, herself invisible, departs to the invisible world — to the divine and immortal and rational . . . and forever dwells, as they say of the initiated, in the company of the gods' (*Phaedo*, 81). '. . . No one who has not studied philosophy and who is not entirely pure at the time of his departure is allowed to enter the company of the Gods, but the lover of knowledge only' (*Phaedo*, 82). Virgil, in his grandiose panorama of the netherworld (*Aeneid*, VI, 129), states: 'Pauci, quos aequus amavit / Juppiter aut ardens evesit ad aethera virtus, / dis geniti potuere. . . .' ('Some few, whom kindly Jupiter has loved, or whom shining worth uplifted to the heaven, sons of the gods, have availed.') Plotinus expands the group of the selected in line with the Pythagorean doctrine of the harmony of the spheres and Plato's conception of love in his *Phaedrus*. Thus, Plotinus says (I, 3): 'The souls capable of ascending and escaping the realm of the senses are those of the musician, of the lover (ἐρωτιχός) and the philosopher.' The Pythagorean heritage, with its doctrine of the harmony of the spheres, made its impact on Filippino's time above all through the 'Dream of Scipio' in Cicero's *De Republica*, Book VI, which through many copies, reprints, and comments became one of the most famous and influential treatises of the Renaissance; in art, it inspired the representation of the choirs of angels in Marian subjects (see Chapter 11 above).

[5] According to Aristotle, *Metaphysics*, I, 1070a, 26: 'Reason, not all of the soul, can survive death.'

role of the Muses as allegories of immortality becomes clear at once. For they, the daughters of Jupiter and Memory and the companions of Apollo-Logos, are the givers and protectors of knowledge,[1] the connoisseurs of the laws of the universe. It is because of this quality that they are represented on sarcophagi, often together with Apollo and Minerva, as sponsors of eternal life for the souls of the knowing ones.

The ardent interest in Roman archaeology and recently excavated works of art, among which were found many sarcophagi, coincided with the intensive revival of Plato's doctrine of the soul, above all in Ficino's *Theologia Platonica de immortalitate animarum* (1480). One of the inevitable problems of the time was to achieve a convincing reconciliation between the pagan and the Christian doctrines of immortality. The first centred on intellectual merit; the second on moral conduct and religion. The Christian Platonist, Ficino, attempted to reconcile these concepts through his theory of contemplation, i.e. the act of contemplation as a state of the soul that prepares for future existence.[2] But even this emphasis on contemplation retains the notion of the élite, the knowing, or in terms of Filippino's fresco, the 'initiati canunt.'[3]

One may argue that such a design, subtly blending pagan and Christian symbolism, may have been too complex for the understanding of the worshippers entering Santa Maria Novella. But easy intelligibility was certainly the least concern of the originator of this scheme, which was addressed to the 'initiati.' This is borne out by the character of the inscriptions, which, far from being explanatory labels, border on enigmas. Actually, subtle and unconventional iconological designs were generally admissable in chapels. They aimed at the humanist, the intellectual élite. Raphael once tried to endow one and the same object, the wind instrument in the hands of Euterpe in his *Parnassus*, with a double meaning: one for the humanist concerned with the ancient monuments and one for the naive beholder.[4] The combination of pagan Muses and ancient instruments with the Christian virtues and the promise of the water of Life may seem a trifle too pagan for a church under Dominican jurisdiction, especially in the days of Savonarola. But such an incompatibility simply did not exist. The Christian heaven had been widely opened to the invasion of pagan myths and images ever since Petrarch's time. Petrarch himself had not men-

---

[1] Virgil, *Georgics*, II, 489.   [2] *Opera omnium*, Turin, 1953, pp. 306, 385.

[3] Chastel, *op. cit.*, p. 391, relates this 'mystic' inscription to a passage in Ficino: 'Les mystères sacrés sont livrés à la foule sous des voiles et révélés aux disciples élus.' On his pp. 165–66, Chastel gives an interesting survey of the traditional styles of Tuscan funerary chapels, leading up to the Strozzi Chapel, but he does not attempt to solve the puzzle of the interrelation of the inscriptions in this chapel, nor of their combination with musical symbols into a homogeneous meditation on immortality.

[4] See Chapter 14 below.

tioned the Bible when he based his hope for immortality on the 'Dream of Scipio,' and it was not cynicism but the prevailing spirit of the times when he said that he did not hesitate as a Catholic to entertain a hope that he found proclaimed by the pagan authorities. And as for the Muses as sponsors of immortality, there was the authority of that great *anima naturaliter Christiana*, Virgil, who invokes the Muses as the great connoisseurs of stars and heaven, the guardians of the knowledge of the causes of things, a knowledge that conquers fear and fate and the noise of Acheron:

> *Felix qui potuit rerum cognoscere causas,*
> *Atque metus omnis et inexorabile fatum*
> *Subjecit pedibus, strepitum Acherontis avari.*[1]

The long contract of 1487 entrusting Filippino with the work says nothing of the questions that interest us in this essay. Thus we may never know how strictly the artist was bound to a scheme devised by a 'litterato come da un pari del Poliziano,' to quote again Vincenzo Galilei. But even if a humanist programme had prescribed many details, there are countless ways, of course, of translating a verbal scheme into the realm of the visually concrete. For this, a poet was required — a poet with a painter's brush. And here Filippino, who was often no more than an imaginative story teller, surpassed himself. He certainly employed the Muses and their instruments in full awareness of their allegorical importance in antiquity and their relation to the doctrine of immortality. He spared no effort in designing them as faithfully and as 'ancient' in style as possible. Instruments seemed the surest way to characterize the Muses; possibly the employment of a majestic giant lyre was suggested to him. One likes to think that perhaps one among the Dominican[2] superiors of Santa Maria Novella, though officially committed to Aristotle and Thomas Aquinas, was a Platonist who treasured *Phaedo* and recalled the passage there about the lyre[3] and its incorporeal divine harmony as a metaphor of the soul; or perhaps he was under the spell of Ficino's astrological studies and thought of the Muses as fitting allegories of the harmony of the spheres.

However this may be, one must admire the way in which Filippino succeeded in fusing all the allegories and symbolic requisites into a convincing artistic

---

[1] 'Blessed is he who has been able to win knowledge of all things, and has cast beneath his feet all fear and unyielding fate, and the howls of hungry Acheron'; *Georgics*, II, 490, transl. by H. Rushton Fairclough, London, 1916.

[2] Filippo Strozzi had been prior of Santa Maria Novella for two years before commissioning his funerary chapel there. Filippino must have had excellent relations with the Dominicans since the Caraffa Chapel decorated by him is in the principal Dominican church of Rome, Santa Maria sopra Minerva.

[3] *Phaedo*, 86, 88, 92.

whole, a homogeneous visual meditation of profound poetry. He also added poetic touches that are not based on humanist archaeological tradition: the Muses have plectra made of human bones and it is these bones that draw music from the golden strings of the lyre, near to other bones held up or trodden upon by the angels of death. It is the music of the Muses, the harmony of the spheres, the music for the initiated, that confirms the Christian promise of the 'DONUM DEI' and the 'NI HANC DESPEXERIS VIVES.'[1]

APPENDIX

[From Vincenzo Galilei, *Dialogo della musica antica e della moderna* (1581), reprinted Rome, 1934, p. 130 ff.]

BAR: (Signor Giovanni Bardi). In qual maniera fatto & di qual forma credete per fede vostra che fusse il Plettro degli antichi Citharisti & Citharedi?

STR. (Signor Pietro Strozzi). Credo che egli fusse un'Archetto simile à quello che adoperano hoggi i sonatori di Viola da gamba, & da braccio, detta modernamente Lira.

BAR. Qui è tutto l'errore.

STR. Come di gratia.

BAR. Il Plettro degli antichi, era uno strumento lungo un palmo, ò un quarto di braccio in circa, della forma che qui vedete il disegno; di che (per quello ne sente Suida) fu autrice Saffo; la qual cosa non so come possa stare, avvenga che Homero che attribuisce l'inventione à Mercurio, fu avanti a Saffo del Mixolydio inventrice.

Il quale strumento s'impugnava con la destra, & con la sinistra si reggeva quella parte della Lira dove erano accomodati i bischeri; & l'altra dove erano attaccate le corde, che era come veduto havete al quanto più larga, si appoggiava al petto; à quella parte però che apportava comodità maggiore: ne tempi poi più bassi, quando si cominciò à sonare in consonāza come si disse che usava Epigonio & Aspendio, si posava in piedi sopra una tavola ò sgabello, & con le due linguette che avanzavano sotto & sopra al pugno ò da lati che ci vogliamo dire, si percotevano & non si secavano le corde di essa Lira; nella maniera che

---

[1] I know of only one other Renaissance chapel in which the relation between music and death is symbolized: it is Lorenzo Costa's *The Triumph of Death*, in the fresco of the Bentivoglio Chapel in San Petronio, Bologna. There, in front of the conventional procession of the dead, is a separate group of large figures standing (not marching) and listening in deep meditation to an Oriental (Orpheus?) who plays the lira da braccio. The quiet faces of the listeners are of unforgettable individuality. It would seem that here, in this counterpoint between music and death, an artist of little depth was inspired to outdo himself.

vi disse poco fa Vergilio & Ovidio: ha vendo altri & questi stessi Poeti, per
mostrare maggior forza nel toccarle, usata questa voce; Ferire le corde, in vece
di percuoterle. i quali strumenti si costumarono in quelli primi tempi, fare di
quelli ossi che hanno le capre tra le ginocchia & l'ugne delle gambe dinanzi;
lavorati & puliti al tornio ò in altra maniera; dàdogli gli artefici quella forma
che havete veduta come più d'altra conveniente all'ufitio suo: ancora che alcuni
altri vogliono, che l'ugna istessa servisse per percuotere le corde, inpugnando il
Zampetto dopo l'essere staccato dalla capra & secco, & volendo vederne un
ritratto molto simile, il quale non vedo mai senza mia maraviglia; ponete
mente nel superbo tempio di Santa Maria Novella, nella cappella d'uno degli
Avi nostri, dipinta da Filippo di Fra Filippo; in faccia della quale dalla parte
sinistra, si vedono due femmine, una delle quali canta, & l'altra sostiene con la
mano una Lira antica fatta secondo che di sopra vi ho dimostrato; & nella
destra ha impugnato una cosa simile al disegno del Plettro mostratovi, quanto
però alla forma & all'attezza dell'ufitio; dal che si può fare argumento, del gran
giuditio di quello eccellente pittore; caso che in quel affare non fusse aiutato da
alcuno litterato, come da un pari del Poliziano che fu in fiore nell'istesso tempo
& luogo; il quale facilmente potette havere qualche lume di tale strumento, poi
che litterato era, & della musica lasciò scritto in diversi suoi propositi alcune
cose di momento, & comunicarlo à detto Filippo. & acciò che sappiate, non e
più di due anni che tale certezza è pervenuta in cognitione di alcuni pochi
particolari; mercè d'un Pilo antichissimo ritrovatosi ultimamente in Roma, il
quale è hoggi nel Palazzo del Cardinale Santacroce; dove si vedono scolpite in
basso rilievo le Muse, & in mano à una la forma di lui con lo strumento appresso,
la cognitione & certezza del quale, fa hoggi che si scorge in più rovesci di
medaglie, che era prima conosciuto per ogn'altra cosa che per un Plettro.
un'altro ancore simile, se ne vede pur in Roma in una scultura antichissima; la
quale è in una nicchia del cortile del Palazzo già del Cardinale Montepulciano,
& hoggi de Cievoli Gentilhuomini Pisani; in mano d'una figura in habito di
donna con uno strumento à canto. che le corde dell'antica lira si percotessero
ultimamente, & non si secassero, ve lo confermo con l'essempio d'uno Evangelo
Nobile Tarentino, raccontatoci da Luciano. . . .'

[TRANSLATION]

BAR. (Signor Giovanni Bardi). How and in what shape, in your opinion, was
the plectrum of the ancient cithara players made?

STR. (Signor Piero Strozzi). I believe it was a bow, similar to that used today
by the players of the viola da gamba and of the viola da braccio, called in
modern times the lyre.

BAR. Herein lies the whole error.

STR. How so, if you please?

BAR. The plectrum of the ancients was a tool of about a palm's length, or approximately one fourth of an arm's length, in the shape which you can see in this illustration; and its inventor (as far as we can learn from Suidas) was

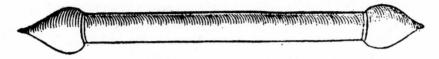

Fig. 23. Plectrum (see also Plate 88b).

Sappho; but I do not know how this could be, since Homer, who attributes the invention to Mercury, came before Sappho, who was the inventor of the Mixolydian mode.

The player grasped this tool in the right hand, while his left held that part of the lyre where the pegs are attached; the other and, as you have seen, much larger part of the lyre, where the strings are attached, was held against the chest where it was most comfortable; but in later times, when people began to play consonances, as allegedly did Epigonius and Aspendios, the lyre was placed upright upon a table or stool, with the two tongue-like ends projecting above and beneath the fist, or from its sides, so to speak; the strings of the lyre were struck — but not stopped — in the way we learned earlier from Virgil and Ovid: since they and other poets, in order to describe the greatest possible force in touching the strings, used the term 'wounding' the strings, rather than 'striking' them. In these early times, the plectra were usually made from those bones which goats have between their knees and the hoofs of their forelegs; they were fashioned and smoothed at the turning-lathe, or in some other way, so that they received from the craftsmen precisely the shape you have seen as most convenient for their function. Still, some others insist that the hoof itself was used for striking the chords, by taking the hoof after it had been removed from the goat and had been dried. And if you want to see a good likeness, which I can never look at without great amazement, then remember the church of Santa Maria Novella and the chapel of one of our forefathers decorated with paintings by Filippo di Fra Filippo; there on the main wall on the left two women can be seen; one of them sings and the other holds with her hand an ancient lyre shaped as I have explained above; and in her right hand she grips an object similar to the design of the plectrum that I have shown above, so adequately shaped for its function that one can draw conclusions about the expert knowledge of our excellent painter; unless he was helped in this matter by some humanist of the rank of Poliziano, who was flourishing at that time and place, and who could easily have had some information about such a plectrum, since he was learned and left us various important statements about music, which he might have communicated to our Filippo. And you must know, it was not more than two years ago that actual certainty was obtained in the knowledge of a few details, thanks to a very ancient sarcophagus recently found in Rome. It is now in the palace of Cardinal Santacroce, and on it in relief one sees the Muses; one of them holds in her hand, near the instrument, the object that we recognize today on the reverse sides of medals, which was earlier identified as something other than a plectrum. Another similar plectrum can be seen, also in Rome, on a very ancient sculpture, standing in a niche of the court of the palace formerly owned by Cardinal Montepulciano and now owned by the venerable gentleman from Pisa: there, it is held by the hand of a figure in female garb, with the instrument nearby. The fact that the strings of the ancient lyre were struck and not stopped in late antiquity, I can confirm by the example of a nobleman from Tarento, named Evangelo, as reported by Lucian.

14 · Musical Archaeology of the Renaissance in Raphael's *Parnassus**

The frescoes of the Stanza della Segnatura do not belong among the neglected works in the history of art, and about the *Parnassus* whole libraries have been written. Especially in the last generation, when the ancient models of Renaissance art were once again brought into focus, the *Parnassus* was examined as to its inspiration by Greek or Roman models. The results of these examinations are comparatively meagre. They are usually limited to such general statements as: 'antiquity is present in Raphael's compositions,' or, at best, they point concretely to some relationship or similarity between the pose or garb of a single figure in the fresco and that of an ancient statue.[1] The present study attempts to prove a direct relationship between the *Parnassus* fresco and a well-known Roman sarcophagus, a relationship that is not limited to certain small details of the figures or their garments, but is revealed by a considerable number of characteristic features taken over from that ancient monument because of the great interest of Raphael or his advisers in the musical instruments of antiquity and in the problem of their reconstruction. It is precisely through my studies in

* I wish to express my gratitude for most valuable help to Dr. Deoclecio Redig de Campos, the late Prof. Ludwig Curtius, Prof. Richard Krautheimer, Dr. Filippo Magi, the late Prof. Charles Rufus Morey, Dr. Olga Raggio, and the late Prof. Martin Weinberger, with all of whom I have had the pleasure of discussing various aspects of this study.

[1] Oskar Fischel, *Raphaels Zeichnungen*, Berlin, 1913–41, p. 255: 'In Marcantonio's engraving, Apollo remained nearer to the ancient model, and the garb of the poets and Muses, after classical models, are not yet conceived in that timeless style which imparts so much poetic lightness to the fresco.' Fischel also calls attention to a similarity between the Muse at the right of Apollo (whom he calls Erato) and the girl playing a kithara on the sarcophagus in the Louvre, with the representation of Apollo in Skyros. Adolf Michaelis, *Geschichte des Statuenhofs im Vatican-ischen Belvedere*, in *Jahrbuch des Kaiserlichen Deutschen Archaeologischen Instituts*, V (1890), 18 ff., observes, as did Passavant before him, a similarity between Raphael's sketch for Calliope in the Albertina and the statue known as Cleopatra in the Belvedere. I wonder whether Erato could not just as well be compared with the type of sitting figure that we find, for example, in the Palazzo dei Conservatori (catalogue by Settimo Bocconi, Rome, 1930, tav. 122). There is a great likeness not only in the pose but in several details of costume, especially if we look at Raimondi's engraving. Later Raphael transformed the whole figure into an image of intense listening and, at the same time, of nervous, passionate devotion, features particularly noticeable in the large sketch in the Albertina, where the ear is strongly accentuated and further emphasized by the encircling coil of hair (Fischel, *op. cit.*, Pl. 251).

the little-cultivated field of musical archaeology that I became convinced of the findings presented here.

To approach this problem, it will be necessary to look at the preliminary steps of the composition, especially Marcantonio's engraving (Pl. 79) and the copy of a compositional sketch in the nude at Oxford (Pl. 80), which are the most important surviving documents reflecting the earlier stages of the painting. An analysis will reveal that the instruments in the *Parnassus* were first treated quite differently, and that certain ancient (*antichi*) models entered the scene in the course of the work and decisively shaped the fermenting imagination of Raphael, at that time a most devoted student of antiquity. These models can all be identified as appearing in a Roman sarcophagus of the Asiatic type from the end of the 3rd century; a close comparison between the details of the sarcophagus and the fresco will reveal not only that all the musical instruments in the sculpture have been transplanted into the fresco, but also that Raphael borrowed other important details, such as the tragic and lyric masks, cloth motives, and coiffures. Thanks to some lucky discoveries, it will, I trust, not be too difficult to show that the sarcophagus was known at Raphael's time and to reconstruct its state of preservation at that time. We are then left with the most puzzling but, at the same time, the most thought-provoking problems: to explain the seemingly anachronistic introduction of Apollo's bowed instrument among those taken from antiquity; and to explain why the latter instruments differ from the ancient models in certain structural details, sometimes to the point of being functional nonsense. The reasons, we will find, are manifold: Raphael's allegorical aims; the blunders of the draughtsman when he copied from the ancient models; the beliefs — and mistakes — of contemporary students of ancient musical instruments; and, last but most revealing, Raphael's didactic intentions — his aim of combining features of modern instruments with those of ancient ones, to make his instruments appear truly antique (that is, archaeologically correct) and at the same time symbolically meaningful for the whole composition, which was to be seen and understood not only by the learned ones, by the Bembos and Castigliones, but by the public as well.

We begin with a quick preliminary look at the fresco itself (Pl. 78). There are five instruments depicted, some ancient, some contemporary, but all afflicted with strange and unorthodox features occurring neither in representations of the ancient instruments nor in the actual instruments of Raphael's day.

The nearest approach to an ancient model is the elaborate and ornate kithara held by Erato[1] on her lap (Pl. 82a). Its sound box actually consists of

---

[1] Or is she Terpsichore? The identification, or rather the naming, of the nine Muses on the basis of their attributes and their functions, according to the canons established by the art and

two boxes, the front of the lower box showing three slits. The arms, decorated with five knobs, curve up gracefully towards the yoke. The latter is inserted into the arms and can evidently be turned by the usual side disks, of which one is visible. Following Terpander's rule, there are seven strings, which spring from the lower box. The projecting rim of the upper box, functioning as a bridge, changes their direction, and at the point where they reach the yoke no fastening device is depicted. In fact, the usual sticks or rolls (*kollopes*; mentioned as early as the *Odyssey*, Bk. XXI), which help to attach the strings to the yoke and to vary their tension for tuning purposes, are absent here (see Pl. 77b, showing a Roman wall painting, for an idea of their shape and location).

No less problematic is the wind instrument held by Erato's counterpart, Euterpe (Pl. 83).[1] It is a single metal tube, swelling slightly towards the top and terminating first in a bulb and then in an unusually flat, small bell. The lower end shows clearly a cup-shaped mouthpiece, like those used in brass instruments of all periods. In short, this instrument would appear to be a trumpet were it not for the four strange protuberances on its right side, below Euterpe's arm; they make no sense in a trumpet or in any other brass instrument.

Most enigmatic is the string instrument held by Sappho (Pl. 82b). A curved sound box, shaped more like a turtle shell than an animal head, carries a complex machinery, a sort of frame with four side disks, three of which are visible. They seem to be of the same nature and function as those on Erato's kithara and thus would serve to turn the crossbar, or, more precisely, the two crossbars. But why two crossbars? Moreover, the way in which this machinery is attached to the turtle shell remains unclear. Certainly two arms grow from the shell, continuing its contour; it seems as if two animal horns are inserted into the two holes for the front feet of the turtle.

---

literature of the ancients, is no easy task. The literature on Raphael's *Parnassus* offers a diverting multiplicity of opinions. To cite one example, the two Muses flanking Apollo: Deoclecio Redig de Campos (*Le Stanze di Raffaello*, Florence, 1930, p. 26) calls the one at the left 'Calliope, la Musa della poesia epica,' and the one at the right 'Terpsichore, quella della poesia lirica,' while Fischel (*op. cit.*, p. 263) calls the former Euterpe — possibly with reference to Ausonius: 'dulceloquis calamos Euterpe flatibus urgit' ('the sweet-voiced Euterpe excites the pipes with her breath') — and the latter Erato — possibly with reference to the same poet: 'plectra gerens Erato saltat pede, carmine, vultu' ('bearing the plectrum, Erato, with expressive face, dances and sings'). But why criticize the modern scholars when even the ancients themselves did not agree? Terpsichore, according to Ovid, plays the *tibiam duplicem* — 'grataque Terpsichore calamos inflare paravit' ('the graceful Terpsichore was engaged in blowing the pipes') — while Ausonius has her play the kithara — 'Terpsichore affectus citharis movet, imperat, auget' ('Terpsichore, with her kithara, moves the passions, dominates and increases them'). Raphael, though full of respect for the iconography of the ancients, paid little attention to pedantries, and the Muse sitting at Apollo's left exchanged, without any apparent qualms, the syrinx that she held in Marcantonio's engraving for the more noble kithara of the Oxford sketch and the fresco.

[1] Terpsichore, according to de Campos (see preceding footnote).

At first glimpse, Sappho seems to hold one of those large plectra that are often depicted in ancient art. But a closer inspection shows that this large horn-shaped object is part of the instrument — without it, the instrument would fall down. Whether the instrument is connected to the bulge below the hand, or whether it is connected to a smaller bulge farther right (which may be another of the disks mentioned above), remains utterly unclear. No doubt the painter was not clear about it himself. The five strings spring from an elaborate string holder with a curved profile, and stop in mid-air shortly before reaching the fastening point, another symptom of the uncertainty of the draughtsman.[1]

There is a third Muse who holds a musical instrument, the wonderful figure with her back to the viewer, the farthest right of the Muses. Her instrument has scarcely been commented upon in the literature. Fischel[2] calls it a lute, and the shading indeed suggests a rounded surface similar to a lute's belly. But the belly of a lute was invariably made of staves, and that Raphael knew how to short-hand such a design is shown by his quick sketch of a lute player (Pl. 81b). In a study for the drapery of this Muse (Pl. 81a), the instrument rapidly jotted down resembles a cetra — that is, the Renaissance cetra rather than the ancient kithara, which was also called 'cetra' in Raphael's time. One might also be tempted to recognize, in the drawing, the front of the lute with the strings sketched in, but the strings of a Renaissance lute were attached to a frontal string holder, not to the tail end of the soundboard.[3] Among the enormous

---

[1] Numerous authors of the 16th century who wrote about the musical instruments of the ancients, and considered Raphael as the great authority in this field, found themselves in an embarrassing situation when they tried to translate obscure regions of a painting into the clear lines of a woodcut or engraving, where they were forced to resolve any confusions and uncertainties. In view of the well-known damage to the fresco (such as that inflicted during the sack of Rome in 1527) and the ensuing restorations, the reader may well inquire whether this section of the painting still retains its original surface, or whether the instrument has been changed by the hand of a well-meaning restorer. One could, in fact, draw up a long list of Renaissance works of art in which the musical instruments have been 'corrected' or 'modernized' in this fashion, for example by suppressing obsolete details such as bourdon strings or pegs. This kind of restoration is found above all in large museums and in famous works; in provincial collections and less famous churches, where zeal and money were lacking, paintings and frescoes have frequently remained intact. Fortunately, Sappho's instrument in the *Parnassus* shows no trace of restoration or overpainting. At this point, I wish to express my thanks to the Administration of the Vatican Museums, especially to Dr. Filippo Magi and Dr. Deoclecio Redig de Campos, who permitted me to spend many hours on scaffolds and to examine the sections of the fresco that were of interest to me. The unrestored condition of this particular section seems also to be confirmed by the words of Bellori, in his *Descrizione delle imagini dipinti da Raffaelle d'Urbino*, Rome, 1695: 'With her right hand Sappho reaches under the horn (*corno*) of the lyre,' a description that coincides perfectly with the instrument as we see it today.

[2] *Op. cit.*, p. 265.

[3] See, for example, the lutes depicted in Giovanni Bellini's altarpiece in the Accademia, Venice; Carpaccio's painting of the Virgin with Christ in Santa Maria de Frari, Venice; and Luca della Robbia's cantoria, in the Museo del Duomo, Florence.

number of extant lutes, and among those appearing in Renaissance painting, sculpture, and prints, I know of not one single exception. It will, perhaps, be better to leave this question open for the moment.

The last instrument to be mentioned is Apollo's. It is a lira da braccio and the only instrument which is being played; the others remain respectfully silent.[1]

So much for the instruments in the fresco. We can turn now to their representation in the engraving by Marcantonio and the drawing at Oxford. Fischel,[2] without directly establishing their chronology, simply states that 'in the grouping of the figures in the Oxford drawing, the composition already approached its final form.' But since this question is essential to my interpretation, we must pause to consider it.

At first glance the problem seems complicated, since Marcantonio's engraving shows seven more figures than the Oxford drawing, of whom most — with many or few changes — have been incorporated into the fresco. But closer inspection of the figures and their grouping reveals beyond doubt that the Oxford drawing is the immediate predecessor of the final work. All figures here have taken precisely the poses that they assume in the fresco: Apollo is seated as in the fresco; the extreme right Muse has turned around, now showing her back; the black-bearded poet on the right, often identified with Baldassare Castiglione, has turned towards the right. This similarity is apparent even in minutiae. In the Oxford drawing, as in the fresco, the seated Ennius is part of the smooth arc formed by Virgil, Homer, and Dante, and this rounded contour is continued through his right arm — quite different from the jagged contour in the engraving. The Oxford drawing also hides Euterpe's left forearm, fully shown by Marcantonio. A special case is the eloquent bearded elder in the right foreground; he appears in the engraving and also, in a more subtle and elegant version, in the drawing, but is omitted in the fresco (however, he reappears, slightly modified, in the right foreground of the *Disputà del sacramento*).

We arrive at the same conclusion if we compare the three compositions with respect to the grouping of the standing Muses. In the drawing, the heads in each group are so arranged that they form descending lines converging towards Apollo, and in the right group the two middle Muses are closely linked to each other and detached from the flanking ones. All this agrees precisely with the fresco but is markedly different from the engraving.

In addition to these incongruities, another aspect of the composition reveals that Marcantonio's engraving is a world apart from the fresco. In the engraving, the single groups are static, isolated from each other, and the figures are

[1] On the evolution and changing shapes of the lira da braccio, see Chapter 5 above.
[2] *Op. cit.*, p. 255.

firmly rooted to the ground. In the fresco all the poets are involved in a soft, almost imperceptible motion from the left foreground, over the hill, and down again.[1] It is like an eternal procession across the ages, from time immemorial and continuing into the future, suggesting the participation of all epochs in the beautiful. In contemplating this image, both profound and nostalgic, we are reminded — as perhaps was Raphael — of Petrarch's beautiful words:

> *E Greci e nostri, che son fatti eredi*
> *Del monte di Parnaso e per quei gioghi*
> *Mosser più tardo, non men presti, i piedi.*[2]

Assuming, on the basis of this comparison, that the Oxford drawing represents a much later stage than Marcantonio's engraving,[3] we can turn to an examination of the musical instruments depicted in both of them.

To begin with the engraving: the same four figures as in the fresco (that is, Apollo and three of the Muses) have instruments, two string and two wind instruments in all. These evidently all pose as ancient instruments, but are not truly so; in fact, they have no more to do with Greek or Roman instruments than do the lyre-guitars, so fashionable for a short time in the French Empire. But these lyre-guitars could at least be played, whereas the vague, pseudo-ancient lyres were unfunctional, lacking, among other things, a sound box. In particular, the two lyres of Marcantonio, one with strings and a short base and the other without strings and with a larger base, are simplified stylizations for allegorical purposes. But one should not blame Raimondi for them; they may very well be Raphael's. These instruments are quite concordant with the usual pictorial representation of ancient lyres around 1500; Mantegna, in his *Parnassus*, gave Apollo a similar lyre,[4] and Raphael himself followed this usage in the decorative, stylized instruments that he gave to the Apollo defeating Marsyas on the ceiling of the Segnatura, to Poesia in the same work (called 'un suono antico' by Vasari), and to the large Apollo in the niche of *The School of Athens*. If one wishes

---

[1] In the literature on the *Parnassus*, only one writer points to this motion: De Campos, whose *Le Stanze di Raffaello*, in the form of a small guidebook, contains many valuable suggestions and original ideas.

[2] 'The Greeks and we Latins, who have inherited the mountain of Parnassus and have traversed these ranges — in later times, but no less swiftly' (*Trionfi*, III, 61; *altra redazione*, publ. in *Letteratura italiana, storia e testi*, VI, Milan, 1951, p. 575.

[3] There is no need to take up here *in extenso* the often-discussed question of whether Vasari's description of the *Parnassus* was based on Marcantonio's engraving or directly on the fresco. Both hypotheses have been maintained in the critical literature; I believe the solution lies in the middle. Vasari admires the *putti* ('an infinity of nude Cupids in the air'), which occur only in the engraving, but at the same time he speaks of the 'dotta Sappho,' who appears only in the fresco. It is more than probable, therefore, that Vasari, who certainly knew the fresco, used the engraving to refresh his memory.

[4] However, he copied Roman military instruments accurately enough for his *Triumph of Caesar*, now at Hampton Court.

to see how accurately Raphael depicts instruments familiar to him, one has only to look at the psaltery in King David's hand in the *Disputà* or at the lira da braccio of the *Parnassus* Apollo, both instruments that he must have seen and heard countless times in Urbino and Rome.[1]

Equally vague and conventional is the syrinx held by Erato. It is the typical pastoral instrument usually depicted at that time in the hands of shepherds, satyrs, and frequently Polyphemus (as, for instance, the languishing Polyphemus by Sebastiano del Piombo in the Farnesina, to cite an example from Raphael's circle). But the real syrinx — one beautiful example is held by the dancing faun of the Capitoline Gallery — has to be graduated, with tapering pipes, and there is no trace of this in Raimondi's print.

Finally, Euterpe's instrument, conspicuously held against the sky, is a typical trumpet, quite common at Raphael's time, and the traditional allegorical attribute of Fama. The mouthpiece is hidden, but the shape of tube and bell leave no doubt.

Thus none of the four instruments shown in Raimondi's print, though in line with the current allegorical conventions, have much to do with instruments of the ancients, nor, to say the least, do they stem from the observation of ancient monuments that became so important at the time of Raphael's work in Rome.

All this changes at once with the phase of Raphael's work that is represented by the Oxford drawing. No longer are there pseudo-ancient instruments: Euterpe holds a double pipe, clearly an indication of the ancient Lydian aulos, although the upper end is not delineated and the lower end is hidden behind the legs, as it was in Marcantonio's engraving. Erato now holds a kithara identical with the one in the fresco, except that her hand here grasps the nearer arm of the kithara. The Muse at the extreme right holds an instrument of which only the lower part is visible. It cannot reliably be identified, but it certainly is not the pseudo-lyre of the engraving; most probably, it is a contemporary cittern. Apollo, finally, has also replaced his pseudo-lyre with a cittern; it is very sketchily outlined, yet clearly recognizable from the characteristic ears that are non-functional yet inevitable features of *quattrocento* citterns, occurring first as large projections and then, towards the *cinquecento*, gradually degenerating into small scrolls.[2]

[1] He also must have seen daily the marvellous and minutely precise intarsia representations by Giovanni da Verona that decorate most of the lower sections of the doors leading into the Segnatura. These intarsias seem to be the last remnants of the decoration that covered the lower part of the walls of the room itself before it was given over to Raphael. The doors include exclusively contemporary instruments — a harp, a spinettino, recorders, krummhorns, a set of viols, and a lute, but not a single lira da braccio, psaltery, or brass instrument.

[2] See Chapter 3 above. Examining the persistence of such elements over the centuries, one could perhaps formulate a hypothesis of some sort of collective memory. And, although this is

This comparison between the fresco and the preliminary stages of its composition has produced a strange result: in the Oxford drawing, although it is, for the most part, merely a compositional study in the nude, two new instruments have been depicted, at a point close to the completion of Raphael's plans. They reveal, for the first time, an intimate observation of ancient Greco-Roman instruments. Where did this knowledge come from, and why did this archaeological interest not enter the work until this late stage?

It is a fact that most of the musical instruments represented in ancient art that could have served as models in Raphael's time have not survived up to our day, or survive only in severely damaged condition (as, for instance, the decorations of the Domus Aurea). Nor is the pre-1511 literature on ancient music very revealing for our problem, as it consists mainly of theoretical matters such as the explication of the ancient modes; there is little about the instruments themselves, and, above all, not a single illustration that might have served as a model for the painter or as a guide for his humanist advisers. Among actual monuments, we have chiefly gems and coins; of real lyres and kitharas little has been preserved. There are also wall paintings, but they were done with impressionistic verve. As for statues of Apollo and the Muses with instruments, almost none exist in which the delicate projecting parts are not broken or — usually incorrectly — restored.[1] These small delicate parts had their best chance for preservation in reliefs, and it is in fact a sarcophagus, almost completely preserved at Raphael's time, that furnished the exact models for the *Parnassus*. This sarcophagus is, I believe, the Mattei Sarcophagus in the Museo Nazionale in Rome (Pl. 85a), a work neither obscure nor unknown, having been published and reproduced repeatedly.[2]

This sarcophagus, one of the most beautiful specimens of the Asiatic Sidamara type,[3] shows the nine Muses with two poets — five Muses on the front and two

not the place to indulge in such theorizing, I should like to point out the strange coincidence that, just at the time when the fanatical revival of antiquity had reached its climax, Apollo, the player of the lyre in antiquity, was given an instrument equipped with an atrophic form of the arms of the ancient lyre.

[1] An example of expert and ingenious restoration is the Apollo Musagetes in the Sala delle Muse of the Vatican. The remaining stump of one of the two arms of the kithara showed, in relief, two small legs, up to the knees; the restorer has completed them by adding the entire body of the suspended Marsyas.

[2] Jakob Sponius, *Miscellanea eruditae antiquitatis*, Lyon, 1679–85; Bernard de Montfaucon, *L'Antiquité expliquée*, Paris, 1724, Tome I, Part II, Tab. LVI, p. 112; Ridolfino Venuti, *Vetera monumenta Matthaeorum*, Rome, 1779, Vol. III, Tab. XVI, XVII; Johann Joachim Winckelmann, *Monumenti antichi inediti*, 2nd ed., Rome, 1821, Lib. V, cap. 3, notes 25 and 37; also Lib. VIII, cap. 3; Edward Gerhard, *Ueber ein Musenrelief des Königlichenu Museums zu Berlin*, in *Archäologische Zeitung*, 1843, p. 115, n. 11g; Friedrich Matz and Edward Friedrich Karl von Duhn, *Antike Bildwerke*, Leipzig, 1881–82, No. 3268, p. 406; Charles Rufus Morey, *Sardis*, Vol. V, Pt. 1: *The Sarcophagus of Claudia Antonia Sabina and the Asiatic Sarcophagi*, Princeton, 1924, p. 26, Plate XVI.

[3] For a comparison with other Asiatic sarcophagi, see Morey, *op. cit.*, pp. 49 ff.

Muses flanking a poet on each side. It is the front that interests us most, for here are all the attributes that characterize each of the five Muses and that, if my hypothesis is correct, must have interested Raphael: the musical instruments and the two masks, tragic and lyric, that emphasize the middle niche. The instruments correspond to those in our fresco, occurring in the same order from left to right: the left instrument was given to Sappho; the right one, an elaborate kithara, to Erato; the Lydian aulos, in a modified form which we will discuss later, to Euterpe, to the left of Apollo. And indeed the masks, too, have been transferred to the fresco in the same symmetrical arrangement, the bearded one carried by the extreme left Muse, the unbearded one by the Muse to the right of Apollo. The latter mask was already introduced in the Oxford drawing, but was there held by the first Muse on the right. The beautiful motif of the bare shoulder of the kithara player is repeated no less than three times in the *Parnassus*: in the figures of Euterpe, Sappho, and the Muse holding the lyric mask. But we look in vain for this motif in Marcantonio's engraving, which is one more proof that the motif was inspired by a subsequent acquaintance with the sarcophagus.

Yet, striking as these parallels may be, they still leave several questions open; not all the details tally. Sappho's instrument has a horn, while the corresponding one in the sarcophagus has none; Euterpe's strange trumpet is no aulos. Moreover, the instruments on the sarcophagus are damaged today — not to mention the four missing heads; in what condition were they when Raphael or his draftsmen saw them? And do we possess any evidence, besides its relation to the Segnatura fresco, that the sarcophagus was known before 1511? The art-historical literature, as far as I can see, does not contain a single word about this.

It is possible, and also advantageous, to answer all these questions together, for good luck makes it possible to refer to depictions of the sarcophagus in earlier, better-preserved states — at least one of them before Raphael's day.

Well known, of course, is the engraving of the sarcophagus in the *Monumenta Matthaeiana* (Pl. 85b). It is rather academic and conventional, but gives some important clues: the instrument at the extreme left has one horn with a hand touching it, as does Sappho's in the fresco; the aulos has four protuberances; the right arm and hand of the kithara-playing Muse and even the large plectrum are still intact. An amusing misunderstanding has afflicted the tragic mask; the fingers holding it by the chin have been misinterpreted by the engraver, so that the mask here spits the sleeve cloth of the Muse out of its mouth. More important is the fact that all the heads except the one at the extreme right are still extant. Although drawn schematically, they at least show the direction of the faces.

An earlier reproduction of the sarcophagus, the engraving in Jakob Sponius, *Miscellanea eruditae antiquitatis*, Sect. II, Art. IX, p. 44, is even more interesting and more precise. Here the original top is shown, with the medallion of the deceased couple, man and wife, which occurs in no other reproduction of the sarcophagus. Also, all the heads of the Muses appear, including the one of the farthest right Muse, which is missing in the engraving of the *Monumenta Matthaeiana*. The same engraving is repeated by Bernard de Montfaucon, *L'Antiquité expliquée et representée en figures*, Paris, 1724, Tom. I, Part II, Tab. LVI, p. 112 (Pl. 85c).

Let us now turn to still earlier evidence: the drawings. The drawing preceding Raphael's is by no lesser hand than that of Francesco di Giorgio (Pl. 88b; Uffizi, Gabinetto dei Disegni, 326 A.R.). Its subject and its relation to the Mattei Sarcophagus have so far not been recognized.[1] It is evidently a leaf from a travel sketchbook, containing ground plans of ancient buildings, with dimensions and an ancient inscription added. At the top left is the kithara-player from the Mattei Sarcophagus; further to the right are the heads of the other four Muses. Over the complete figure is the remark 'a san Pauolo', over the four heads again 'a san Pauolo.' The right head, graciously bent, evidently belongs to the extreme left Muse (compared with the engraving from the *Monumenta Matthaeiana*). Francesco was evidently particularly interested in the coiffure, and his shorthand is admirably precise, as we see if we compare the third head from the right with its model, the head of the centre Muse on the sarcophagus. This head has an elaborate double coiffure with a ribbon between the lower and higher part. Raphael, it seems, liked it too, and it found its way into the Oxford drawing, applied to the Muse at the extreme left; later, in the fresco, it was given to the standing Muse to the right of Apollo.

The full figure of the kithara-player is a model of delicate shorthand innuendo. No wonder Francesco was struck by the graceful pose of the lifted leg, and the smooth neckline with one shoulder exposed by the diagonal rim of the peplum. This figure was a favourite in antiquity and was used as a single figure, independent of the circle of the Muses. The right hand with the larger plectrum and, above all, the left hand plucking with strongly arched fingers are delineated with sharper, more determined strokes.

[1] A. S. Weller, *Francesco di Giorgio*, Chicago, 1943, p. 263, comments on this drawing: 'In the upper left corner is a sketch of a figure in transparent flowing drapery playing a lyre, labelled "*a sanpavolo*." In the Uffizi Catalogue, Ferri says that this is an Apollo on a sarcophagus at San Paolo fuori le Mura. It appears, however, that the figure is no Apollo but one of the Muses. Four other female heads, in various attitudes, also appear. The heads have proportion lines added, in a fashion found also in many of the *Trattato* illustrations. . . .' R. Papini, *Francesco di Giorgio architetto*, Florence, 1946, Vol. II, fig. 26, reproduces only the upper part of the page, with the comment: 'Donna che suona la cetra, studii di teste e di una pianta di Villa.'

By a lucky coincidence, the other two Muses with instruments from the sarcophagus are also represented in a drawing, a page of the Wolfegg Sketch-book, attributed to Amico Aspertini.[1] This page shows in its four sections various scenes from ancient reliefs, all containing musical instruments, although this may not have been the principle of choice. The lower scenes are of maritime character; the upper ones have larger figures, evidently copied from sculptures in diverse places, for they are accurately labelled 'in santo paulo.' Interesting to us are the two figures in the upper left (Pl. 89c), evidently sketches after the left and middle Muses of the front of the Mattei Sarcophagus. The instrument of the left figure is sketched with considerable detail, and tallies in many details with Sappho's lyre in the fresco. But realistic observation and fantasy are mixed a little differently and less timidly than by Raphael. There is again the complex machine on top, but it includes the little *kollopes*. Thus we have to assume either that they were intact on the sarcophagus at that time or that the draftsman reconstructed them from the remains, which are still preserved today. Moreover, the instrument has only one horn, the one in the rear, as in the engraving of the *Monumenta*; the draftsman did not take the trouble to supply the other horn, the stump of which is still visible today. The player's hand does not hold the horn, as in the *Monumenta* engraving, but reaches down to the 'machine', and consequently the arm turned out much too long. The round sound-hole, drawn in by analogy with a lute, is sheer imagination. The three strings are drawn in, but they cross the horizontal projection of the soundboard and thus transform it into something like a bridge.

More reliable is the aulos; obviously, it was still preserved when the draughts-man saw the sarcophagus. The upper ends with the bulbous swellings are indicated, and so are the six cup-shaped protuberances, of which three still remain today while the other three are broken. The lower ends of the pipes beneath the left hand were neglected by the draughtsman, although they still survive today.

By comparing the drawings of Francesco di Giorgio and Aspertini, and the prints from Sponius and the *Monumenta* with the sarcophagus itself, the reader will now be able to reconstruct the successive states of preservation of the sarcophagus and acquire an approximate picture of the condition in which Raphael or his draughtsmen saw it; only now is it possible to judge how much

---

[1] Professor Richard Krautheimer, who kindly read the Italian version of this chapter, drew my attention to two articles, one by Cornelius von Fabriczy (*Un Taccuino di Amico Aspertini*, in *L'Arte*, 1905, p. 401), attributing the *taccuino* to Aspertini, and the other by Carl Robert (*Ueber ein dem Michelangelo zugeschriebenes Skizzenbuch auf Schloss Wolfegg*, in *Mitteilungen des Kaiserlichen Deutschen Archaeologischen Instituts, Römische Abteilung*, XVI, 237, n. 1); both articles suggest a relation between the Wolfegg sketch, the Mattei Sarcophagus, and the drawing by Francesco di Giorgio.

Raphael borrowed from the sarcophagus, and whether his deviations from this model resulted from damage, misunderstanding, or other reasons.[1]

Gathering together the results of our inquiry, we can now turn back to the instruments in the fresco. The simplest case is that of the kithara: it is an example of almost literal transplantation. The only functional differences between Raphael's instrument and that of the sarcophagus concern the *kollopes*: some of them have survived until today in the sarcophagus instrument (Pl. 88a). Francesco's drawing shows them all, and this was evidently the condition at Raphael's time, since he accurately depicts the front arm of the kithara with the side disk of the yoke (in both the Oxford drawing and in the fresco). Thus we have here simply a lack of technical-functional understanding, and Raphael's way out of the dilemma was to omit what he did not comprehend.

The problem is solved differently in the case of Sappho's lyre. Here too, the ancient model (Pls. 86 & 87b) is an accurate copy of a real instrument: the points where both horns broke off are still visible; the yoke, completely preserved, is the usual one; rudiments of the *kollopes* on both sides of the yoke are preserved. But evidently there was only one horn remaining in Raphael's time, and this must have perturbed the copyist, who interpreted it as a plectrum, without noticing that the Muse holds a plectrum in her right hand (Pl. 85a). In short, the result is a fantastic machine for 'la dotta Sappho,' and Raphael, embarrassed by this pictorial reconstruction, did not even dare to sling the strings around the yoke.

Much more complex is the case of Euterpe's trumpet. We observed at the beginning of this essay that the shape of the tube, and especially of the cup-shaped mouthpiece pressed against Euterpe's thigh, belongs clearly to a trumpet. But the bell is strangely small and flat, and even stranger are the bulb beneath it and the four dark protuberances growing out of the tube. Comparing this with the sarcophagus (Pl. 87a), the solution is obvious: the features, inexplicable in a trumpet, are taken from the aulos. The result is acoustical nonsense: no

---

[1] There are, of course, other sarcophagi with representations of the nine Muses, but only one of them, that from the Villa Montalto (now in the British Museum), is in many respects similar to that from the Mattei collection. Its front shows the Muses in niches: the central one in a small niche, the other eight, in pairs, in four larger niches. The Muse with the lyre at her feet is the third from the right; the one holding the tibia is in the centre; and the one with the kithara is on the right. All these Muses are strikingly similar to those of the Mattei sarcophagus, and the same is true of their instruments. Nonetheless, I do not believe it was this sarcophagus that inspired Raphael or the sketches of Francesco di Giorgio and Aspertini. The attire of the Muse with the lyre differs from that of the corresponding Muse on the Mattei sarcophagus, and the Wolfegg sketch corresponds perfectly with the latter and not with that from the Villa Montalto. Also, the Montalto Muse with the tibia raises her right hand up to head level, while in the Mattei sarcophagus and the Wolfegg sketch the hand reaches only to shoulder height. Finally, the Muse who plays the kithara bends backwards in the Montalto sarcophagus but slightly forward in the Mattei version and the sketch by Francesco di Giorgio.

trumpet had soundholes to be stopped by the fingers, while no aulos had a cup-shaped mouthpiece. Moreover, the aulos had its mouthpiece, with oboe reed and bulb, on top; the trumpet in the fresco had its mouthpiece on the lower end. Here ignorance can hardly be the explanation; instruments of the oboe type — and the aulos was a double oboe — were quite common at that time, and even double oboes were frequently depicted in angel concerts. Furthermore, not only contemporary double oboes were known; the ancient aulos itself was evidently well understood in the Raphael circle. Perin del Vaga, for instance, who had worked in the Segnatura to replace the intarsias of Fra Giovanni da Verona by more up-to-date frescoes,[1] made a drawing (now in the Gabinetto dei Disegni of the Uffizi) showing Muses with masks and musical instruments; one of the Muses holds a mask and two pipes, strikingly similar in shape to the instrument held by Euterpe in the *Parnassus* — but functionally correct and with the lateral protuberances sketched in. Still more important, Raphael himself, according to the Oxford drawing, depicted a double pipe, and therefore the apparent absurdity of Euterpe's instrument cannot be explained by ignorance. We must assume rather that functional logic was intentionally subordinated to allegorical aims. Up to now, we have called the Muse carrying the strange wind instrument Euterpe[2] because, according to ancient iconography, it was Euterpe who carried the aulos. But in the fresco there was also needed a heroic-epic Muse — 'Calliope gesta canens' — and her traditional attribute, at least in Raphael's time, was the trumpet. Perhaps, too, the presence of two wind instruments would not have been appropriate on the Parnassus that echoes with the silvery sound of Apollo's lira da braccio.[3] Thus the aulos was fused with the trumpet, and the appearance of archaeological authenticity was combined with allegorical persuasion: Euterpe merged with Calliope.

Apollo's instrument presents no archaeological problems;[4] except for the number of strings, it is a life portrait of the common lira da braccio (Pl. 84a). The body, the heart-shaped head with frontal pegs, the two drone strings, etc., are all of typical shape. The instrument is identical with the lira da braccio played by one of the angels in Raphael's *Incoronazione* in the Vatican Pinacoteca.

Raphael has often been criticized for including in the *Parnassus*, and

[1] See Vasari, *Vite*, ed. Milanesi, IV, 337, and V, 130. About the intarsias, see fn. 1, p. 191 above.

[2] See fn. 1, p. 186 above.

[3] With admirable logic and iconographical taste, Raphael also abandoned the all-too-bucolic syrinx that appears in Marcantonio's engraving.

[4] For the figure of Apollo, the Mattei sarcophagus offered no model. The Apollo of Marcantonio's engraving seems to bear some resemblance to the type of seated player (Apollo or Orpheus) in the centre of another sarcophagus reproduced in the *Monumenta Matthaeiana*, Tab. XIII, under the title 'Metropolis cum diis tutelaribus.' It is not without interest that this relief shows, in the group of figures that surround the player, two persons in profile, crowned with laurels and comparable to Virgil and Dante in Raimondi's engraving.

especially in the hands of Apollo, a contemporary instrument,[1] the more so because it is a bowed fiddle, and bowing was a technique unknown to Greco-Roman antiquity. But this anachronism is in fact specious, for was it not Raphael's purpose in the Segnatura, and especially in the *Parnassus*, to merge antiquity with contemporary life, to show the noble figures of the past in conversation with their followers, to show 'Greci ed Eredi' as strands of the very same fabric of history? Dante had no qualms about letting himself be guided by Virgil. Why should not Petrarch and Ariosto be assembled with Sappho? In *The School of Athens*, the fusion is even more intense: Plato appears in the likeness of Leonardo, Bramante as Euclid, Michelangelo as Heraclitus; and in the Stanza d'Eliodoro, Julius II opposes Heliodorus, while Aeneas, travelling in the other direction, saves Anchises from the 9th-century *Incendio di Borgo*.

Moreover, the lira da braccio is often mentioned in Renaissance literature as an instrument of the ancients. This was also believed of the viola and, later, of the violin; in fact, the invention of the bow was attributed to the ancients and frequently to Sappho.[2] This belief went as far as to include archaeological fakes. Sylvestro Ganassi's *Regola Rubertina*, Venice, 1542, Pt. I, Ch. VIII, refers to ancient statues as the source of information for bowed instruments in antiquity:

[1] One recalls, for example, Goethe's *Wilhelm Meisters Theatralische Sendung*, Bk. 6, Ch. 9. After praising the beauty of the violinist Horatio, the poet observes: 'and when he at last grasped his instrument, one forgave Raphael for showing his Apollo with a violin instead of a lyre.'

[2] Bernardi, *Ragionamenti musicali*, Bologna, 1581, p. 45: 'Il violino fu inventato da Orfeo, figliuolo d'Apollo, e di Calliope. Safo Erista Poetessa antica inventò l'Arco con li crini di Cavallo e fu la prima, che suonasse il Violino, e Viola, come s'usa hoggidi, e questa fu 624 anni avanti la ventura del Signor Nostro Giesù Christo.' ('The violin was invented by Orpheus, son of Apollo and Calliope. The ancient poetess Sappho invented the bow fitted with horsehair, and was the first to use the violin and viola in the way they are used today; and this happened 624 years before the coming of Our Lord Jesus Christ.') The emblematic literature of the 16th and 17th centuries, when speaking of the lira, frequently quotes ancient and contemporary sources indiscriminately, and, even where a distinction is made between the 'lira col archeto' and the 'lira toccata dal plettro,' both forms are said to be ancient (see, for instance, P. Abb. Picinelli, *Del Mondo simbolico ampliato*, Lib. XXIII, Cap. V). In an Italian plaquette of the late 15th century (E. R. D. McLagan, *Catalogue of the Plaquettes of the Victoria and Albert Museum*, No. 95, 1865, Pl. IX), Apollo contending with Marsyas plays the kithara, but also keeps a bowed fiddle in reserve. The question of whether antiquity actually knew the fiddle bow remained quite undecided until well into the 18th century; Leopold Mozart, in the introduction to his *Versuch einer gründlichen Violinschule*, Salzburg, 1756, after quoting Zarlino and Tevo, says sceptically: 'Und wenn endlich Merkur ... das Recht zu seiner Leyer behält, solche auch nach ihm erst in die Hände des Apollo und Orpheus gekommen ist: wie lässt sich solche mit einem unserer heutigen Instrumenten vergleichen? Ist uns denn die eigentliche Gestalt dieser Leyer bekannt? Und können wir etwa den Merkur zu dem Urheber der Geiginstrumenten angeben... ?' ('And if, finally, Mercury ... is left with his claim to the lyre, and if this instrument only after him comes into the hands of Apollo and Orpheus, how can we compare it with one of our modern instruments? Do we really know the actual shape of that lyre, and are we really entitled to consider Mercury the inventor of the fiddle?')

Notice how the violone is made with six strings. I often wondered which was more ancient, the lute or the violone, when I wanted to describe its origin. Having discussed the question with various people, I recalled having seen among the antiquities of Rome, in a history with many marble figures, one figure who had in his hands a bowed viola similar to those mentioned above. There I immediately recognized that the violone was more ancient than the lute, on the evidence of the story of Orpheus, who is not mentioned as using the lute, but rather the instrument with strings and bow that is the lira, which with its strings and its bow is like the violone. But as to its name, it was lira or lirone, although most people call it violone. But it is more correct to call it lirone, and, in the plural, lironi, rather than violone or violoni; our evidence is based on Orpheus and his lyre. . . .[1]

Also Pierius Valerianus, in his *Hieroglyphica*, Basel, 1567, p. 346, includes, in an extensive chapter on the lira, a woodcut showing an ancient altar with a lira da braccio sculptured in relief on each of the four sides (Fig. 1 in Chapter 1 above),[2] evidently an imitation of the ancient type of altar with a lira or kithara on each of the four sides (such as that found in Vejo, now in the Lateran Museum). This confusion was no doubt facilitated by the name 'lira' and the presence of the two open strings. Accordingly, Pinturicchio's Musica in the Appartamenti Borgia and Pollaiuolo's Musica on the tomb of Pope Sixtus IV each hold a lira da braccio, as does a long line of Orpheuses, Apollos, King Davids, and countless angels in celestial concerts (for example in Perugino's *Assumption of the Virgin* in the Accademia, Florence). In all these cases — apart from the angel concerts, which follow their own iconographical tradition — the lira da braccio is the instrument of the solo player, usually accompanying his own song or recitation. This was precisely the case with recitation to the lyre or kithara in antiquity, and the Renaissance was fully aware of this. In this respect, Raphael was not deviating from convention.

But he was diverging in *one* respect: his lira da braccio has nine strings in place of the usual seven. The common *accordatura* consisted of five melody strings to be stopped against the fingerboard, and two open strings, running

---

[1] 'Nota bene come il violone è composto di sei corde, et più volte io pensava qual fosse più antico o il leuto o il violone per poter discrivere l'origine della cosa del che parlando con più persone sommi arricordato da uno haver visto nelle antighità di Roma in una historia di molte figure sculpite in marmo essergli una delle figure che haveva in mano una viola d'arco simile a queste, et subito conobbi ch'l fosse più antico il violone che il leuto per l'autorità ancora cavata d'Orfeo non si dice che lui usasse il leuto: ma ben lo istromento di corde, et arco che è la lira laqual è conforme di corde, et archetto come è il violone: ma ancora nel suo nome che è lira o lirone a ben che il più diceano violone: ma molto più è conforme al suo suggetto il nominarlo lirone et lironi molti insieme, che viole nè violoni: perchè l'autorità si cava di Orfeo per la sua lira. . . .'

[2] The text reads: 'huic autem a singulis angulis Lyrae appensae sunt, corymbis et sertis medio intervallo dependentibus. . . .'

outside the fingerboard and vibrating in their full length when plucked or bowed. We have mentioned above how familiar Raphael must have been with the lira da braccio, and thus a mistake concerning the number of strings is out of the question. The explanation can be found only on the allegorical plane: nine was frequently given as the number of Greek modes[1] as well as of the Muses. Baldassare Castiglione, if he was Raphael's adviser then, was probably too musical to symbolize the nine modes by nine strings; it would have been a superficial metaphor.[2] The Musagetes, inspiring the nine noble sisters, would not be beyond *cinquecento* concepts of allegorical numbers.

> *Mentis Apollinea vis has movet undique Musas,*
> *In medio residens complectitur omnia Phoebus.*[3]

In view of these problems, it seems less important whether Raphael, as has often been said, gave Apollo the likeness of Giacomo San Secondo, the famous virtuoso on the lira da braccio at the Court of Leo X. It is a fact that, at the time, solo players like San Secondo were among the most famous and most generously paid musicians,[4] but this, as far as I can see, is the only evidence

[1] Actually, different numbers are given in the ancient literature and, consequently, in the Renaissance writings. It is interesting that Zarlino in his *Istitutioni harmoniche*, Venice, 1558, p. 367, imputes to the philosopher Gaudentius the numbering of nine modes in music.

[2] In the Renaissance, symbolic significance was frequently attributed to the lyre. A long list of examples taken from ancient as well as modern sources is found in P. Abb. Picinelli, *op. cit.* (see fn. 2, p. 198 above). An example of number symbolism concerning the strings of the ancient lyre is found in Zarlino, *Istitutioni harmoniche*, Venice, 1573, p. 21: 'Questa tale harmonia troppo bene conobbero Mercurio et Terpandro; conciossia che l'uno havendo ritrovata la Lira, overamente la Cetra, pose in essa quattro chorde ad imitatione della Musica mondana (come dice Boetio et Macrobio) la quale si scorge ne i quattro Elementi, overo nella varieta de i quattro tempi dell'anno; et l'altro la ordino con sette corde alla similitudine de i sette Pianeti.' ('Such a harmony was well known to Mercury and Terpander, since the former invented the lyre or rather the cetra, and attached to it the four strings in imitation of the *Musica mondana* [i.e. the Pythagorean harmony of the universe] — according to Boëthius and Macrobius — that is, the music that we perceive in the four elements or in the difference between the four seasons; and the latter fixed it with seven strings, with reference to the seven planets.')
The same kind of symbolism is pointed out by Lanfranco (*Scintille di musica*, Brescia, 1533), who speaks of the correspondence between the seven strings of the lyre and the seven planets. Another kind of parallel we encounter in G. C. Capaccio, *Trattato delle imprese*, Naples, 1592, p. 23 verso: 'L'impresa di Napoli e rappresentata da una Sirena che si spreme latte dal petto con una lira da braccio in primo piano.' ('The emblem of Naples shows a Siren who squeezes milk from her breasts, with a lira da braccio in the foreground.' See Fig. 24 in Chapter 15 below.) The text explains that the lyre is symbolic, and that its six strings signify the union of 'cinque piazze di Nobili, e una Popolare' ('five piazzas of the nobility and one of the common people').

[3] Natalis Comes, *Mythologiae libri decem*, Padua, 1616, p. 583: 'The spirit of Apollo forcefully moves these Muses; residing among them, he embraces the universe.' See also Franchino Gafurius, *Theorica musice*, Bk. I, p. 2.

[4] On this point, see E. P. Rodocanachi, *La première renaissance, Rome au temps de Jules II et de Leon X*, Paris, 1912, p. 107; Jakob Burckhardt, *Die Kultur der Renaissance in Italien*, Leipzig, 1926, p. 342; Jan Lauts, *Isabella d'Este*, Hamburg, 1952, p. 55 ff.

proferred for this alleged identification.[1] A portrait of San Secondo has not survived, as far as I know, although the portrait of a musician in the Galleria Sciarra has occasionally been connected with San Secondo.[2]

It may be found surprising, by the way, that neither the *Parnassus* nor the *Scuola*, both so liberal in the inclusion of contemporary thinkers, admit any composers, though masters such as Ockeghem, Obrecht, Isaac, Josquin des Près, Pierre de la Rue, Brumel, Agricola, Orto, and Mouton were then in the flower of their glory. Two reasons seem probable: first, the great contemporary composers were famous chiefly for their *musica sacra*, which, as polyphony, could hardly have sounded well on Parnassus; as for the profane frottolas and madrigals, they were also polyphonic, as well as too light to be represented by composers of such fame. Secondly, Raphael's archaeological advisers may have felt, and rightly so, that ancient musical life gravitated around poetry and that it was the rhapsodists, the solo recitalists, who were the prototypes of the ancient musician. The allegorical figure on the ceiling of the Segnatura over the *Parnassus* shows the winged Poesia with a book in her right hand, a lyre in her left, and the bust of Homer decorating her throne.

In this gigantic allegory of the Beautiful, so radically and ingeniously departing from the traditional and still basically medieval cliché of Musica (as one of the *artes liberales*), Raphael, the Pope's new Superintendent of Antiquities, intuitively found his way back to the ancient conception. This was the first systematic attempt to employ ancient models with *intenzione antichizzanda*. It was not only an important step in pictorial symbolism, but also in humanist archaeology, long before the contemporary literature on the subject had advanced to this point, and before precise woodcuts or engravings have been made of the ancient instruments. Not before the literature of the Baroque was this subject tackled seriously and systematically, and wherever the instruments of the ancients are treated there, it is done with explicit references to the instruments in Raphael's *Parnassus*. But that is another story.[3]

[1] Such an identification must have already seemed suspect to Burckhardt, who wrote: 'Anyone who finds the violin objectionable should blame only Raphael himself; in no case is the present anachronism the result of an instruction to celebrate a famous contemporary virtuoso, who, by the way, is considered by some authors to have been also a valet of the Pope. In all probability, the violin offered the painter a more lively and telling motif than an ancient lyre' (*Cicerone*, Leipzig, 1925, p. 865).

[2] Cf. E. P. Rodocanachi, *op. cit.*, p. 108.

[3] As for the enormous impact made by Raphael's *Parnassus* on later painters, see above all the interesting study by A. P. de Mirimonde, *Les Concerts des muses chez les maîtres du Nord*, in *Gazette des beaux-arts*, March, 1964, which also deals with the problem of 'realistic' depiction of ensembles, complicated in concerts of Muses by the symbolic significance of instruments as attributes.

15 · The Inspired Musician: A 16th-Century Musical Pastiche

In the unending stream of combinations and recombinations that is the life of forms, two main types can be distinguished. An artist may borrow two or more images, combining them into a new composition, without however changing their content or significance. Or he may change a borrowed or inherited image to make it carry a new meaning. Both types occur frequently, but we do not often find a combination of both procedures, namely, a fusion of borrowed images into a new unity which is the carrier of a new message. Such a case can be seen in the picture which is the subject of this chapter (Pl. 91). It was evidently painted by an Italianate Dutch or Flemish artist towards the middle of the 16th century.[1]

A youth and a girl face each other against the background of a deep, luminous mountain landscape. Both have serious, deeply absorbed expressions, but, unlike lovers, avoid each other's gaze. The youth is evidently a musician, holding in his left hand a typical 16th-century viol, and in his right hand, with awkward grip, the bow. The girl, half-nude and crowned with laurel, also holds the viol with her left hand, while the right squeezes from her breast milk, which falls upon the instrument in four thin silver streams. This certainly is no love scene. Their glances do not meet, and the instrument separates them. The meaning is apparent: we have here an allegory of the creative artist together with the crowned Muse who inspires him by baptizing the instrument of his art with the nourishing liquid.

The allegory is quite unusual considering its date. It represents the inspiration of the artist, the musician in the act of receiving the divine afflatus at a time

[1] This picture was illustrated in *The Burlington Magazine*, Dec. 1950, p. 366, in the advertising supplement under 'Notable Works of Art now on the Market,' with the title '*Allegory* by Jan van Hemessen.' I was so intrigued by the allegory, its connection with Titian and other prototypes, and by the musical instrument, that I wrote to the owner, the Arcade Gallery Ltd., which kindly supplied me with a photograph. Since then I have found the painting in excellently cleaned condition in the collection of my former colleague at the Metropolitan Museum of Art, Mr. Theodore A. Heinrich, now Director of the Royal Ontario Museum, who attributes the painting to Jan van Scorel and dates it 1525–30. Earlier attributions which I encountered while studying the painting were to Gossaert, Massys, and Swart van Groningen; however, as a teacher of the history of music and curator of musical instruments I am in the fortunate position of being able to leave the crossing of the attributional Rubicon to others.

when it was not yet customary to depict a contemporary musician as an inspired being, as *ingegno*, as pioneering genius, as creator.

Images of Apollo, Orpheus, King David, with their various instruments — changing from period to period — come down through the centuries in an almost unbroken line from antiquity; the noble figure of Musica appears among the *quadrivium* as one of the *artes liberales*.[1] Mythological figures, such as the Muses, Pan, and Marsyas, became familiar again in the *quattrocento*. But it was not before the Romantic movement of the early 18th century and the age of Shaftesbury that musical genius — that is, a contemporary musician in the state of inspiration — became an accepted subject.

In other fields, the portrayal of inspiration is a different story: St. Matthew's stylus was inspired by the angel in countless medieval illuminations. The poet already appeared among the Muses on numerous Roman sarcophagi, a motif which is retained and intensified in the wonderful 5th-century ivory diptych in the cathedral of Monza, where in one tablet the poet is shown listening attentively to the music played on the kithara by the Muse in the facing tablet (Pl. 89b). Homer and Virgil, Dante and Petrarch, Ariosto and Pietro Bembo are admitted to the company of the Muses in Raphael's *Parnassus*, but no musicians, not even a Josquin or a Dufay; and the artisans — sculptors, painters, or architects — do not fare any better. Even Michelangelo could only make his appearance in Raphael's *School of Athens* when camouflaged as Heraclitus.[2] Similarly, Bramante needs the garb and pose of the prophet Joel to be admitted to the Sistine ceiling.

And when artists insert their self-portraits into frescoes or paintings to be near their painted saints or to secure visual immortality, they do so modestly. This is the case, for instance, with Ghiberti peering out of the frame of the Porta del Paradiso, with Masaccio in the Brancacci Chapel, with Orcagna who put his likeness into the marble relief of the *Death of the Virgin* on the tabernacle in Or San Michele, and with Raphael modestly sharing the company of the philosophers in the *School of Athens*. In these and many more cases it is the likeness of the artist which is immortalized, but he is never shown in the act of creation or in a state of inspiration.

It cannot, of course, be the purpose of this study to sketch the changing iconography of the inspired musician, but a few words may not be amiss on the ideas and the spiritual climate that determined the early formation of this image.

[1] There she is often accompanied by that bearded man with hammers who stands sometimes for Tubalcain, the inventor of musical instruments, sometimes for the blacksmith whose hammer sounds led Pythagoras to make his acoustical investigations, sometimes even for Pythagoras himself.

[2] See Deoclecio Redig de Campos, *Raffaello e Michelangelo*, Rome, 1946, p. 155.

The Pythagorean philosophy of numbers as modified by the Platonists and the Stoa conceived of Musica as the theory of proportions, as the rational science of the divine order of the cosmos, and therefore put music in the *quadrivium* together with arithmetic, geometry, and astronomy. In Augustine's famous definition of music as *scientia bene modulandi*, the term *modulari* signifies not only 'mode' as form of the musical scale, but also and chiefly the mathematical term 'modulus.' In the medieval treatises Musica retained — if not augmented — her noble position among the liberal arts. Or so one would believe if one reads in Giraldus de Cambrai that 'sine Musica nulla disciplina potest esse perfecta,' and finds in Aquinas that 'Musica inter septem artes liberales sola tenet principatum.' In fact this esteem had by that time increasingly become lip service: the Platonic-Stoic rational inquiry into the laws of the universe by investigating its mathematical proportions no longer had any place within Christian cosmology; the *ars musica* could no longer serve as a main road towards cognition of God and His creation, and therefore was gradually reduced to a theory of the musical intervals and to technical rules for making music *ad majorem Dei gloriam*.[1] This notion of Musica was absorbed by *quattrocento* humanism and — at least for sacred music — retained authority in the treatises of the theorists for more than two centuries and well into the Baroque.

The position of music in the *quadrivium* could not fail to give scholarly standing to the musicians — theorists, organists, and choirmasters. But it left little chance for a conception of the musician as creator in the deeper sense of this word. The emphasis was on the rules of composition, not on free creation. The customary musical images were the figure of Musica itself, usually depicted on her throne in the *quadrivium*; the twenty-four elders with their musical instruments; and above all the multitude of musical angels singing, dancing, and playing. King David, the musician, is an exception in that he is often shown as a solitary, sometimes even enraptured instrumentalist, but this is due in all likelihood to the affiliation of his early depictions with those of Orpheus in late antiquity. At any rate, it is significant that of the multitude of Renaissance portraits of musicians, hardly a single one shows more fire, let alone rapture, than would befit a master or teacher. Apart from the portraits, all with serious or pensive

---

[1] It is remarkable that the doctrine of the *quadrivium* had a quite different and in a certain sense contrary effect on the visual arts and the social status of the artists. While Musica as a science of proportion gradually lost her cosmological importance and thereby her central position in philosophical speculation, it was just the doctrine of proportions which became the preoccupation of the draughtsmen of the *quattrocento* and their rational-mathematically 'correct' portrayal of nature. Perspective became the new science-art and the vogue of the century, and consequently the painter ascended from the level of artisan to the rank of scholar. And Pollaiuolo merely put the seal on a completed evolution when — in need of an eighth figure for the decoration of the tomb of Sixtus IV — he added the figure of Prospettiva to the figures of the *quadrivium* and *trivium*.

expression, we find the master teaching, or at the organ, or offering his compositions to the Pope or to a secular patron. It would be grossly anachronistic to imagine a portrait of Palestrina in the transfigured pose that Gluck attains in Duplessis's grandiose painting, or in the pose that Ingres gives to Cherubini, with the monumental muse holding her blessing hand over the composer's head.

At the beginning of the Renaissance a new road opens toward the conception and depiction of the inspired musician through the direct turn to the mythological imagery of the ancients and the influence of neo-Platonic theories developed in Florence. Now pictures of Orpheus, Apollo, and Homer abound as allegories of poetic and musical inspiration. But characteristically this was not in the field of church music, where the medieval world of rules continues to prevail, but where invention and execution coincided: in the field of improvisation. It is no accident that the countless images of mythological musicians appear precisely in an age of celebrated virtuosi who improvise the accompaniment to their recitation on the lira da braccio or viol or lute. Understandably and lamentably not one note of their admired performances is preserved; neither do we know exactly how many paintings and prints of Apollo and Orpheus were portraits of actual musicians or poets of the day,[1] but in some cases the identity is established.[2] All the mythical musicians, however, whether they charm animals, or force the gates of Hades, or meditate, fiddle in hand, against the melancholy of the evening sky, are mere symbols of the power of music, and some, the solitary fiddlers and lutenists, possibly signify inspiration. Yet there is not another example of the scene shown in our painting, the allegorical baptism of the musician's instrument by the maternal muse.

If we find the content of our picture to be quite exceptional for its time, it may be even more surprising to find that this allegory is, in fact, composed of elements borrowed almost literally from other sources. One of these sources is evidently the famous mirror back, the *Patera Martelli* (Pl. 89a), or, more precisely, its right half. The correspondence between the bacchante there and our muse is quite obvious: the same profile view, the same nude torso with drapery falling from the right shoulder over the back, the same jets of milk. In the *Patera*, however, the milk flows into a drinking horn, evidently to be offered to the satyr opposite her. Streams of ink have been shed over the *Patera*, its meaning

---

[1] Raphael's enraptured Apollo playing the nine-stringed lira da braccio in the Segnatura has repeatedly been considered as a portrait of Giacomo San Secondo, the celebrated virtuoso on the lira da braccio at the court of Leo X, but this assumption has little basis in fact; see Chapter 14.

[2] See, for example, the print of the poet-musician Giovanni Filoteo Achillini playing the guitar, in Adam Bartsch, *Le Peintre graveur*, Vienna, 1802–21, Vol. XIV, 349, 469; Arthur M. Hind, *Marcantonio and Italian Engravers and Etchers of the 16th Century*, London, 1912, Pl. XI; Henri Delaborde, *Marcantoine Raimondi*, Paris, 1888, p. 252.

and its maker,[1] and this is not the place to augment this flood except to discuss two details that may have interested our painter. The *Patera* contains two musical instruments: the syrinx made of seven pipes in the centre and a small double oboe, the Lydian aulos, suspended beneath, both wind instruments and of Dionysiac connotation. The *Patera* also includes other symbols of generation and of the orgiastic realm of Dionysus: the little priapic herm and the *thyrsoi* tipped with pine cones behind the satyr and in front of the bacchante. Perhaps the gesture of the satyr's left hand[2] belongs to the same realm.

The artist who painted our picture was led to adapt the female figure to a new function. Laurel has replaced the vine, the animal skin has become a very civilized silk. The inclination of the head is less marked since her eyes are no longer fixed on the drinking horn. The left arm of the bacchante in the *Patera* was thrown back to enable the hand to squeeze the breast; now the upper arm falls so that the hand may grasp the viol.

The allegory of the muse inspiring the creative mind with her milk is of course an old one. Dante (*Purg.* XXII, 101) in the Poet's Limbo refers to no less a poet than Homer with the words, 'siam con quel Greco che le Muse lattàr più ch'altro mai,' and since then, it seems, this allegorical motive has lived on. Capaccio, *Trattato delle imprese*, Naples, 1592, p. 23, illustrates as the emblem of the city of Naples a siren squeezing milk from her breasts which falls on a lira da braccio (Fig. 24).[3]

---

[1] The *Patera Martelli* exists in several casts, of which the best belongs to the Victoria and Albert Museum (8717–1863). Another is in the Museo Nazionale at Florence (Pl. 89a). Its attribution to Donatello by Bode and others has been unanimously rejected in the last decades. The satyr and bacchante exist in separate Renaissance plaquettes: the Berlin Museum has plaquettes of both subjects (293, 294); the Victoria and Albert Museum, the bacchante (A48–1912). These plaquettes are copied after ancient models, a number of which still exist in various museums. (See *Catalogue of Italian Plaquettes*, Victoria and Albert Museum, London, 1924, p. 11.) I cannot exclude, of course, the possibility that our painter saw only a plaquette with the bacchante, although the connection with musical instruments and symbolism exists only in the *Patera*.

[2] Familiar still to Italians today as one of the protective magic gestures against *malocchio*.

[3] Capaccio's text explains the instruments as a symbol of Concordia: 'La Lira, significò la Concordia, che per quel celeste Simolacro se la dipingono propria i Napolitani in braccio d'una Sirena, e di sei corde, per l'unione di cinque piazze di Nobili, e una Popolare. Ma non parue a me buona mai l'Impresa di Sirena, mai di cosa buona significatrice, sempre fraudolenta, e che inganna; e direi che più tosto e Impresa per significar le delitie, e i gusti della Città, alludendo alla dolce, e delitiosa Partenope.' A true iconologist will not fail to consult his sacred books — Ripa, Cartari, etc.— and he will find direct relations not only with 'benignity,' but also with 'fecundity of the inventive mind.' Cesare Ripa, in his *Iconologia*, Rome, 1603, includes a woodcut showing Poesia, with the upper half of the body nude and with several musical instruments, among them a syrinx and a lirone (a large lira da braccio). The text explains that the breasts full of milk signify the wealth of ideas and inventions that are the soul of poetry ('mostrano la fecondità de' concetti & dell inventioni che sono l'anima della poesia'). In a similar pose, though with a different meaning, Charity (*Benignità*) is depicted and explained (see Ripa, 1618 ed., pp. 43, 66). I am indebted to Mr. Benedict Nicolson for drawing my attention to

Fig. 24. Emblem of the City of Naples. From Capaccio, *Trattato delle imprese*, Naples, 1592.

While the right half of the *Patera* thus provided the model for the right half of the picture, one can hardly say the same of the left half, and it would probably be an over-estimation of the rejuvenating power of milk to relate the elderly satyr in the *Patera* to the youth in the picture. In any case it is quite obvious that the youth is not a free invention, but is borrowed from some other source. One has only to look at the unnatural position of the right hand that holds the bow. The model is apparently the naked youth at the left of Titian's *Three Ages of Man* in the Ellesmere Collection, exhibited in the National Gallery of Scotland (Pl. 90).[1] Here again, pose and contours, even the unruly hair, are almost identical; variations occur only so far as they help to adapt the figure to its new emotional and allegorical purpose. Complete clothing makes him a contemporary musician and therefore emphasizes the gap between a mortal musician and his mythological counterpart. The left arm now holds the viol, the right the bow. The right knee is lifted a little higher to support the instrument. One is tempted to assume that if the painter of our allegorical canvas did not see the

Giovanni Serodine's allegorical painting in the Ambrosiana as another possible example of lacteal baptism. On close inspection, I could detect only two very short stripes reaching upwards from the nipple of the right breast, but no trace of milk falling on the instrument. This instrument, by the way, is not a lute (as it is called in Schoenenburger, *G. Serodine*, Basle, 1957, p. 63), but a cittern (*cetra*), which sometimes has a symbolic connotation different from that of the lute.

[1] An attribution of our musical allegory to Van Scorel would coincide quite well with the date of Titian's *Three Ages*; Van Scorel went to Venice in 1520 and in 1522 to Rome, and Titian's *Three Ages* was painted early in his Giorgionesque period. Vasari dates the painting 1515. When I discussed the painting with Mr. Heinrich, I was glad to find that he also had related this figure to the Titian painting.

Titian painting itself, he was at least familiar with a print of it, and, though to my belief no print of it is known, one may assume that one existed because Titian's painting evidently served as a model through a print for other works of art — for example, the right side of an ivory relief of the *Infancy of Bacchus* in the Bavarian National Museum. Characteristically, the borrowed group appears there in reverse.[1]

Since our picture is a musical allegory and the musical instrument appropriately takes the centre of the scene (as the tool of a sacred art) between the symbolic figure and the artist from our world, a few words on the instrument itself and those in the *Patera* and in Titian's painting may be added.

As in our painting, in both the *Patera* and Titian's *Three Ages of Man* musical instruments are placed between the male and female figure. But these are wind instruments, while our painting shows a string instrument. This is quite in line with the symbolism connected with these instruments ever since antiquity and retained throughout the centuries in manifold modifications. The dichotomy between the two realms of strings and winds — with its emotional, aesthetic, religious, and social implications — is one of the most interesting chapters of the history of music and especially of musical instruments, and can only be hinted at here.[2] However, a few comments on the instrument in our painting and in its models may not be amiss and may even help to throw light on the allegorical intentions of our painter.

The syrinx and the aulos in the centre of the *Patera* do not appear in the two oval Renaissance plaquettes each of which shows separately one of the figures from the *Patera* (*e.g.* 645, 646 of the Berlin Museum).[3] It is evidently only in the original *Patera*, itself a *pasticcio*, that these two instruments appear, quite appropriately so between the satyr and the bacchante, together with other Dionysian attributes. The simpler of the two instruments is the syrinx, the traditional attribute of Pan, satyrs, shepherds, and the languishing Polyphemus of countless representations which were then adapted by *cinquecento* artists.[4]

---

[1] See Rudolf Berliner, *Die Bildwerke des Bayerischen Nationalmuseums*, Augsburg, 1926, IV, p. 93, Pl. 418 and 420.

[2] See Chapters 2, 4, and 14 above.

[3] See *Königliche Museen zu Berlin, Katalog, Bildwerke der christlichen Epoche*, Berlin, 1918, Pl. XLVII; *Catalogue of Italian Plaquettes*, Victoria and Albert Museum, 1924, xv.

[4] See, for example, the *Polyphemus* by Sebastiano del Piombo in the Villa Farnesina, and the one by Annibale Caracci in the ceiling frescoes of the Palazzo Farnese. Raphael, in one of the early stages of his *Parnassus* known to us in Marcantonio's engraving, gave the syrinx also to Erato, contrary to ancient tradition. Only later did he correct this deviation from ancient models when the strong current of humanist musical archaeology led him to borrow the instruments directly from an authentic ancient source, a Roman sarcophagus of the Muses, and to replace the syrinx by an aulos (see Chapter 14 above). Refer also to the seven-pipe syrinx carefully depicted by Filippino Lippi in his monochrome fresco on the window wall of the Cappella Strozzi in Santa Maria Novella. Strangely enough it is a musical treatise, Vincenzo

The more complicated instrument is the aulos (tibia), the attribute of Marsyas and the traditional requisite of revelry and Bacchic processions; in the Rome of the emperors it was also the never-absent accompaniment of animal sacrifice. Curiously, both the syrinx and the aulos of the *Patera* deviate in their design from their usual ancient representation. The syrinx, contrary to ancient tradition,[1] consists of two rows each of five pipes; in the two pipes of the aulos the fingerholes continue up the extreme end of each pipe, which acoustically is nonsense.

Small as these details may seem, they imply that the artist of the *Patera* was not entirely familiar with the ancient instruments he represented; an ancient sculptor would not have made such errors, even in a small background representation. But it is quite interesting that the Italian sculptor who united the two ancient figures in the *tondo* filled in the vacuum in the centre with appropriate ancient Dionysian attributes.

It is no less in the spirit of the ancients that Titian in his allegorical picture furnishes the loving couple with double pipes. The double pipes are not only symbolic of the vague association of Eros with music in a general sense, but actually link the two figures. He substitues 16th-century recorders for ancient oboes and thus is able to combine the seeming antiquity of the instruments with the actual contemporary technique of playing.[2]

Finally, our painting with the baptism by milk does not show an ancient instrument nor the reinterpretation of an ancient one, but represents instead a modern string instrument. It is a typical viol of the time, clearly recognizable by its deep body, its sloping shoulders, and its five strings. Viols of this shape with rounded contours without corners were not uncommon (specimens are preserved in the collection of the Vienna Kunsthistorisches Museum[3]), and the

---

Galilei's *Dialogo*, in a chapter on the plectrum of the ancients, which states that Filippino borrowed directly from ancient statuary and was advised by a humanist of no lesser stature than a Poliziano (see Chapter 13 above).

[1] See, for example, the bronze satyr from the Villa of Hadrian, now in the Museo Capitolino, who dances while the syrinx made of seven pipes hangs from the trunk of a tree. As one of many examples of the accurate use of the orthodox classical form of the syrinx in 16th-century symbolism, see Cartari, *Imagini*, 1581, with its beautiful woodcut of Pan holding a syrinx of seven pipes.

[2] This practice was quite common in the 14th and 15th centuries. One could enumerate a long line of examples, from Cossa's Schifanoia *Triumph of Venus*, in which a lady holds a double recorder in aulos fashion, to the double recorders in Rubens' *Triumph of Silenus* in the National Gallery, London. A similar adaptation is to be seen in Giulio Romano's *tondo* in Mantua in the Palazzo del Tè, Sala delle Medaglie, showing the sacrifice of a bull. Two musicians blow shawms which are so close to each other and held at such angles as to give the precise appearance of the two pipes of the aulos required by the ritual scene.

[3] See J. von Schlosser, *Die Sammlung alter Musikinstrumente*, Vienna, 1920, Nos. 71, 73, 74 (all 16th century). These specimens came from the famous Hapsburg Collection in the castle of Ambras in Tyrol.

four *C* holes also appear frequently, for instance in the viols played by angels in Grünewald's Isenheim Altar, in an engraving of a musician by Altdorfer, and in the instruments played by Apollo and one of the Muses in Luca Penni's *Parnassus*. The choice of a string instrument for our symbolical scene is quite significant, for these string instruments (lute, lira da braccio, viol) in the hands of the great virtuosi and *improvvisatori* were the tools of the most subtle and refined province of musical art.[1]

[1] On the subject of this article, see also my review of Günther Bandmann, *Melancholie und Musik, Ikonographische Studien* (Cologne, 1960), in *The Burlington Magazine*, April 1962; this work takes over the material of the present essay, but unfortunately with the addition of some misinterpretations.

16 · Musical Instruments for the Stage in Paintings by Filippino Lippi, Piero di Cosimo, and Lorenzo Costa

Italian feasts of the 15th and 16th centuries were full of music, both vocal and instrumental. Anyone who browses through the documents and *carteggi* will be overwhelmed by the profusion of details concerning the solo instruments and whole orchestras used in the *sacre rappresentazioni, intermedii*, and at many other festival occasions such as *trionfi*, weddings, funerals, and the spectacles that were the immediate precursors of the opera of the 17th century.

A concise interpretation of this material requires the synoptic study of numerous documents, such as records of the plans for spectacles and reports about them; the texts of plays; the visual material — paintings, drawings, and prints depicting the spectacles for posterity, as well as sketches made for their preparation; and the scores of the music that accompanied the spectacles. It may very well have been the complexity and variety of this material that has hampered systematic exploration. Often contemporary historians left detailed reports but no visual records came to us; in other cases, we have paintings or engravings that probably represent *feste* or were inspired by them, but we have no verbal reports by contemporaries to match them.

What the historian of music could hope to learn from this material would be the types of orchestras and ensembles used, the principles of alternation of vocal and instrumental groups, the fashions of accompaniment of solo singers and choirs, the various devices of *cori spezzati*, echo effects, and the like. With such ends in view, he could, for instance, approach such a painting as the Carpaccio *Ascension of the Virgin* (National Gallery, London), where we find no less than five different groups of angels with instruments distributed from the middle ground over the death bed up to the heavens, and relate it to reports such as that by Niccolò della Tuccia on the festivities of the Corpus Domini in Viterbo in 1462, where one could hear 'a singing of the hosts of the heavenly spirits, playing of magic instruments, frolicking, gesturing, laughter of all the heavens.'[1]

For the present study, we are interested only in a very small segment of this

[1] Sebastiano Ciampi, *Cronache e statuti di Viterbo*, Florence, 1852, Lib. VIII, p. 384 ff., quoted in Alessandro d'Ancona, *Origini del teatro in Italia*, Florence, 1877.

instrumental world: the bizarre instruments frequently represented in paintings of the *quattro-* and *cinquecento* that do not seem to fit into the gradual evolution of instruments from the *quattrocento* to the beginning of the Baroque. They are sometimes utterly fantastic in shape, sometimes more or less authentic reconstructions of ancient Greco-Roman instruments, and other times bastard forms between the latter and contemporary instruments. Some of the instruments so depicted seem unplayable, constructed by the painter's brush with no attention paid to functional or acoustical requirements; others, in spite of their unconventional nature, seem so well thought out that one has to consider them as instruments either portrayed after actual specimens or, at least, designed with so much musical and technological understanding that they might have been played.

For our purpose, we may single out paintings by Piero di Cosimo, Filippino Lippi, and Lorenzo Costa. The painting by Lippi that interests us here is his *Dance Before the Bull* (National Gallery, London), usually called — or, rather, misnamed — *The Adoration of the Golden Calf* (Pl. 93). This painting has provoked various iconographical interpretations.[1] One thing is certain: the dancing crowd adoring the bull is Oriental or Greek, judging by their garb, especially the turbans.[2] The numerous instruments represented are a strange mixture of contemporary and ancient shapes. The wind instrument at the left is a trumpet, coiled in S-shape, the form imported to Europe from the Near East and still frequently appearing in the *quattrocento* (for instance, in Fra Angelico's *Madonna dei Linaiuoli*, in the convent of San Marco in Florence). Likewise of oriental origin and frequent in the *quattrocento* is the pair of small kettledrums (*nacchere*) at the right of our painting; we find similar drums in the grandiose and, I believe, not sufficiently studied fresco of an angel concert by Michele Lambertini, in the large arch that separates the apse from the central vault in the Baptistery of the Cathedral of Siena. Another frequent *quattrocento* instrument is the tambourine or, more precisely, jingle drum, played in our painting by the second figure from the left. It is one of the few instruments that lived virtually unchanged from antiquity, where we find it depicted in numerous Bacchic sarcophagi, until the Renaissance and even later.

This leaves three instruments depicted *all'antica* but reconstructed with various degrees of reliability. The large coiled brass instrument towards the

[1] Katherine B. Neilson, *Filippino Lippi*, Cambridge, Mass., 1938, p. 153, gives a tentative interpretation of this scene; Otto Kurz, in his very interesting article, *Filippino Lippi's 'Worship of Apis*,' in *The Burlington Magazine*, LXXXIX (1947), p. 145 ff., explains the subject of painting as the adoration of Serapis by the Egyptians, as narrated in Petrus Comestor, *Historia scholastica, liber exodi*, Cap. IV (Migne, *Patrologia latina 198*, 1143).

[2] Greeks are frequently depicted with turbans; see the Pythagoras in Pinturicchio's fresco showing Musica, in the Borgia Apartments.

right (Pl. 94b) is a true Roman *buccina*, so accurately depicted in shape, proportions, and essential details, including its characteristic crossbar, that it must have been modelled after one of the Roman reliefs showing military processions. Roman military instruments were frequently depicted in the triumphs of the Renaissance, often with great archaeological precision, as for instance in Mantegna's *Triumph of Julius Caesar* (now in Hampton Court): '. . . when he painted in Mantua the triumphs of Julius Caesar, a rewarding topic for revealing the profound archaeological erudition he possessed in his time and his inclination to learn from ancient statuary.'[1] Another *Triumph*, following ancient models but with remarkable archaeological fidelity, is the relief made for Alphonso I, in the Castel Nuovo, Naples.

Much freer is the rendering of the kithara to the left of the buccina (seen also in Pl. 94b). While its design also stems fairly directly from ancient models (probably from sarcophagi of Muses or Marsyas), and while its functional character is evident, its shape has been simplified and, furthermore, it is embellished with typical Renaissance leaves.

The most puzzling instrument is the complex brass instrument played by the third figure from the left in the painting (Pl. 94c). This consists of two parallel metal tubes connected by two crossbars, both tubes ending in small bells; the player blows into the longer of the tubes. No instrument of this fantastic construction existed in antiquity or in the Renaissance. Still, the origin of the design can easily be detected. The instrument is a pictorial substitute for the ancient aulos, that double oboe required in ceremonial or sacrificial scenes. Similar more or less fantastic attempts to create the visual appearance of the aulos, which was not always functionally understood at that time, are quite frequent in Renaissance imagery. In Giulio Romano's *tondo* in the Palazzo del Tè, Mantua, representing the sacrifice of a bull, the appearance of an aulos is simulated by two large shawms played in the background by two different players, in such a way that the two tubes diverge at the same angle as the two pipes of an aulos usually do. A very subtle fusion of the aulos with the trumpet of Fama, for allegorical reasons, appears in Raphael's *Parnassus*.[2]

Yet the instruments depicted in Filippino's *Adoration of the Bull*, especially the 'ancient' ones, do not seem to be merely pictorial *staffage*, made to characterize the crowd as a musical one; they are painted with such a degree of realism that the spectator would expect to see their backs if he could only turn them around. One can hardly resist the belief that the painter must have seen them as real three-dimensional objects. Actually, such real instruments, however bizarre or fantastic, were used in the mythological plays or allegorical representations

[1] Milanesi, in his comments to his edition of Vasari, *Vite*, III, 458.
[2] See Chapter 14 above.

occurring in *intermedii*, *sacre rappresentazioni*, and other forms of theatrical display. Here, especially the kithara would point in this direction. Its simplified shape omits the resonating body; it could therefore have provided only very little volume of tone and was employed for its evocative appearance rather than for its sound.

The instruments are by no means the only details in Lippi's painting that remind us of the stage. The two symmetrical hills form stage wings, sharply dividing the foreground from the background and opening the vista on the distant sea. The straight line of dancers in the foreground, all equally near to the beholder, also strongly evokes stage design. Last but not least, the appearance of the bull in the sky corresponds strikingly to the numerous figures appearing in or descending from the sky that were quite routine in Renaissance stage machinery. It would have been easy to move the bull across the sky with the help of wires or ropes stretched between the two artificial hills, or with the help of unseen levers.

These strange features appear even more pronounced in Piero di Cosimo's famous *cassone* painting of *The Liberation of Andromeda* in the Uffizi (Pl. 92). This painting shows two successive phases of the liberation, with Perseus appearing in both. On the right, he is shown descending from the sky, in precisely the same manner as did many angels and deities on the Renaissance stage with the help of special machines (of which perhaps the most famous example is Brunelleschi's *macchina* devised for the descent of the Archangel Gabriel and eight other angels in the spectacles for the *Festa della Nunziata*[1]). In the centre of our picture, Perseus appears again, standing on the sea monster's shoulders[2] and reaching out to deliver the mortal blow. At the left, Andromeda is fainting, while the crowd averts its glance. At the right, however, we find the same crowd jubilant over her delivery and, in addition, there are two exotic musicians with strange instruments (Pl. 95a). The instrument at the left is held by a kneeling youth; it has a small sound box, which continues in an extremely long neck that termin-

[1] See Vasari, *Vite*, ed. Milanesi, II, 375 ff. Similar *macchine* were designed by Il Cecca for the *sacre rappresentazioni* on the Piazza del Carmine in Florence, where the cherubim and seraphim came down from heaven to announce to Christ 'il suo dover salire in cielo' (Vasari, *op. cit.*, III, 198). See also Sabbatini, *Pratica di fabricar scene e machine ne' teatri*, Ravenna, 1638, where these machines are explained in every technical detail, with illustrations, especially in Chapters 44 and 50.

[2] Similar sea monsters, dragons, and large serpents were extremely frequent on the Renaissance stage, and even outside, in processions such as the Provençal *tarrasca*. The *certamen pithicum* was a persistent element on the stage in Renaissance pageants. Gioseffo Zarlino, in his *Istitutioni harmoniche*, Venice, 1573, Pt. II, p. 79, mentions among the subjects recited by the ancients in their musical performances, 'la Battaglia di Apolline col serpente Pithone.' This combat was later the subject, for instance, of the third of the six *intermedii* performed in 1589 for the wedding of the Grand Duke Ferdinand I de' Medici to Christina of Lorraine, a spectacle of which we will speak later.

ates in a sickle-shaped peg box with side pegs. The upper end of the sound box tapers into a shape resembling the breast, neck, and head of a swan. Three strings run across the soundboard and over the neck to the peg box. This instrument, notwithstanding its fantastic shape, has a perfectly functional construction; its player is shown tuning it.

The other instrument, played by a dark-skinned musician in exotic garb, is much more complex: it has a large sound box, with seven strings running over two bridges. The upper end of the sound box continues in what seem to be two tubes, one short and the other a long one, bent back to run parallel to the side of the sound box. After this bend, the tube develops a bulbous extension in the shape of an animal head. Further down, we notice five side-holes and then a round bulb like that of a platerspiel (a simple form of bagpipe well known in the Renaissance; through its bulb, the tube receives air from the player's mouth by means of a short blow-pipe). While the left hand of the player plucks the strings, the right hand stops the fingerholes of the long tube. Curiously, the fingerholes are not between the blow-pipe and the mouth of the tube; thus the entire wind attachment is functional nonsense. However, as a combination of string sound with wind sound, it is only one example of a whole line of such instruments that seem to fulfil an old dream of musicians — the one-man orchestra.[1]

Piero's instruments, fantastic as they are, seem also to have been modelled after existing instruments, for which the obvious occasion may have been the *feste*. And, as in Lippi's painting, not only the instruments but the whole painting — its perspective, the theatrical dragon, the people shown both as a frightened and a jubilant 'chorus,' and the sky-born Perseus — indicates stage design. In this context it seems not unimportant that Piero was actively engaged in inventing and preparing *feste*.[2] And, what is even more important, there is evidence that painters of *cassoni* and similar decorative paintings were directly inspired by scenes from the theatre and from *feste*. It is, again, Vasari who, in a passage in his life of Dello Delli, emphasizes how widespread was the fashion to depict actual 'jousting, tournaments, hunts, *feste*, and other public entertainments. . . .'[3]

If, then, paintings like those discussed above are portraits of real *intermedio* scenes, or are at least influenced by actual stage performances, we should expect to find information on our fantastic and pseudo-ancient instruments in the

[1] Instruments blown and bowed at the same time appear in, for example, the recently restored angel concert by Gaudenzio Ferrari in the cupola of the Santuario at Saronno. In Praetorius's *Syntagma musicum*, Plate XXXI, an Arab spike fiddle is shown, the spike of which is a recorder (*flute douce*); the caption says: 'Monochordium, is a pipe and also has a string attached, which is bowed with a fiddle bow; common among the Arabs.'

[2] According to Vasari (*op. cit.*, IV, 135), he was the author of the *Carro della morte*.

[3] Vasari, *op. cit.*, II, 149.

literary reports describing such *feste*. In fact, these reports mention a bewildering number and variety of musical instruments designed for the stage. It is to this problem that we now turn.

One of the richest and most variegated spectacles of which we have a detailed report is the wedding of Francesco de' Medici and Giovanna d'Austria in Florence in 1565, described by Vasari.[1] A short analysis of the 'apparato' and of 'tutte le ceremonie ed effetti e pompe' may give us an idea of the manifold use of music and musical instruments. In Vasari's report we encounter, first of all, an enumeration of the decorations in various squares, streets, and bridges, and a description of the monuments such as portals, arches, obelisks, and equestrian statues, together with their surrounding scenery and with all the allegorical details employed. There is no lack of music and musical instruments in all these descriptions. Among the sculptures, we find that of a Muse with her flute, *amorini* singing odes, and other figures which appeared to sing, such as the three Graces ('pareva che cantassero con una certa soave armonia'), tritons blowing wind instruments (*buccine*), a whole choir of beautiful little angels engaged in singing, and so forth.[2] If Vasari considered it worthwhile to attribute these musical effects[3] to statues, we can easily imagine how many more musical activities were represented in all these decorations, and how much actual music was performed while the festival procession moved from one place to the next. But this was only the upbeat. The procession went to the Grande Sala del Palazzo, where an extraordinary spectacle was prepared for the guests. It was as if 'Paradise with all its angelic choirs had opened in this moment: an effect that was marvellously enhanced by a most sweet, masterly, and rich concert of instruments and human voices' (p. 572).

Then followed, as the main entertainment, d'Ambra's comedy *La Cofanaria*. Between the acts there were intermedii played, 'taken from that tender novel of Psyche and Cupid' by Apuleius. In the six intermedii, which were accompanied with real music by Corteccia and Striggio, we find a wealth of instruments. I will quote only some of the most interesting for the purpose of this study: the first intermedio showed Olympus with numerous Gods, which gave opportunity for 'soavissima armonia' (p. 573) and for 'un piacevolissimo coro' of the Hours and the Graces around Venus; in the second intermedio there appeared 'a little Cupid, who seemed to carry a lovely swan in his arms: in this swan, an excellent viol was hidden, and while the Cupid seemed to caress the swan with a swamp reed for a fiddle bow, it began to produce sweet music,' and soon after, the

---

[1] *Ibid.*, VIII, 519–622.   [2] *Ibid.*, pp. 523 (Muse), 534 (*amorini*), etc.

[3] Vasari was a remarkable connoisseur of music, as one can judge from the numerous expert technical remarks in many of his *Vite*, and from the frescoes with which he decorated his own palazzino in Arezzo.

allegorical figure of music, 'recognizable by the musical hand [the symbolic Guidonian hand] on her head, and the rich garb decorated with her various instruments and various cards showing all the musical notes and tempos prescribed by her; but, even more, one could see her playing in sweet harmony a beautiful large lirone.'[1] Then four other cupids entered the stage, carrying 'four richly decorated lutes, also producing lovely sounds.' These cupids sang a madrigal describing the love of Amor and Psyche; the accompaniment was executed by 'lutes and many other instruments hidden backstage.' Thus we see here a variety of instruments. Some, like the lirone, are instruments *all'antica*; others are contemporary instruments, such as the violone, disguised for allegorical purposes, or beautifully decorated, such as the lutes.

The intermedii III, IV, and V used more dressed-up instruments. Intermedio III introduced Fraud and Deceit with their allegorical attributes, which could not help but produce a comical effect: 'they carried traps, fish hooks, or deceptive hooks under which were hidden, with singular ingenuity, curved pipes for the music they were supposed to produce'; and they also, like the cupids before them, performed a madrigal.

The description of the fourth intermedio mentions a rather subtle camouflage: two antropophagi or Lestrigones played trombones disguised as trumpets. In all probability, this especially interesting passage means that the martial significance of the trumpets had to be retained for the eye, although the ear was to be treated to the music of the much more flexible slide trombones.

Intermedio V included the most complex disguise. Four allegorical figures, Jealousy, Envy, Worry, and Scorn, had to defend themselves against four terrible serpents. Each grasped one of the snakes and beat it with thorny twigs. But, as soon as Psyche began to sing a madrigal, sweet instrumental music was heard; 'for in the snakes were cleverly hidden four excellent violins,' and in the twigs were four fiddle bows. In addition, four trombones furnished accompaniment from backstage.

The sixth and last intermedio brought Pan to the stage, with nine other satyrs, all 'holding various pastoral instruments beneath which other musical instruments were hidden.'

The intermedii were by no means the end of the festivities. They were followed by a 'Triumph of the Dreams,' which took place on the squares before Santa Croce and Santa Maria Novella. Here again, musical instruments were played, for instance, 'two beautiful sirens who, sounding two large trumpets instead of small ones, marched in front of all the others.' Then Fame appeared, with the customary attributes: 'carrying on her head a ball representing the

---

[1] For the lirone — the same instrument held by Armonia in one of the illustrations in Ripa's *Iconologia* of 1603 — see Chapter 5 above.

universe, and appearing to blow a large trumpet with three mouths.'[1] This fantastic trumpet reminds us somewhat of the brass instrument in Filippino Lippi's painting (Pl. 94c).

After the Triumph of the Dreams, there followed a procession of decorated cars, which had as their theme the genealogy of the gods. There were no less than twenty-one cars, of which I mention only those with interesting musical instruments. The fourth car, representing the Sun, showed, among many other figures, that of Orpheus, 'appearing to play a very ornate lira'; then the nine Muses, with various musical instruments; the tenth car again exhibited Fama, 'sounding a very large trumpet'; the fifteenth car showed Pan 'with a large *zampogna* of seven reeds.' *Zampogna* here does not mean a bagpipe, but the ancient syrinx (*syringe polycalume*). The twentieth car, devoted to Bacchus, was a boat of silver which carried, among other figures, several bacchantes and satyrs, 'playing various harpsichords and other similar instruments.'

The finale of the *festa* was a 'buffolata,' consisting of ten squadrons with various deities and allegorical figures. After all these secular spectacles in celebration of the wedding, there followed, in front of the Church of Santo Spirito, a performance of the traditional and famous *festa* of San Felice, as a religious finale to all the wedding festivities, 'with a very large apparatus, and with all the ancient instruments and not a few new ones added.' It is a pity that this interesting differentiation between old and new instruments is not elaborated by further details.

These occasional references by Vasari to instruments would in themselves permit us to judge what care must have been taken to make them appear convincing and realistic, and at the same time to adapt their shape to the allegorical meaning of the scene. And it goes without saying that wherever instruments *all'antica* were needed, they also were made to look realistic and, with the help of archaeological models and information, as authentic as some of those in Filippino's painting. In the case of disguised instruments, Vasari does not tell how the masking was actually done. Fortunately we find sufficient information on this point in the documents that report numerous details of the *feste* for the wedding of Grand Duke Ferdinand I de' Medici to Christina of Lorraine in 1589.[2] Artists of great reputation participated in the preparation of

---

[1] A four-pronged trumpet with four bells is blown by a winged Fama in a Flemish or northern French tapestry of the early 16th century, *The Triumph of Fama*, in the Metropolitan Museum of Art [A.N. 41.164.2].

[2] We selected the *Nozze* of 1565 for the description of the entire typical *feste* because they were more extensive and variegated, and because the reporter, Vasari, was a musical connoisseur. For details of performance, however, we prefer the *Nozze* of 1589, not only because of the excellent study of Aby M. Warburg (*I Costumi teatrali per gli intermezzi del 1589*, in his *Gesammelte Schriften*, Leipzig and Berlin, 1932, I, 259–300), with the important comments by Dr.

these spectacles: Giovanni Bardi as chief organizer, Emilio de' Cavalieri as stage and music director, Bernardo Buontalenti as stage architect and engineer of the theatrical machines, and Marenzio, Malvezzi, Peri, and again Bardi and Cavalieri, as composers. In addition to several comedies, a football game in costume, and animal fights on the Piazza Santa Croce, a *sbarra* (rope-dancing) and a *naumachia*, a *corso al Saracino*, and a masquerade of Rivers, there was a performance of six intermedii from the comedy *La Pellegrina*, 'nel gusto antico.' Unlike the six intermedii of 1565 described above, which represented in sequels one single theme — the story of Amor and Psyche — the intermedii of 1589 were only loosely connected, but all celebrated the power of music. Their titles were: 1) *L'armonia delle sfere* (The Harmony of the Spheres); 2) *Lo gara fra Muse e Pieridi* (The Contest of the Muses and the Pierians); 3) *Il combattimento pitico d'Apollo* (The Pythian Combat of Apollo); 4) *La regione dei demoni* (The Region of the Demons); 5) *Il canto d'Arione* (The Song of Arion); 6) *La discesa di Apollo e Bacco insieme col Ritmo e l'Armonia* (The Descent of Apollo and Bacchus with Rhythm and Harmony).

There is no need for a detailed analysis of these intermedii since they have been examined minutely from the iconographical point of view in Warburg's excellent study. What chiefly interests us here are the instruments, their types, their manufacture and, in many cases, their disguises. On this point we receive information from the *Memorie e ricordi* of Girolamo Serjacopi, Provveditore delle Fortezze di Firenze,[1] in which is contained, among other things, the technical instructions given by Bardi for each single instrument — instructions that were forwarded to the theatre workshop (*guarda roba*).

Stage instruments were disguised with papier-maché (*cartapesta*) or covered with veils, taffeta, or other cloth to fit the scenes and their allegorical functions. One of the instructions reads: 'other papier-maché to cover instruments' (*strumenti da sonare* — thus, real instruments!), and again, similarly: 'Decorate the instruments of the musicians with taffeta and veils.' The first intermedio (*L'Armonia delle sfere*) required instruments to fit (visually) the celestial rays: 'Decorate the harps, lutes, and other instruments so that they look the same as the celestial rays,' and 'Attach to the lutes, harps, and other instruments some ribbons and pieces of papier-maché or other material to make them look like rays of stars.' There was evidently much gilding.

In the second intermedio (*Lo gara fra Muse e Pieridi*), the instruments were adapted to the pastoral setting by covering them with foliage. The fourth intermedio, which presented Hell, required instruments posing as snakes.

Gertrude Bing (*ibid.*, p. 394 ff.), but also because there exists a great wealth of technical information on their stage details, including the musical instruments.

[1] Archivio di Stato, Florence, Arch. Magistrato delle Nove, fa. 3679.

Accordingly, viols[1] as well as trombones were camouflaged: 'Signor Bernardo says to give to the keeper of costumes the designs of the four viols that look like serpents . . . the wrapping of taffeta around the trombones to make them look like serpents is the duty of the keeper of costumes,' and also: 'four violoni should be covered with taffeta painted green, and scales, and gilded to look like serpents. . . .' The fifth intermedio, which introduced the singing Arion, required instruments appropriate for tritons and nymphs (following the ancient Roman representations, in the manner used before by Raphael and Giulio Romano), and wind instruments had to be masked as conch shells: 'Decorate the instruments of the goddess and the nymphs to make them look like sea shells, and do not forget the dolphin,' and 'it will be necessary to make the instruments look like sea shells and other things from the sea.'

These examples could of course be multiplied *ad infinitum*. It is not without interest that one can find many analogous ones in the *sacre rappresentazioni*. The abundance of instruments used there is documented, for instance by a text describing the transportation of the head of St. Andrew in Rome in 1462: 'one saw boys in the form of angels; some of them sang sweetly, others played organs; no instrument of the art of music was lacking. . . .'[2] The reports on the procession of the Corpus Domini, in the same year in Viterbo, mention the representation of paradise: 'singers, representing angels, intoned sweet chants . . . now one could hear lovely melodies sung by human voices, now delightful chords played by musical instruments. . . .' Later, in the course of the procession: 'sounded the trumpets, the organs, and innumerable musical instruments. . . .' And during the enacting of the Assumption of the Virgin, which was also part of the celebrations, there was 'a singing of the hosts of the heavenly spirits, playing of magical instruments, frolicking, gesturing, laughter of all the heavens. . . .'[3] Nor were the disguised instruments absent in the *sacre rappresentazioni*. D'Ancona[4] mentions 'una mascherata' in Florence, described in the diary of San Gallo (p. 153), having a representation of Hell and its devilish monsters: 'Thereupon came twelve standard-bearers on horseback, disguised as dragons . . . and trumpet players disguised as dragons with muted trumpets, and with wings, a fearful sight indeed.'

If we review these examples, we notice the careful attention given to the instruments in the course of the *feste*, and the precision with which they are adapted to the mythological or allegorical topics of the spectacles. These instruments can be classified into two main categories: on the one hand, instruments that are transformed into fantastic ones, thereby losing their musical

[1] In the fifth intermedio of the wedding of 1565, there were four serpent viols.
[2] Pius II, *Comentarii*, Rome, 1584, Lib. VIII, p. 365.
[3] Ciampi, *op. cit.*, VIII, 384 ff.	[4] *Op. cit.*, I, 273.

function, as in the case of the trumpet of Fame with its three bells; and, on the other hand, instruments that retain their function but are adapted to the scene by appropriate masking, as the violoni disguised as serpents and the bows disguised as twigs.

The subjects of the profane *feste*, whether intermedii or trionfi, were (almost without exception) mythological. Only the more vulgar spectacles, such as tournaments *a la Saracena* or animal fights, were free of classical influence. But for mythological subjects, the *gusto antico* demanded 'ancient' instruments for the stage, especially when protagonists such as Apollo, Orpheus, Amphion, and the Muses had to recite in the ancient manner, playing their own accompaniment. But the organizers of the spectacles found themselves in difficulties, for if they tried to follow the instructions given by the humanists and proceeded with archaeological precision, they must have realized that the 'ancient' instruments could not be played, because the playing technique of the Renaissance differed radically from that of the ancients. In fact, the ancient kithara and lyre were instruments with 'open' strings, each sounding their full length without being stopped against a fingerboard as is done on the lute or violin. The kithara and lyre, lacking a neck, had no fingerboard at all. The open-string technique of the Greeks, whether with plectrum or fingers, was totally different from the Renaissance stopping technique. And, in spite of all humanist research and attempts to rediscover and reconstruct Greek music, it was, after all, contemporary polyphonic or chordal music that was to be played in the *feste*. The interesting dilemma which resulted was solved in various ways.

The easiest way around the problem, and at the same time the most musically satisfactory way, was based on a falsification of history: this was the employment of the lira da braccio,[1] an instrument eminently suited by virtue of its five melody and two drone strings to polyphonic solo recital (*bicinia* and *tricinia*, according to Praetorius) and to recitation by singers who accompanied themselves. In texts of the Renaissance, this instrument is often called 'lira' and sometimes 'lira antica,' to distinguish it from the 'lira moderna.' According to a widespread belief, it was invented by Sappho and, in view of this, its appearance in the hands of countless representations of Apollo, Orpheus, and allegories of Music was not considered an anachronism. Even as late as the 17th century, the large statue of Apollo standing at the right of the left-hand Fontana dell Organo, in the garden of the Villa d'Este in Tivoli, holds a life-size lira da braccio. There is no doubt that the instrument was used in stage performances. Peruzzi, who gave the instrument to all the musical heroes in his frieze of Ovid's *Metamorphoses* in the Villa Farnesina, would certainly have had no qualms about having it used on the stage and in the plays that he helped to prepare.[2] It occurs often

---

[1] See Chapter 5 above.   [2] Vasari, *Vite*, ed. Milanesi, IV, 600 ff.

in paintings, with fantastic and elaborate decoration, as in the *King David* of Bartolommeo Passerotti, in the Galleria Spada (Pl. 32a). A lira da braccio decorated with plant-like curves and curls, in Gaudenzio Ferrari's *Virgin with St. Anne* (Pinacoteca, Turin; Pl. 34b), reminds us of the decoration of a lira 'alla boscareggia [*sic*]' mentioned in the description of the second intermedio in the *feste* of 1589. It is not without interest that two twigs spiralling away from the sound box in the latter example seem to suggest the arms of the ancient lira.

The second way out of the dilemma was to show unplayable instruments on the stage, instruments made to conform to archaeological standards or mythological tradition, and to supply the real sound by other instruments backstage.[1] We have encountered instruments of this type before, in the descriptions of *feste*, and we should here like only to refer to one example in painting, the stag-head lyre in Filippino Lippi's *Allegory of Music* (Kaiser Friedrich Museum, Berlin; Pl. 96b). Among the traditional attributes of Musica in the Renaissance were the swan and the stag. The latter, as traditional symbol of the speed of sound, is represented here not as a living animal (as it is in the allegory of Music engraved by Cornelis Floris), but only by its head, which serves as the body of an ancient lyre. This lyre is a strange mixture of completely fantastic elements and elements borrowed from ancient models with almost pedantic care. The yoke, with its elaborate form, and the strings — seven, with one of them broken — are archaeologically correct, as is the use of animal horns for arms to carry the crossbar. On the other hand, the second crossbar, beneath the first one, is sheer invention, and so is the way in which the upper and lower ends of the strings are attached. Last but not least, the instrument could not have produced much sound,[2] for the stag's head is not a real resonator or sound box. And even if it were, the strings do not reach it. Thus the instrument is entirely unfunctional, but, since it is conceived with the pretension of reality, it seems closely related to the theatrical showpieces used in the intermedii and other spectacles. The large bone plectrum beneath the lyre and the syrinx comprised of seven canes are faithfully copied after Roman sarcophagi, and the little pipe beneath the syrinx combines the appearance of a small contemporary shawm with that of an ancient aulos, for it has at least two of the rings with projecting cups that are the standard equipment of the fully developed Roman tibia. While this

[1] In pictorial representation, we often find instruments *all'antica* mixed indiscriminately with modern instruments. In a Flemish tapestry of about 1585 in the Uffizi (Pl. 95c), showing a festival given for the Polish ambassadors, we see Parnassus, upon which is Apollo with an ancient lyre, while the Muses beneath him play a *cornetto curvo*, a lute, and an ensemble of viols. Vasari, however, in his costume sketches, usually showed more archaeological ambition, and furnished Muses with even wind instruments *all'antica* (Pl. 95b).

[2] Leonardo's famous lira (Vasari, *Vite*, ed. Milanesi, IV, 18, 28, 29), shaped like a horse's skull and decorated in silver, was no doubt a lira da braccio used by him to accompany his recitation. See my article in *Die Musik in Geschichte und Gegenwart*, XIII, Kassel, 1966, col. 1664.

pseudo-aulos is not a functional instrument, it reveals the respect paid to the musical practice of the ancients.

This leads us to a third possible solution of the dilemma of combining archaeological precision with modern playing techniques: the invention of bastard instruments shaped to some extent after ancient models but incorporating modern functional elements that permitted the actual performance of Renaissance music. Here again, we find an example in the work of Filippino Lippi, namely in the wonderful grisaille frescoes on the window wall of the Cappella Strozzi (Pl. 74b) in Santa Maria Novella, Florence.[1] Of the four musical instruments depicted around the figure of Parthenice, the large string instrument held by Parthenice interests us most. Its lower part is precisely that of an ancient kithara: a large sound box with two gracefully curving arms that would normally carry the crossbar. But here they carry no crossbar, at least not directly; two columns are grafted on them, and it is only their capitals that carry the crossbar — or, rather, what poses as a crossbar, for the strings are attached not to it but to a three-leafed flat head that resembles the leaf-shaped flat head of the common lira da braccio. This head is connected with the sound box by a neck with fingerboard, and it is this fingerboard over which all the strings run. Thus we can say that this instrument is a kithara adapted to the Renaissance technique of stopping the strings by the addition of a neck like that of a lute, viol, or lira da braccio. Another contemporary feature is the round sound-hole in the soundboard, which resembles that of a lute. The bone plectrum in Parthenice's right hand follows ancient models. For want of a better term, we may call this instrument a lyre-guitar, simply because it resembles those lyre-guitars that became fashionable for a short time as ladies' instruments in the French Empire.

Thus this bastard instrument, constructed to reconcile Greek appearance with modern playing style, was a logical if fanciful compromise between the old and the new; and its inventor, whether Lippi or perhaps a stage designer before him, in fact repeated only the transitory stage in an evolution that took half a millenium, from late antiquity to the *trecento* — the gradual transformation of ancient string instruments into the fingerboard instruments of the Middle Ages. In this light it does not seem an accident that Lippi's lyre-guitar strikingly resembles the lyre-guitars in the Utrecht and Cambridge Psalters, where they are frequently depicted side by side with their immediate predecessors, the kitharas of antiquity.

This example of adaptation of ancient instruments to modern playing technique is by no means unique. We find such bastard instruments frequently in other paintings, and I believe they must have been used on the stage. Two of the

---

[1] See Chapter 13 above.

most carefully constructed instruments of this type are found in two mysterious paintings by Lorenzo Costa, both painted for the studiolo of Isabella d'Este in the Palazzo Ducale in Mantua, and now in the Louvre. It is not likely that these two paintings represent actual stage scenes, for we know the accurate and even pedantic instructions given by the Marchesa when she commissioned some of the other paintings for her studiolo from Giovanni Bellini and Mantegna, and in all probability similar instructions were also given for the two paintings by Costa. Nevertheless, if one examines these two paintings, one can hardly fail to be struck by their resemblance to actual stage sets; and, among the accessories, it is precisely the musical instruments which make us think of the theatre and can, in fact, hardly be explained if they are not considered as stage instruments. After all, Costa, like Piero di Cosimo before him, was engaged in the preparation of actual *feste*.[1] In all probability, he must have been familiar with the brilliant *feste* in Ferrara, such as those of 1503 which were honoured by the presence of Isabella d'Este and Lucrezia Borgia. Much ink has flowed concerning the meaning of these two allegorical paintings, but again we do not need to touch on their iconographical significance here, and may restrict ourselves to the instruments important to our study, the lyre-guitars in each of the two paintings.

In the painting frequently referred to as *The Court of the Muses of Isabella d'Este*, four musicians encircle the central scene. The two bearded figures nearer the front are evidently Greek or Oriental; their instruments can be seen only in part. The two figures towards the background, however, are evidently classical mythological figures. The left-hand figure (Orpheus?), enraptured, plays a lira da braccio. The one on the right (Sappho?) holds a lyre-guitar (Pl. 96a). Here the classical form of the kithara, with its arms, is precisely retained; but instead of one crossbar there are seven, and none of them is functional. A neck is grafted on to the sound box, ending in a long thin peg box with side pegs, and a square flat head with three additional frontal pegs. This instrument could certainly have been played in guitar fashion, although it may not have been comfortable to stop the strings on its neck, which could not be easily grasped. The other allegorical painting also contains a lyre-guitar, in addition to a lira da braccio, psaltery, syrinx, and other wind instruments. The lyre-guitar is held by a youth crowned with laurels (Pl. 96c), and consists, again, of the body of a kithara with a neck grafted on it. Here we have only one crossbar, but this penetrates the arms and the sound box at the middle and therefore cannot carry any strings, since the strings run the length of the soundboard and the neck. Costa is also not very consistent here: there are seven strings in all, but only six pegs on the flat head. Unlike the other lyre-guitar, this one has seven frets on the fingerboard.

[1] Vasari speaks of 'due trionfi, tenuti bellissimi, con molti ritratti,' in the frescoes for San Jacopo Maggiore in Bologna (*Vite*, ed. Milanesi, III, 135).

PLATE I

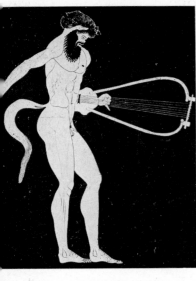

a. *(left)*. Silenus with lyre, from red-figured Greek amphora, c. 490 B.C.

b. *(right)* Illustration from Fétis, *Histoire générale de la musique*, III, 549. Misinterpretation of a Greek original.

c. Illustration of a harp, from Fétis, *Histoire*, I, 255, after a reliable archaeological drawing of the wall painting in the tomb of Ramses III.

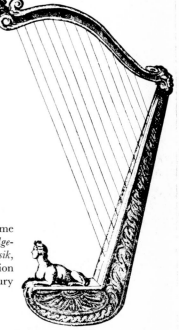

d. Illustration of same harp in Forkel's *Allgemeine Geschichte der Musik*, I, Tab. 5. An adaptation to please 18th-century taste.

e. Upper margin of an illustration from a Florentine choirbook, showing four trumpets in symmetrical duplication, overpowering the string instruments. Cleveland Museum of Art, J. H. Wade Collection.

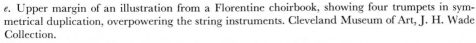

PLATE 2

Giovanni Bellini, *The Feast of the Gods.* National Gallery, Washington, D.C.

PLATE 3

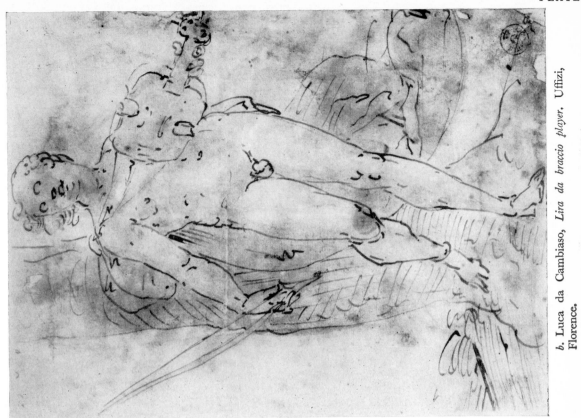

b. Luca da Cambiaso, *Lira da braccio player.* Uffizi, Florence.

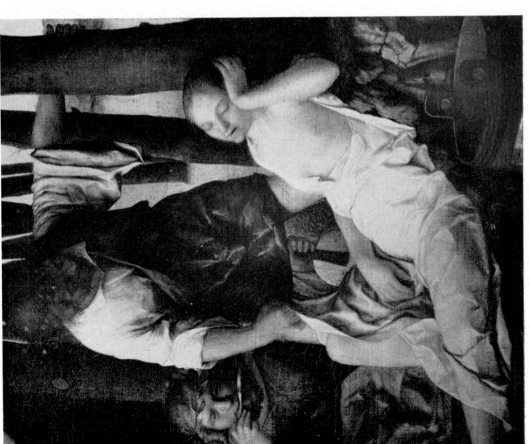

a. Detail of Plate 2.

PLATE 4

PLATE 5

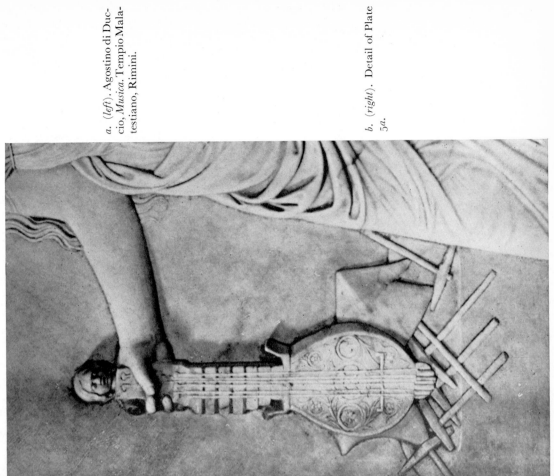

a. (*left*). Agostino di Duccio, *Musica*. Tempio Malatestiano, Rimini.

b. (*right*). Detail of Plate 5a.

PLATE 6

b. Paolo Veronese, *Allegory of Music*. Palazzo Ducale, Venice.

a. Francesco Cossa, detail from the frescoes in the Palazzo Schifanoia, Ferrara.

PLATE 7

Titian (Giorgione?), *Concert champêtre*. Louvre, Paris.

PLATE 8

Titian, *Bacchanal*. Prado, Madrid.

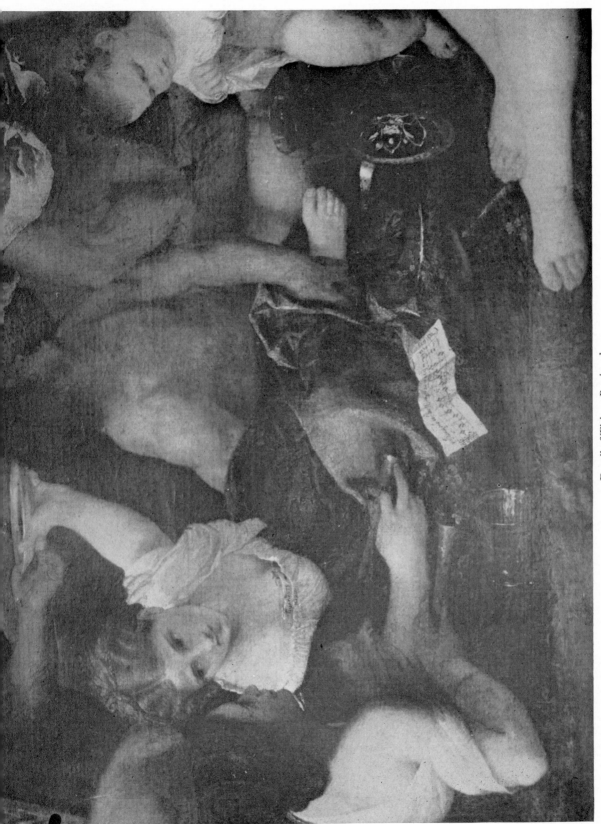

PLATE 9

Detail of Titian, *Bacchanal.*

PLATE 10

Titian, *Venus and the Lute Player*. Metropolitan Museum of Art, New York.

PLATE II

b. Apocalyptic elder holding a vielle, showing a bourdon not appearing in contemporary sculptural representations of the same subject. Detail from fresco in St.-Martin de Fenollar, Roussillon.

a. Romanino, detail of fresco in the Castle of Trent.

PLATE 12

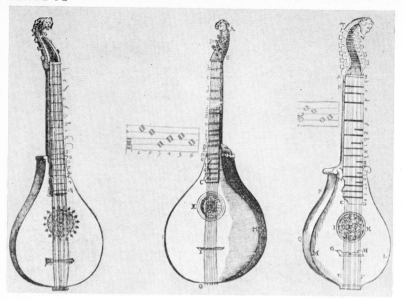

a. Three citterns, from woodcuts in Mersenne, *Harmonie universelle* (1636)

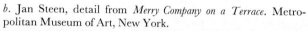

b. Jan Steen, detail from *Merry Company on a Terrace.* Metropolitan Museum of Art, New York.

c. Cittern made by Girolamo de V
Brescia, 1574. Kunsthistorisches Mu
Vienna.

PLATE 13

Two citterns, from Praetorius, *Syntagma*, *Theatrum instru-torum* (1618).

b. Luca della Robbia, *Cantoria*, detail of angels playing citterns. Museo del Duomo, Florence.

Fra Giovanni da Verona, cittern in intarsia. Choir stall, onte Oliveto Maggiore, Siena.

d. Andrea Previtali, detail from *Scenes from an Eclogue of Tebaldeo* (previously attr. to Giorgione). National Gallery, London.

PLATE 14

b. Gaudenzio Ferrari, detail from fresco, show angel with cittern. Santuario, Saronno.

a. Musicians with cittern and vielle, from Queen Mary's Psalter. British Museum, London.

c. Raffaellino del Garbo, *Madonna*, detail showing angel with lyre-guitar. Dahlem Museum, Berlin.

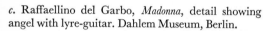

d. Lyre guitars. Metropolitan Museum of Art, Crosby Brown Collection.

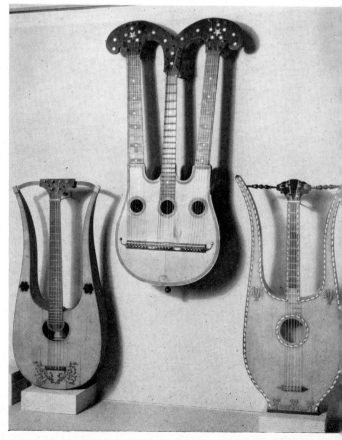

PLATE 15

a. Musician, from Bible of Charles the Bald. ...liothèque Nationale, Paris.

b. Detail from Stuttgart Psalter, f. 4or.

c. Musicians. Strasbourg Cathedral, west portal, middle section.

d. Benedetto Antelami, cittern player. Baptistery, Parma.

PLATE 16

b. Psalm 150.

d. Psalm 92.

a. Psalm 147.

c. Psalm 71.

DETAILS FROM UTRECHT PSALTER

a. Detail from Utrecht Psalter, Psalm 108.

b. Detail from Utrecht Psalter, Psalm 43.

c. Detail from mosaic, Qasr el-Lebia.

PLATE 18

a. Hurdy-gurdy in lute shape (France, 18th century).
Metropolitan Museum of Art, Crosby Brown Collection.

b. Hurdy-gurdy in guitar shape (France, 18th century).
Metropolitan Museum of Art, Crosby Brown Collection.

PLATE 19

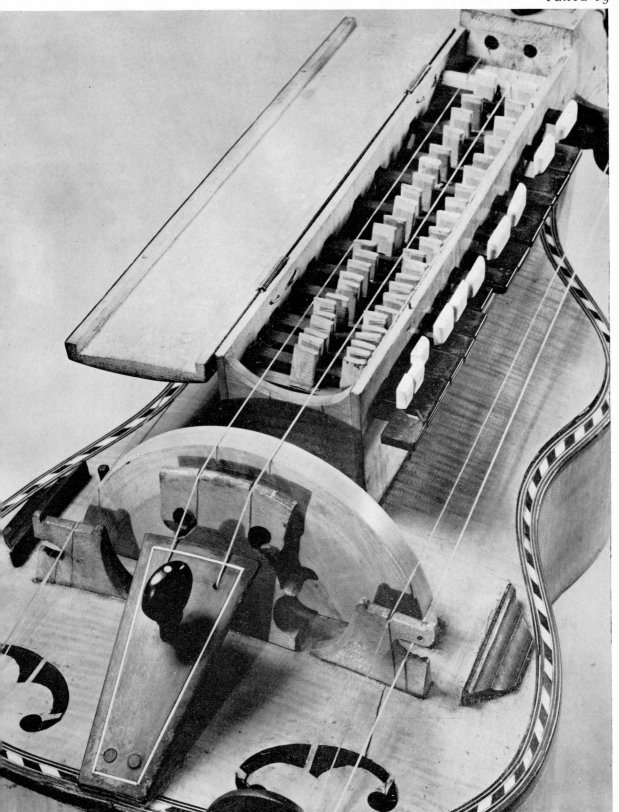

Wheel and stopping mechanism of the hurdy-gurdy shown in Plate 18*b*.

PLATE 20

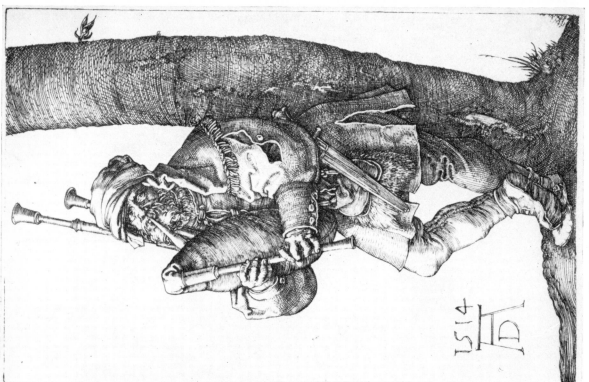

b. Georges de la Tour, *The Hurdy-Gurdy Player*. Nantes Museum.

a. Albrecht Dürer, *The Bagpiper* (engraving).

PLATE 21

c. Gaudenzio Ferrari, detail of angel playing a bagpipe with two one-hand chanters and two drones. Santuario, Saronno.

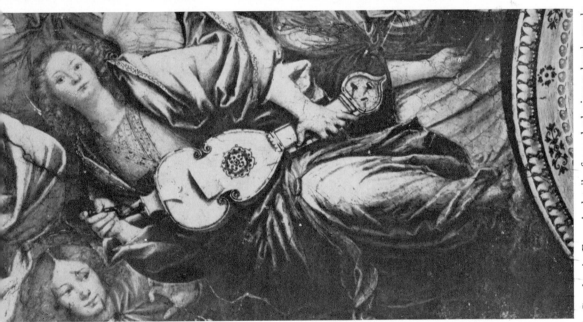

b. Gaudenzio Ferrari, detail of angel playing a hurdy-gurdy. Santuario, Saronno.

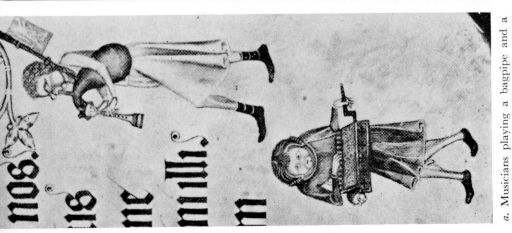

a. Musicians playing a bagpipe and a symphonia. Marginal illustrations from the Loutrell Psalter (14th century). Lulworth Castle, Dorset.

PLATE 22

a. Musicians playing hurdy-gurdies.

b. Musician playing a bagpipe with two pairs of drones and a double chanter.

MINIATURES FROM THE *CANTIGAS DE SANTA MARIA* (13TH CENTURY)

c. Musicians playing bagpipes with single chanters, no drones.

d. Musicians playing bagpipes with double pipes.

PLATE 23

a. Organistrum played by two elders (end of 12th century). Portico de la Gloria, Cathedral of Santiago de Compostela.

b. School of Giotto, *Glorification of St. Francis*, detail. Church of San Francesco al Prato, Pistoia.

PLATE 24

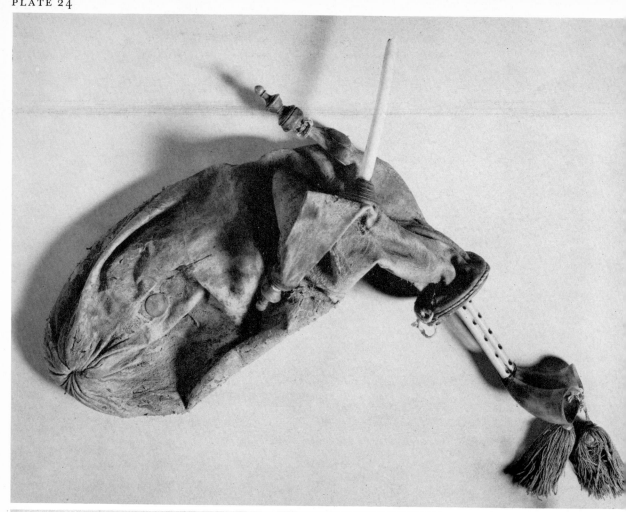

a. Bagpipe of Near Eastern type (Turkey, 19th century). Metropolitan Museum of Art, Crosby Brown Collection.

b. *Above*: Zampogna (Italy, 19th century). Length of longest drone, 4 feet. *Below*: Musette (France, 18th century). Length of chanter, 9½ inches; of bourdon cylinder, 5½ inches. Metropolitan Museum of Art, Crosby Brown Collection.

PLATE 25

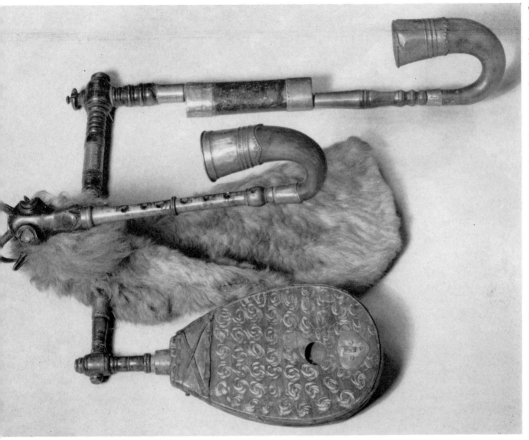

b. Bock with bellows (Germany, 19th century). Length of chanter, 1 foot 9 inches; of drone, 3 feet 6 inches; both are fitted with single-beating reeds. Metropolitan Museum of Art, Crosby Brown Collection.

a. Bock (Germany, 18th century). Length of chanter, 2 feet 5 inches; of drone, 5 feet 4 inches. Metropolitan Museum of Art, Crosby Brown Collection.

PLATE 26

a. Musette player with other musicians, from Watteau's *L'Amour au théâtre français.*

b. Watteau, *Fête champêtre*, detail showing muse player.

c. Watteau, *L'Accordée de village*, detail showing musette and vielle played for dancing.

d. Engraving after Watteau, showing Chinese musici with a vielle.

PLATE 27

a. Angel playing a three-stringed hurdy-gurdy (c. 1500). St. Thomas Altar, Cologne.

b. Van Dyck, *Portrait of François Langlois*. Private collection. Note the bellows straps on the right arm, and the single chanter.

c. Player with zampogna.

d. Street singer with hurdy-gurdy, from the case of a South Tyrolean psaltery (18th century). Metropolitan Museum of Art, Crosby Brown Collection.

PLATE 28

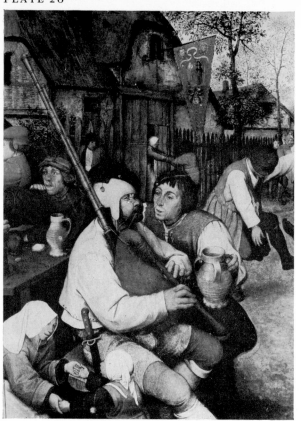

a. Peter Bruegel, *Dance of the Peasants*, detail.

b. Engraving after Peter Bruegel, *The Fat Kitchen*, detail.

c. Vielle player from a woodcut (c. 1570) entitled *Les Noces de Michaud Crouppière: Histoire d'une drollerie facécieuse du Marriage de Lucresse aux yeux de boeuf et Michaud Crouppière son mary, avec ceux qui furent semouz au banquet.*

PLATE 29

23

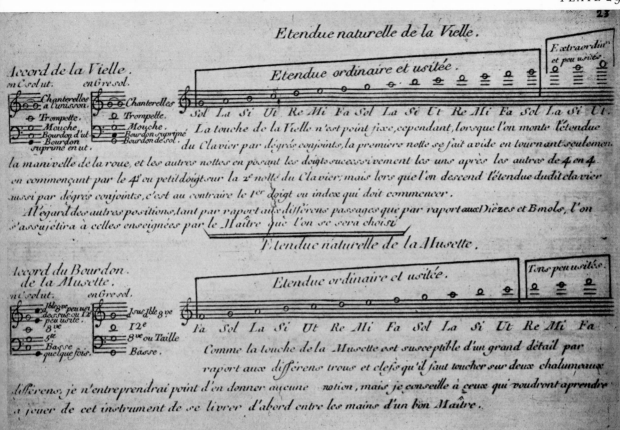

a. Page from Bordet's *Méthode raisonnée*, Paris, c. 1755.

b. Cornemuse with ivory pipes (France, 18th century). Length of chanter, 10 inches; of drone, 7 inches. Metropolitan Museum of Art, Crosby Brown Collection.

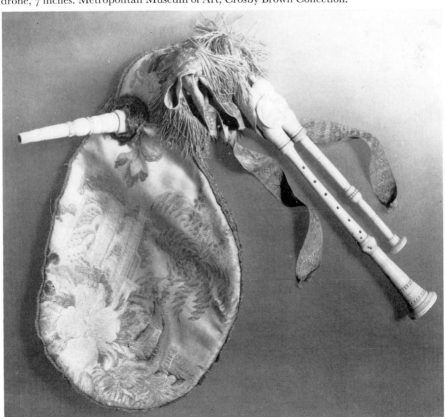

PLATE 30

a. Plaque for the musical scholar Ercole Bottrigari (early 17th century).

b. *Orpheus in Hades*, after a bronze plaque by Moderno.

PLATE 31

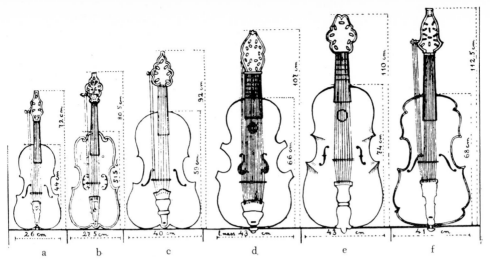

Examples of various lire da braccio and lire da gamba (after sketches by Disertori in *Rivista musicale italiana*, XLIV [1940]):
a. Lira da braccio, Brussels Conservatory, Mahillon Catalogue 1443. *b*. Lira da braccio, Kunsthistorisches Museum, Vienna, Schlosser Catalogue 94. *c*. Lirone, Heyer Collection, Kinsky Catalogue 780. *d*. Lira da gamba, Heyer Collection, Kinsky Catalogue 784. *e*. Lira da gamba, Brussels Conservatory, Mahillon Catalogue 1444. *f*. Lira da gamba, Kunsthistorisches Museum, Vienna, Schlosser Catalogue 95.

g. Lira da braccio by Giovanni d'Andrea, Venice, 1511; front and back views (same as *b* above).

h. Lira da gamba by Wendelin Tieffenbrucker, Padua, c. 1590 (same as *f* above).

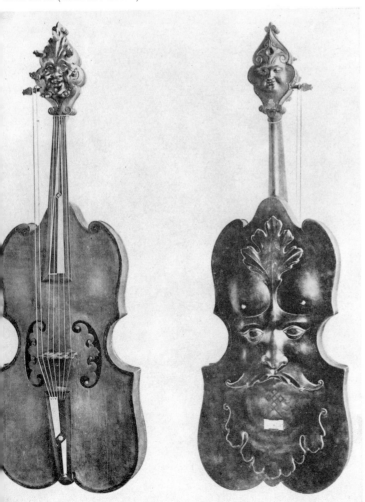

PLATE 32

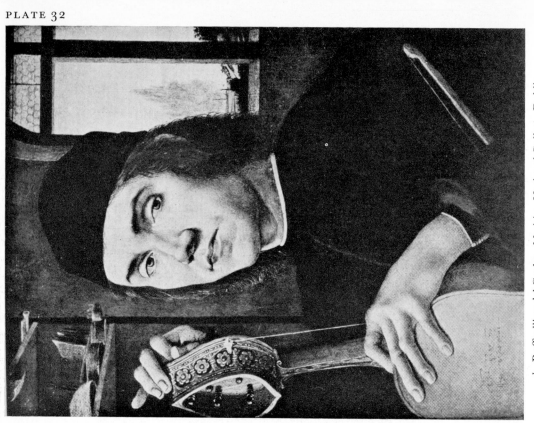

b. Raffaellino del Garbo, *Musician*, National Gallery, Dublin.

a. Bartolommeo Passerotti, *King David*. Galleria Spada, Rome.

PLATE 33

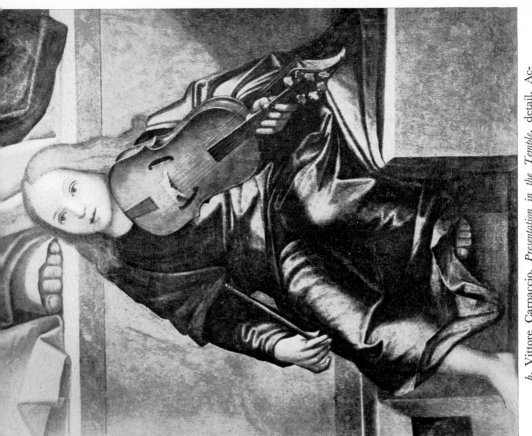

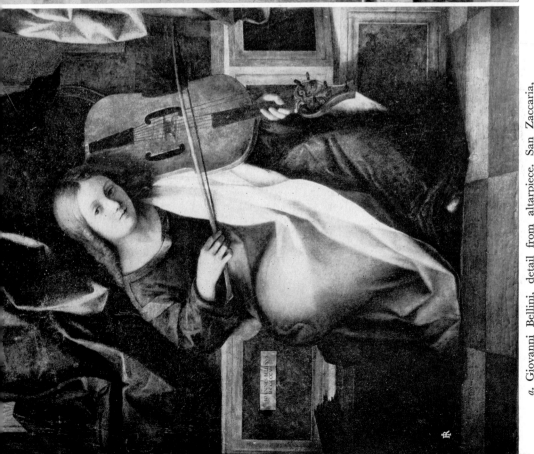

b. Vittore Carpaccio, *Presentation in the Temple*, detail. Accademia, Venice.

a. Giovanni Bellini, detail from altarpiece. San Zaccaria, Venice.

PLATE 34

b. Gaudenzio Ferrari, detail from *Virgin with St. Anne.* Pinacoteca, Turin.

a. Lira da braccio in wood intarsia. Choir stall in Santa Maria in Organo, Venice.

PLATE 35

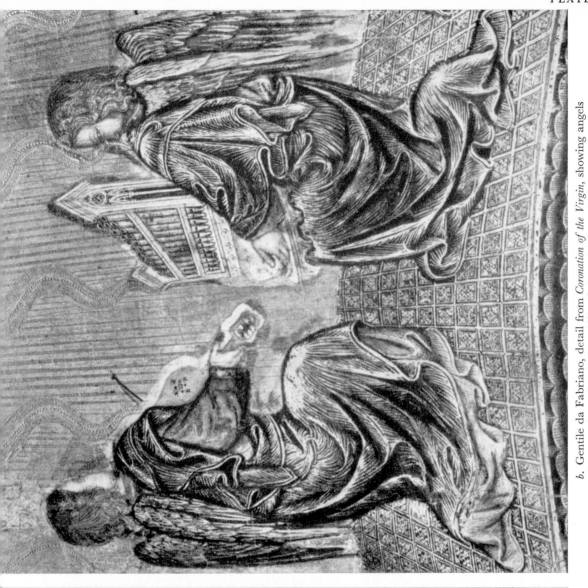

b. Gentile da Fabriano, detail from *Coronation of the Virgin*, showing angels with portative and early form of lira da braccio. Brera, Milan.

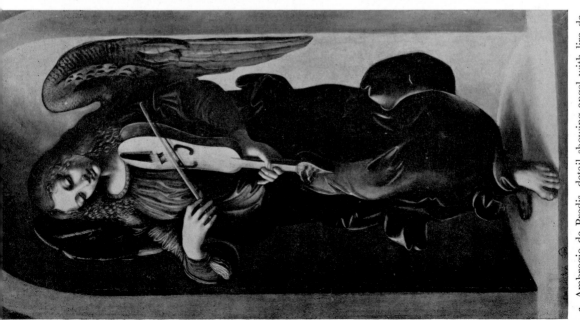

a. Ambrogio de Predis, detail showing angel with lira da braccio. National Gallery, London.

PLATE 36

Palma Vecchio, *Sacra conversazione*. San Zaccaria, Venice.

PLATE 37

a. Jan Bruegel the Elder, detail from *Allegory of Hearing*. Prado, Madrid.

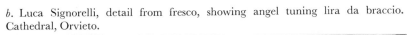

b. Luca Signorelli, detail from fresco, showing angel tuning lira da braccio. Cathedral, Orvieto.

PLATE 38

b. Detail of Plate 38*a*.

PLATE 39

a. Gaudenzio Ferrari, detail of *La Madonna degli aranci*, Church of San Cristoforo, Vercelli.

b. Bernardino Lanini, detail of *Sacra conversazione*, Raleigh Museum, Raleigh, North Carolina.

PLATE 40

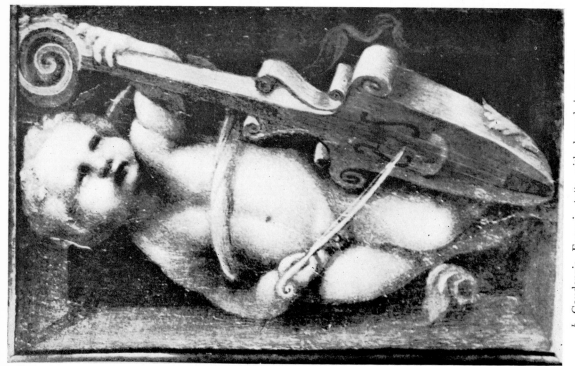

b. Gaudenzio Ferrari, *putto* with bowed instrument. Collection of E. Schweitzer, Berlin.

a. Gaudenzio Ferrari, study for an angel concert. Staatliche Graphische Sammlung, Munich.

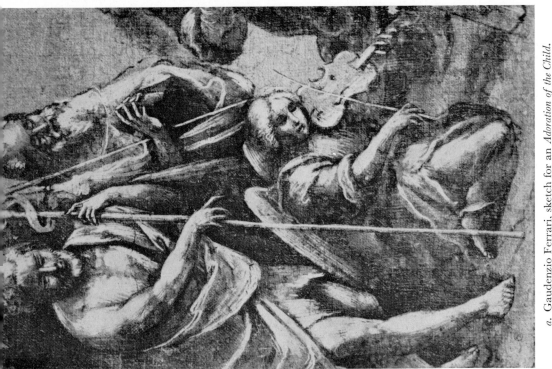

PLATE 41

b. Gaudenzio Ferrari, detail from fresco. Santuario, Saronno.

a. Gaudenzio Ferrari, sketch for an *Adoration of the Child.* Palazzo Reale, Turin.

PLATE 42

a. Harpsichord, supported by tritons and sea nymphs, with companion figures of Polyphemus and Galatea (Roman, 17th century). Metropolitan Museum of Art, Crosby Brown Collection.

b. Detail of harpsichord, with frieze showing triumph of Galatea.

PLATE 43

a. Small clay model of harpsichord, in partially assembled state. Palazzo Venezia, Rome.

b. The model of the harpsichord, in completed state.

PLATE 44

a. Detail of frieze on harpsichord.

b. One of the tritons at the front of the harpsichord, beneath the left end of the keyboard.

c. *Putto* riding sea shell, at end of harpsichord.

PLATE 45

a. Schematic view of an exhibition room in Todini's music museum in Rome, with a musician (perhaps Todini himself) playing one instrument and, magically, three others at a distance. From Kircher's *Phonurgia nova*, 1673.

b. Another view of the same room, evidently drawn on the spot. Four keyboard instruments are attached to a structure hiding their mechanical connection. From Buonanni's *Gabinetto armonico*, 1722.

XXXIII *Prospetto della Camera detta Galleria armonica nel Palazzo delli Signori Verospi in Roma in cui sono molti Strumenti sonori, fabricati con prodigioso artificio dà Michele Todino*

PLATE 46

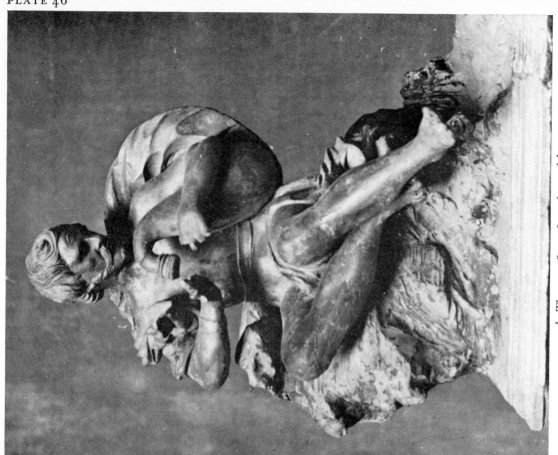

b. The same figure from the model.

a. Figure of Polyphemus playing a bagpipe, from the harpsichord.

PLATE 47

b. Renaissance lute, from a Bolognese intarsia, Metropolitan Museum of Art, New York.

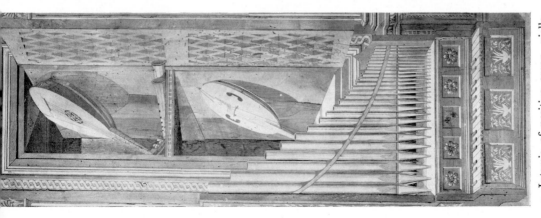

a. Intarsia of positive organ, vielle, and zinks, from the Gubbio Study, Metropolitan Museum of Art, New York.

PLATE 48

b. Intarsia of lutes. Stanza della Segnatura, Vatican.

a. Intarsia of cittern, recorders, and lute. Monte Oliveto Maggiore, Siena.

PLATE 49

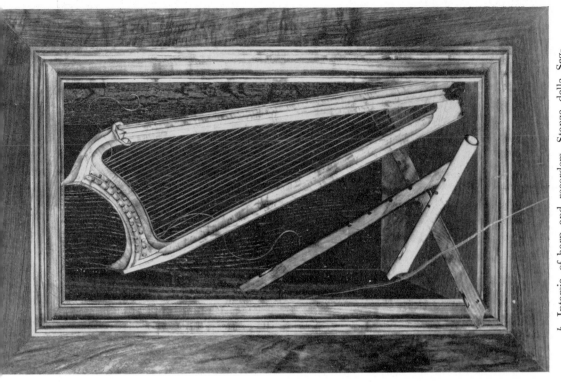

b. Intarsia of harp and recorders. Stanza della Segnatura, Vatican.

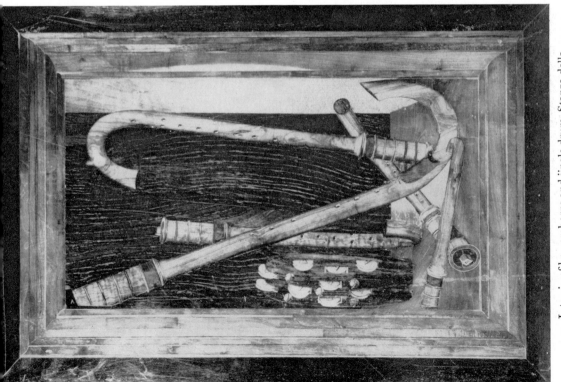

a. Intarsia of krummhorns and jingle drum. Stanza della Segnatura, Vatican.

PLATE 50

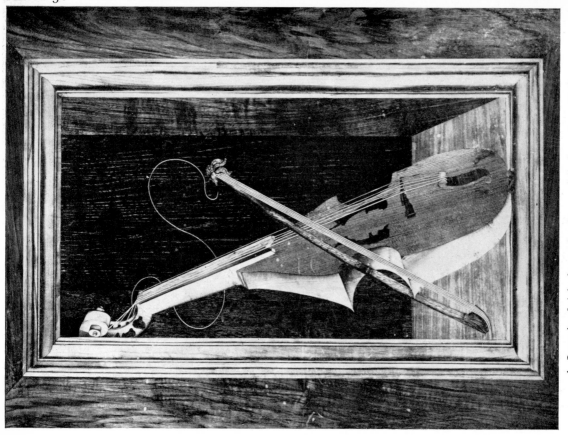

b. Intarsia of viola da gamba. Stanza della Segnatura, Vatican.

a. Intarsia of spinettino. Stanza della Segnatura, Vatican.

PLATE 51

a. Intarsia of clavichord. Studiolo of Federigo da Montefeltro, Urbino.

b. Intarsia of harpsichord, from a choir stall. Cathedral, Genoa.

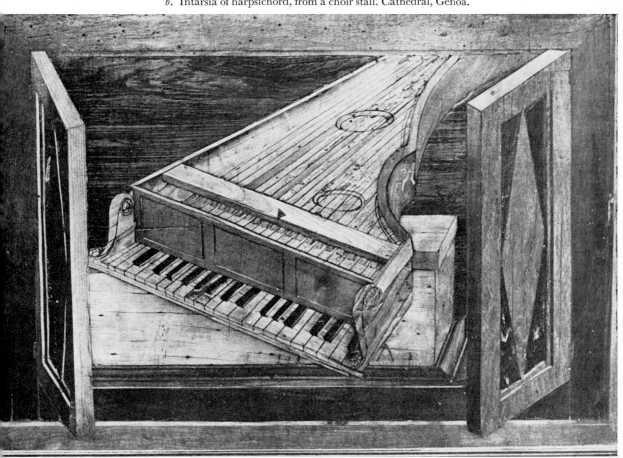

PLATE 52

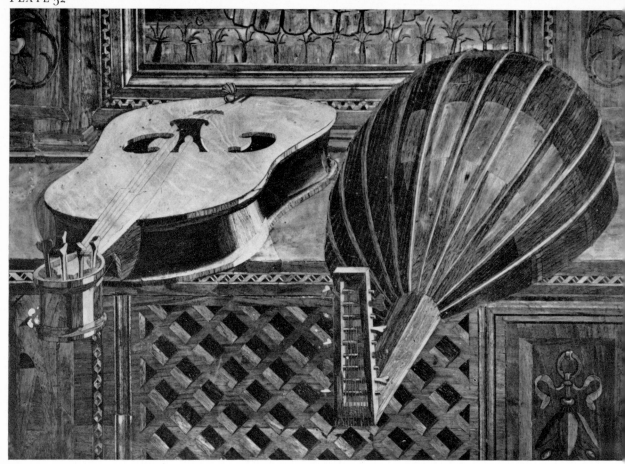

a. Intarsia of lute and lira da braccio. Studiolo, Urbino.

b. The Gubbio Study of Federigo da Montefeltre. Metropolitan Museum, New York.

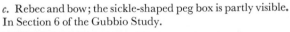

a. Cittern with pair of dividers and hourglass. In section 9 of the Gubbio Study.

b. Cosimo Tura, detail of *Madonna and Child*. National Gallery, London.

c. Rebec and bow; the sickle-shaped peg box is partly visible. In Section 6 of the Gubbio Study.

d. Fiddle with four melody strings and one drone. In Section 5 of the Gubbio Study.

PLATE 53

PLATE 54

a. Signorelli, detail of a painting, showing an angel playing a fiddle. Church of the Casa Santa, Loreto.

b. Pinturicchio, detail of a fresco, showing an angel playing a rebec. Santa Maria in Aracoeli, Rome.

c. Shadow cast on mouldings by the lectern. In Section 1 of the Gubbio Study.

d. Celestial globe, books, and quadrant. In Section 2 of the Gubbio Study.

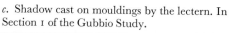

PLATE 55

a. A corner of the Gubbio Study, showing the treatment of the baluster shadows.

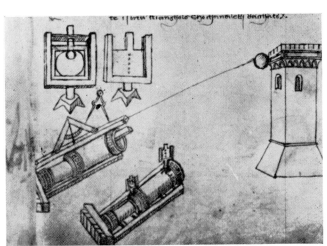

b. Francesco di Giorgio, drawing showing bombards and their sights. Ducal Library, Turin.

c. Albrecht Dürer, *The Designer of the Vase* (woodcut).

PLATE 56

a. Border patterns with geometrical bodies. Centre wall of the Gubbio Study.

b. Geometrical border, from a panel attributed to Francesco di Giorgio. In the pavement of the Cathedral, Siena.

c. (*below*). Mazzocchio, or turban ring. On a bench in Section 7 of the Gubbio Study.

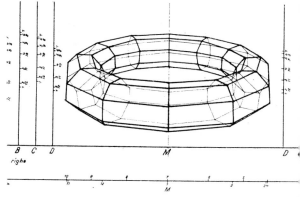

d. Ring of twelve sections with octagonal cross-section. From Piero della Francesca's *De prospectiva pingendi*, 1469.

PLATE 57

a. Florentine woodcut with disc border pattern, from *Il Savio Romano.*

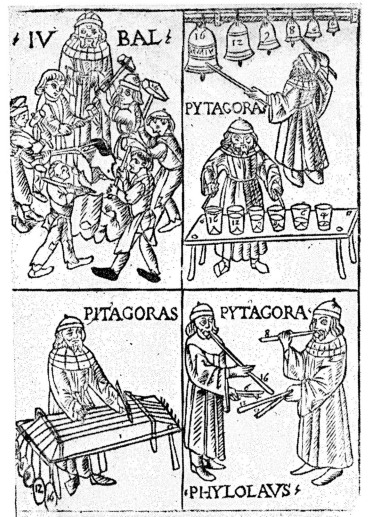

b. Woodcut from Gaffurio's *Theorica musice*, 1492.

c. Border ornament around cupboards flanking window. In the Gubbio Study.

PLATE 58

b. Page showing an old man with a harp in the large initial, and a monster playing a transverse flute in the space below the text.

a. The Annunciation to the Shepherds. The musician in the initial is playing a bagpipe, the shepherd beneath him a pastoral shawm.

FROM THE BOOK OF HOURS OF JEANNE D'ÉVREUX, METROPOLITAN MUSEUM, NEW YORK

PLATE 59

b. Scene representing the education and chastisement of the young St. Louis. At the bottom of the page, a youth sitting on a bearded monster is bowing a vielle.

a. The Nativity. The main scene shows two angels with cymbals and a vielle; below is a monster plucking a jawbone.

ROM THE BOOK OF HOURS OF JEANNE D'ÉVREUX, METROPOLITAN MUSEUM, EW YORK

PLATE 60

b. The Adoration of the Magi. Little angels in the background are playing a trumpet, bells, a psaltery, a vielle, and kettledrums. The scene

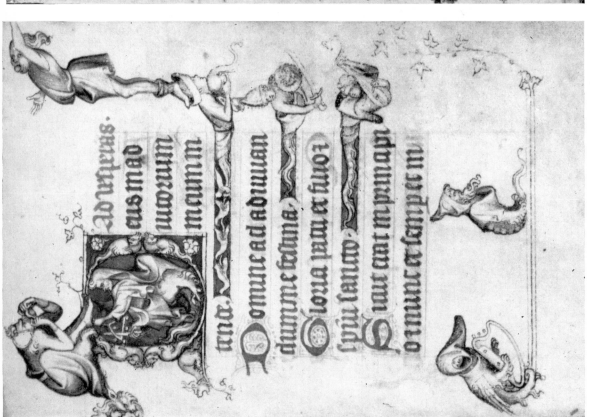

a. Page showing a monster with a triangle in the initial, and another with a harp below; a long-tailed monster is playing a mandola with a

FROM THE BOOK OF HOURS OF JEANNE D'ÉVREUX, METROPOLITAN
MUSEUM, NEW YORK

PLATE 61

a. Page showing, in the initial, a monster wearing a monk's robe and plucking bellows with a plectrum; the little monk above him holds his music. In the lower right corner a long-tailed creature is playing a psaltery with his fingers.

c. Initial with a monster playing a vielle in a rather awkward position.

b. Page showing, at left of Annunciation scene, a figure playing a mandola.

FROM THE BOOK OF HOURS OF JEANNE D'ÉVREUX, METROPOLITAN MUSEUM, NEW YORK

PLATE 62

a. Initial with a woman playing cymbals.

b. A musician playing a bagpipe with a very large chanter and drone.

c. A mandola of medium size.

d. A tailed monster playing a bagpipe.

e. The 'training' of a bagpipe.

f. A fantastic creature playing a dog as a bagpi[pe] and another blowing a large shawm with a cowh[orn] bell.

FROM THE BOOK OF HOURS OF JEANNE D'ÉVREUX, METROPOLITAN MUSEUM, NEW YORK

PLATE 63

a. A snare drum and fife.

e. A triangle.

f. Bells and a reed pipe.

g. A snare drum.

b. A rattle.

h. A bell hit with a stick.

c. A monster blowing a bellows like a wind instrument.

d. A bellows played as a trumpet.

i. A goat bowing a jawbone with a rake.

FROM THE BOOK OF HOURS OF JEANNE D'ÉVREUX, METROPOLITAN MUSEUM, NEW YORK

PLATE 64

Detail of Geertgen tot Sint Jans, *Virgin and Child*. Van Beuningen Museum, Rotterdam.

PLATE 65

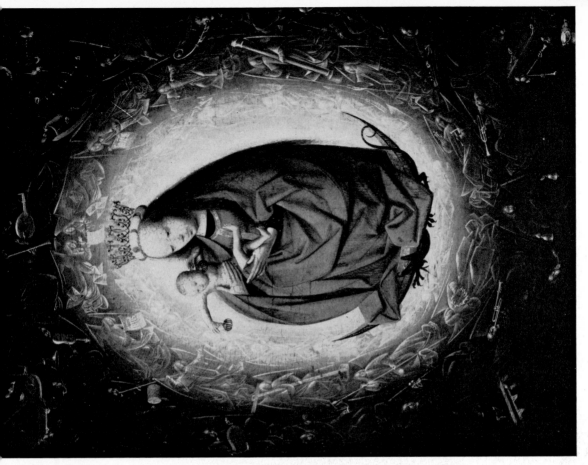

a. Glorification of the Virgin. Collection of Baron Heyl, Worms.

b. Geertgen tot Sint Jans, *Virgin and Child.* Van Beuningen Museum, Rotterdam.

PLATE 66

Master of the St. Lucy Legend, *Ascension and Coronation of the Virgin*. National
Gallery, Washington, D.C.

PLATE 67

DETAILS OF PLATE 66

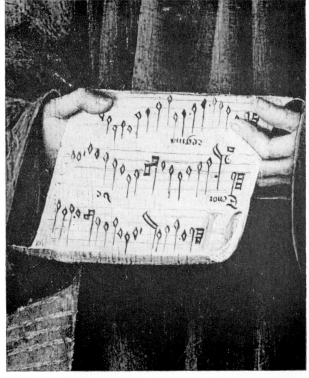

PLATE 68

Zanobi Machiavelli, *Coronation of the Virgin*. Museum, Dijon

PLATE 69

a. Detail of Plate 70*a*, showing Apollo.

b. Detail of Plate 70*a*, showing Apollo flaying Marsyas.

c. Detail of Plate 70*a*, showing Pallas Athena.

d. Benedetto da Majano, sarcophagus. Cappella Strozzi, Santa Maria Novella, Florence.

PLATE 70

a. Contest between Apollo and Marsyas. National Gallery, Washington, D.C., Samuel H. Kress Collection.

b. Benedetto Montagna, *Contest between Apollo and Marsyas* (engraving).

c. Benedetto Montagna, *Contest between Apollo and Pan* (engraving).

PLATE 71

a. Andrea Schiavone, *The Judgment of Midas*. Accademia, Venice.

b. Details of window wall in Cappella Strozzi, Santa Maria Novella, Florence.

left: Angels to left of window.   *right*: Angels to right of window

PLATE 72

Burial chapel for Filippino Strozzi. Santa Maria Novella, Florence.

PLATE 73

a. Window wall, showing round plaques at top.

c. Lower part of window: St. John
the Evangelist and St. Philip.

b. Upper part of window: Madonna.

CAPPELLA STROZZI, SANTA MARIA NOVELLA, FLORENCE

PLATE 74

a. Detail of window wall in Cappella Strozzi, showing Caritas and angel.

b. Parthenice, with palm tree and *putti* with instruments. Cappella Strozzi.

c. Detail of window wall in Cappella Strozzi, showing two muses with pedestal lyre.

PLATE 75

NI
HANC
DESPEXERIS
VIVES

FIDES

a. Detail of window wall in Cappella Strozzi, showing Fides and angel.

b. Anonymous drawing of figures in Pl. 74*c*. Uffizi, Florence.

SACRIS
SVPERIS
INI
TIATI
CANVNT

c. Left tablet, with inscription. Cappella Strozzi.

PLATE 76

b. Filippino Lippi. *Jesus and the Woman of Samaria.* Seminario, Venice

a. Detail of book held by St. Philip. Cappella Strozzi

PLATE 77

a. A sarcophagus of the Muses, showing left part of front. Kunsthistorisches Museum, Vienna.

b. (*below*). Kithara player, from Roman wall painting.

c. (*right*). Detail of Plate 77a.

PLATE 78

Raphael, *Parnassus.* Stanza della Segnatura, Vatican.

PLATE 79

RAPHAEL PINXIT IN VATICANO

Engraving by Marcantonio, after an early study by Raphael for the *Parnassus*.

PLATE 80

Early copy of a compositional sketch by Raphael for the *Parnassus*, Oxford.

PLATE 81

b. Early copy of a sketch by Raphael of a lute player. Chantilly.

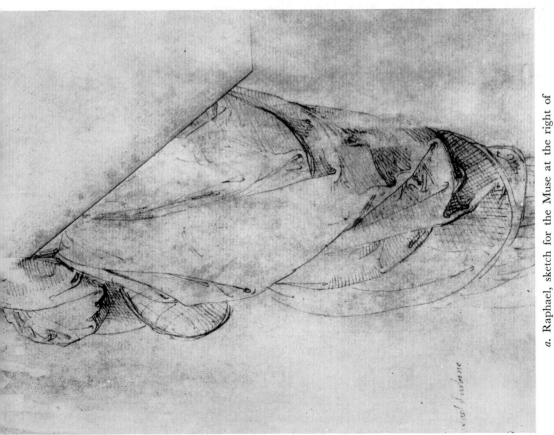

a. Raphael, sketch for the Muse at the right of Apollo. Albertina, Vienna.

PLATE 82

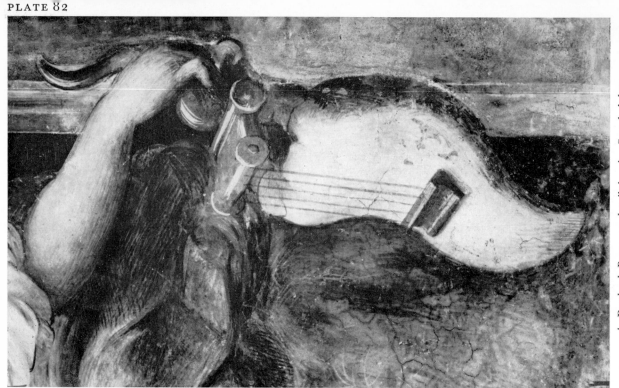

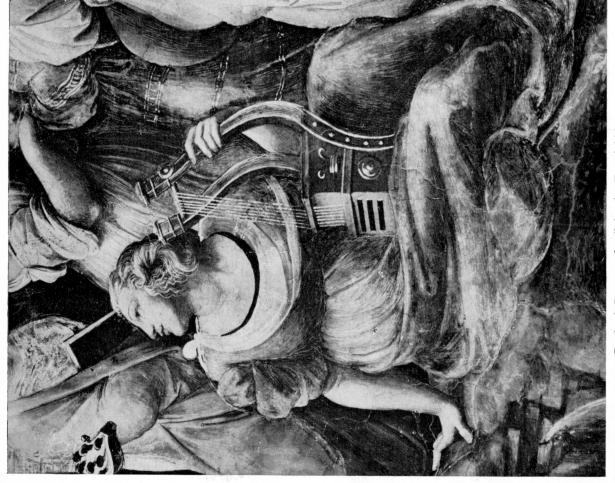

PLATE 83

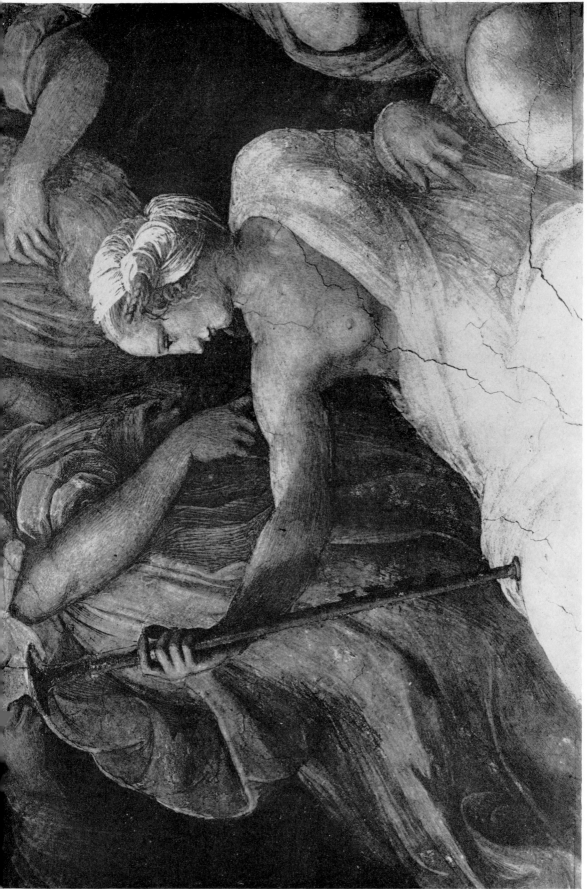

Raphael, *Parnassus*, detail showing Euterpe's wind instrument.

PLATE 84

b. Raphael, sketch for the figure of Apollo playing the lira da braccio.

a. Raphael, *Parnassus*, detail showing Apollo.

PLATE 85

a. Sarcophagus of the Muses (formerly in the Mattei collection). Museo Nazionale, Rome.

b. Sarcophagus of the Muses, in an engraving from the *Monumenta Matthaeiana.*

c. Sarcophagus of the Muses, in an engraving from Montfaucon, *L'Antiquité expliquée et representée en figures.*

PLATE 86

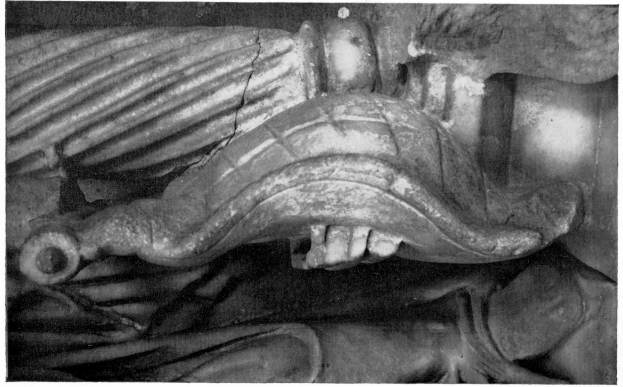

PLATE 87

b. The lyre.

a. The tibia.

TWO DETAILS OF THE SARCOPHAGUS OF THE MUSES. MUSEO
NAZIONALE, ROME

PLATE 88

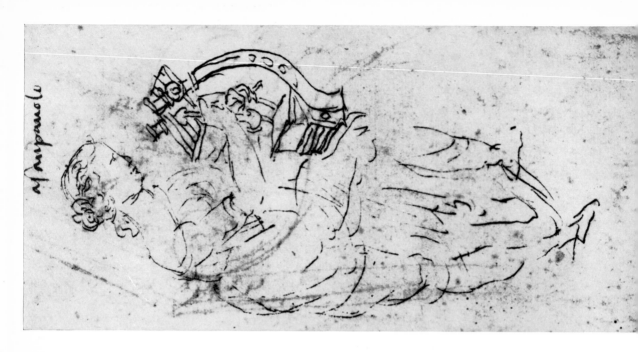

a. (above). Detail of the kithara on the Sarcophagus of the Muses. Museo Nazionale, Rome.

PLATE 89

a. Patera Martelli. Museo
Nazionale, Florence.

c. Amico Aspertini (?), detail from a
drawing in the Wolfegg sketchbook.

b. The Poet and His Muse (ivory diptych,
5th century). Cathedral, Monza.

PLATE 90

Titian, *Three Ages of Man*, National Gallery, Edinburgh.

PLATE 91

Allegory of Inspiration (Flemish, 16th century). Collection of Mr. Theodore A. Heinrich.

PLATE 92

Piero di Cosimo, *The Liberation of Andromeda*. Uffizi, Florence.

PLATE 93

Filippino Lippi, *The Adoration of the Golden Calf*. National Gallery, London.

PLATE 94

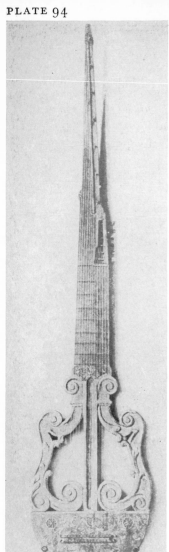

a. Theatre instrument. Kunsthistorisches Museum, Vienna.

b. (*upper right*). Detail of Plate 93.

c. Detail of Plate 93.

PLATE 95

a. Detail of Plate 92.

b. Giorgio Vasari, *Muse with Phrygian Aulos.*
Uffizi, Florence.

c. Parnassus, detail of a Flemish tapestry showing a fête in honour of the
Polish ambassadors, c. 1585. Uffizi, Florence.

PLATE 96

a. Lorenzo Costa, *The Court of the Muses of Isabella d'Este*, detail. Louvre, Paris.

b. Filippino Lippi, *Allegory of Music*, detail. Kaiser Friedrich Museum, Berlin.

c. Lorenzo Costa, detail from an allegorical painting. Louvre, Paris.

While my hypothesis that the instruments represented in the paintings discussed above, and possibly in many others, were actual stage instruments is, I believe, supported by some internal evidence, it would be immeasurably strengthened if real stage instruments of this sort had survived. Unfortunately, like most other tools designed for special use, these seem to have perished when their usefulness ceased. Francesco Sansovino, in his *Venezia, città nobilissima*, Venice, 1580, mentions, in the chapter on Venetian 'studi di musica,' the collection of Agostino Amadi, which included 'instruments not only *alla moderna*, but *alla Greca et all'antica*, in rather large numbers.' One would hardly be mistaken is assuming that these instruments *all'antica* were theatre instruments.

However this may be, we are lucky to find at least one instrument still surviving that could hardly have been anything but a theatre instrument. It is a curious bastard instrument (Pl. 94a), probably from the beginning of the 16th century, now in the Vienna Kunsthistorisches Museum;[1] it belonged to that part of the Habsburg collections that originally came from the famous Obizzi di Catajo collection. The body of this instrument, painted blue and gold, imitates in baroque patterns the form of the ancient kithara; like Costa's and Lippi's lyre-guitars, a long neck has been grafted on. This neck has eight divisions of brass and, like the contemporary chitarrone, two peg boxes — one for the six shorter strings and the other for the eight basses. The flat sound box produces only a limited sonority and this makes us think that it served largely a decorative function on the stage, at the same time permitting the illusion that it could be played.

We hope that the result of this little study may be of interest to the historian of music, since it may help to establish a clear distinction between functional and nonfunctional instruments — a line not easy to draw without relating instruments represented in paintings to those used on the stage, especially since even real and playable instruments were often cast in bizarre shapes and decorated in fantastic manners. Moreover, it may be of value to the historian of Renaissance music to find that the interest of the *quattro-* and *cinquecento* in antiquity extended also to the reconstruction of ancient instruments and to their representation in paintings as well as on the stage. A by-product of this study might be the suggestion that some Renaissance paintings that have not been connected with pageants for the stage should be considered as visual records of actual *feste*, or at least as closely related to theatrical imagination of the time, especially through the very instruments which appear in both.

[1] J. Schlosser, *Die Sammlung alter Musikinstrumente*, Vienna, 1920, item C. 94. In this catalogue, the instrument is called a 'Lyra-Cister.'

Index